Wine
A Global Business

Edited by

Liz Thach
and
Tim Matz

MIRANDA
PRESS

D1214517

Wine
A Global Business

Miranda Press
An imprint of Cognizant Communication Corporation

U.S.A.   3 Hartsdale Road, Elmsford, New York 10523-3701

Library of Congress Cataloging-in-Publication Data

  Wine : a global business / Liz Thach and Tim Matz, editors.
    p. cm.
Includes bibliographical references and index.
  ISBN 0-9715870-2-7 (alk. paper)
  1. Wine industry. 2. International trade. 3. Globalization — Economic aspects.
I. Thach, Liz, 1961- II. Matz, Tim, 1959-

H9375.3.W56 2004
663'.2'0068—dc22

                        2004013870

Printed in the United States of America

Printing: 1 2 3 4 5 6 7 8 9 10 Year: 1 2 3 4 5 6 7 8 9 10

Contents

List of Figures

List of Tables

Foreword

Forty years ago, when living and working in Japan, I was introduced by a mutual friend to Akio Morita, then a rising engineer and executive at a young Japanese company named Sony. Akio Morita went on to build Sony Corporation into a world-class global business, one of the best known brands in the world, and a company listed on both the Tokyo and New York stock exchanges. He and I met many times subsequently as we both served on our respective national commissions trying to reconcile the serious trade deficit between Japan and the United States. It was Akio Morita who first coined the well-known phrase, "Think globally, act locally."

Nowhere is "Think globally, act locally" more appropriate today than the wine business. The last 40 years have seen an enormous growth in global wine consumption and wine growing in the temperate regions all around the world. Many credit the post-World War II wine boom in California with igniting this expansion, but it has certainly accelerated with vast new plantings in South America, Australia, New Zealand, and South Africa. Wines from the Southern Hemisphere rival the quality of those from the Northern Hemisphere just as California wines challenge the traditional wine-growing regions of Europe. More to the point, wine consumers are now found in all the developed economies of the world whether in wine-growing regions or not. Japan and indeed all of East Asia are excellent examples of new, important, and growing wine markets for which there is relatively little domestic supply of quality wine.

Every serious participant in the wine business today must take into consideration the global market and global competition for wine customers. No one in this business, even relatively small wineries such as our own Quivira Estate Vineyards and Winery pursuing a "niche strategy" focused on a few select grape varietals, is immune from the economic forces of global supply and demand, brand proliferation, and very competitive pricing.

On the other hand, few businesses are as intensely local as the wine business. Almost all participants in the wine business are literally "rooted" in very specific locations. The nature and quality of our wines are, in large measure, dictated by our location. "Acting locally" in the wine business requires paying careful attention to specific soil composition and chemistry, drainage, exposure, and microclimate conditions, all of which, singly and in combination with the chosen grape varietals, dictate the "terroir" (the essence of specific vineyard location apparent in wine flavor) of our wines. Particularly with regard to smaller wineries pursuing "niche strategies," our brands bring a specific "terroir" to our customers. In Akio Morita's words, we are literally delivering our "local action" to our global customers.

The Dry Creek Valley in Sonoma County, for example, has been known for many decades for the quality of its Zinfandel. We believe Zinfandel was first planted here in the Dry Creek Valley in 1864 just as Agoston Haraszthy was arriving in the southern part of Sonoma with his boatload of 100,000 cuttings of 300 *vinifera* varietals from Europe. Indeed, Zinfandel came to North America much earlier in the 19th century before Haraszthy's boatload, and gradually made its way west with the early settlers. Its origins have recently been traced, after elaborate genetic detective work, to the Dalmatian Coast of Croatia, from which it has now almost totally disappeared, thus truly making it America's wine grape varietal. Zinfandel is clearly as much at home in the specific locale of Dry Creek Valley as Cabernet Sauvignon is along the banks of the Gironde River in Bordeaux or on the Rutherford Bench in Napa. Perhaps more than any other decision, "acting locally" in the wine business means choosing the right wine grape varietal for a specific location. Especially in the New World wine-growing regions, this is often a process of trial and error that can take a very long time.

Because winegrowers are as much or more farmers as winemakers, "acting locally" is of the first importance. And we are finding that the learning process never ends with regard to effective farming. In this day and age, that means learning globally. Many of us are now seriously turning our attention to organic farming, and in our case at least, to biodynamic farming (a practice that in modern parlance might be termed "extreme organic"). As we walk down the road of organic and biodynamic farming, we find many have gone before us, especially in Europe. We are studying their practices, mistakes, and successes. To paraphrase Akio Morita, we are learning globally and acting locally.

This is the first book to tackle the global wine business in a comprehensive manner. The ambitious and talented editors, Liz Thach and Tim Matz, together with the contributions of their judiciously selected expert authors, have carefully woven all of the strands noted above and many more. *Wine: A Global Business* will help all of us, whether we are already firmly rooted in the wine business or young aspirants, to understand the forces at work, the winning strategies, and the decisions necessary for success in the wine business of the 21st century. I know that if he were alive today, Akio Morita (a man who incidentally enjoyed a glass of good wine) would be pleased to see his now famous slogan so elegantly elaborated in this important book.

Henry Wendt
Founder and CEO
Quivira Estate Vineyards and Winery

Acknowledgements

We would like to thank all of the very supportive people who have encouraged us in the creation, writing, and editing of this book. Special thanks to our publisher, Robert Miranda, of Cognizant Communication Corporation, for all of his advice and patient response to our hundreds of questions. We extend deep appreciation to all of the authors who contributed chapters to this book, as well as the many members of the wine community who encouraged and supported us along the way. And very special heartfelt thanks to Henry Wente for his inspiring foreword, and to all of the other wine executives and managers who wrote endorsements for this book.

We are also extremely grateful to our families for their support through long days and nights typing away at the computer. To Liz's family: her husband Michael Thach, 6-year-old daughter Zia Thach, mother Vivian Olsen, sisters Celeste and Michelle Drewien, and father Rod Drewien. To Tim's family: his wife Ruth, 13-year-old daughter Marie, and 9-year-old son Theo.

Finally, a very special thank you and acknowledgement to all of the wine business students at Sonoma State University (SSU) who asked for a book like this for their studies, and provided helpful suggestions in its editing. Also we extend special recognition to the faculty and staff of the SSU School of Business & Economics for supporting this project with their writing efforts and encouragement.

Most Appreciative,
Liz Thach and Tim Matz

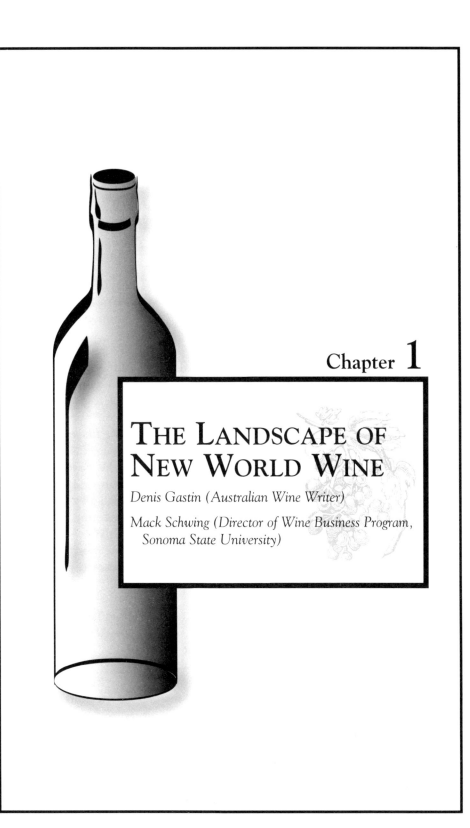

Chapter 1

THE LANDSCAPE OF NEW WORLD WINE

Denis Gastin (Australian Wine Writer)

Mack Schwing (Director of Wine Business Program, Sonoma State University)

What is New World wine? In a word, New World wine represents *freedom*. It means freedom to imagine new wine styles and innovative varietal combinations, to experiment with new practices in the vineyard and new winemaking methods, and, above all, freedom to interpret what the drinker wants and then to go ahead and do it. In this world, the market is the ultimate arbiter. If the consumer likes your product, you have a business; if not, you are on your own.

This chapter introduces the concept of a New World wine model. It provides some basic definitions and identifies the drivers. It discusses formative trends, presents some important statistics, and discusses the response of Old World wine players. It concludes with an overview of the challenges and opportunities in the current and future landscape for New World wine.

Defining New World Wine

When asked what New World wine represented to her, Jancis Robinson, one of the world's most widely published wine commentators (www.jancisrobinson.com) and editor of the *The Oxford Companion to Wine*, as well as co-editor of the *World Atlas of Wine*, described it as follows:

> Without an inherited model such as the centuries of tradition in European wine production, the New World has been able to identify what's important for business survival: successful selling of a product designed for the consumer rather than the producer. So sought-after grape varieties have been planted and then farmed efficiently, often sold to large wine producers with the muscle and sophistication required to actively sell those products into the major retailers, wherever in the world they may be. From my perspective in Britain, the stereotypical contrast is between one of the dominant Australian wine companies that parachutes its sales force into the UK supermarkets' buying offices with all the equipment needed (targeted price points, regular promotions, vast marketing budgets, etc.) to secure long-term co-operation, on the one hand, and, on the other, the typical French vigneron, one of tens of thousands, who makes wine more or less as his father did and waits for potential customers to drive up. (D. Gastrin, personal email interview, August 2003)

Free of the burden of history, liberated from geographic boundaries, and uninhibited by onerous regulations designed principally to preserve tradition, New World wine producers have drawn the most out of what the grape has to offer in the finished wine. They have experimented creatively with new grape varieties—and indeed have commercialized their own signature varieties. They have experimented judiciously with varietal blending, and have found inspired flavors and textures forbidden in the Old World. They have pioneered new viticultural and winemaking techniques and technologies that have been replicated far and wide, including, more recently, in the traditional heartland of wine.

Most importantly, the consumer is in their sights from the vineyard through to the table—not just at the end of a heavily regulated process. And the consumer has rewarded this diligence handsomely—initially in their home markets where consumers were won away from other beverages to wine, but in the traditional wine markets too, where consumers have been increasingly attracted by the alternatives on offer from the New World producers (see Figure 1.1).

The leaders in this wholesale change to the world of wine were Californian, quickly followed by Australians, then more recently New Zealanders, Chileans, Argentineans, and South Africans.

On the back of the successes by the New World pioneers, wine is now being exported to world markets from countries that would never have contemplated it even a decade ago—like Mexico, Peru, and Uruguay. And in this "emerging New World" there are some dazzling new wine experiments and nascent new players—like China (now the world's 11th largest wine-producing nation), and even India and Thailand.

The Drivers

Historically, the drivers of the New World wine phenomenon were closer to the soil than to high commerce. They were farmers looking for new crops or ways to create value beyond traditional farming. But it was also, fundamentally, influenced by immigration. Settlers and clergy from the "old" countries still wanted to enjoy the pleasures and traditions of wine in their adopted homelands: the only way to do this, in most cases, was to make it themselves. And from this impulse many businesses were spawned.

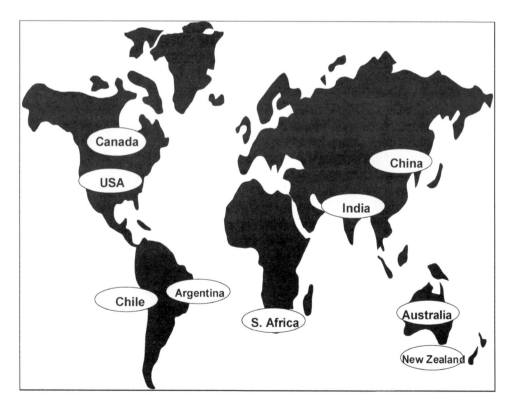

Figure 1.1. Map of major New World wine countries.

But no business is a success without a market. Few businesses are "born global," and New World wine businesses were no exception. The domestic market was the core of the original business rationale. In fact, it is really only in the last 20 years that New World wine producers began to make an impression on a global market scale. But what began as a market extension maneuver quickly became an industry phenomenon.

Corporatization of the Wine Sector

The growth of family businesses is one thing, but the corporatization of an entire industry sector is quite another. And this has been perhaps the most distinguishing feature of the New World business model: despite their relatively recent origins, six of the world's top ten producers and marketers of wine in 2003 were New World corporations (see Table 1.1).

Corporatization of the industry brought an overlay of technological, business, financial, and organizational skills on Old World tradition—without extinguishing it. This has been reinforced by regulatory frameworks that permit and even encourage change. At the basic level this has introduced:

Table 1.1. The Major Wine Players

		2002 Wine Sales		
Rank	Company	Millions of 9-L Cases	US$ (millions)	Remarks
1	Constellation/ Canandaigua/BRL Hardy	59.0	1700.0	includes Canandaigua, Hardy's, and Franciscan
2	E & J Gallo Winery	66.7	1428.0	includes spirits
3	Allied Domecq	21.0	1200.0	after acquisition Mumm Perrier, Buena Vista, Argentina (2x), Montana, and BYB
4	LVMH	7.0	1140.0	mainly champagne
5	Foster/Beringer Blass	17.0	1050.0	after acquisition Beringer
6	Southcorp	20.9	824.0	after merger with Rosemount
7	Diageo Chateau & Estate Wines	12e	700e	after acquisition of Seagram wines
8	Castel Frères	48.0	666.0	negociant, also in beer and water
9	Henkell & Co	12.7	619.0	mainly sekt
10	Freixenet	16.6	528.0	after acquisition Yvon Mau and Wingara

Source: Rabobank International (2002). Reprinted with permission.

- broad acre cropping, adapting practices and techniques previously developed for grains and other crops to a traditionally small-scale agricultural industry;
- adding mechanization to tradition in picking and processing grapes;
- a constant striving for productivity enhancement (e.g., through clonal selection and innovations in production and storage equipment);
- focused market research and deliberate market responsiveness;
- effective linking of production through to retail;
- modern distribution practices;
- conscious brand-building cachet;
- effective exploitation of media as a business resource;
- open-market capitalization;
- creating "shareholder value."

Naturally, corporatization has also broadened the definition of "market." Whatever the limits to the market ambitions of farmers, corporations see their market as global. However, in spite of this trend to corporatization, the wine industry remains highly fragmented as only 12.8% of the world's wine is produced by the top 10 wine companies (Shanken, 2003). Most of the world's wine is still produced and sold by small wine companies. This will continue to change as consolidation occurs in the future, but there will always be small, passionate producers of high-quality wine.

Constructive Industry Regulation

Regulation has also been a positive factor supporting the internationalization of the New World wine industry. In some cases this has amounted to officially conceived and validated quality assurance. In the Australian model, for example, the Australian Wine and Brandy Corporation (AWBC) applies a quality control system to reassure consumers (and the industry itself) that faulty or low-quality wine, or indeed dishonorable exporters, will not be allowed to damage their confidence in "brand Australia." No wine can be exported from Australia other than by a licensed exporter, and, as licenses are renewed annually, any holder behaving in any way that could bring the "brand" into question can quickly be removed.

Furthermore, no wine can be exported without an export approval number issued by the AWBC after the wine meets basic technical standards and is individually assessed and approved by an AWBC sensory assessment panel. The regulations are certainly onerous but widely applauded by the industry. Although the AWBC is the industry regulatory body created by federal statute, it is jointly administered with and funded by the industry. The effect of this model is that maximum creative freedom is provided for in the growing and production phase but the consumer is totally protected at the end point of wine in the bottle.

The Emergence of New Signature Varieties

Consumer imagination (and, ultimately, consumer loyalty) was stimulated by winemakers doing vastly different things with classic Old World grape varieties (such as Shiraz/Cabernet blends in Australia, Fume Blanc in California) and discovering new styles with less well-known varieties from Europe (such as Verdelho as a dry white table wine in Australia and Petite Sirah/Durif in California and Australia).

But consumer *loyalty* was most effectively forged with special "signature" varieties that have come to typify particular wine countries or wine regions: the locally evolved varieties, such as Zinfandel in California and Pinotage in South Africa, or the reinterpretation of some of the more obscure varieties, such as Carmenère in Chile, Malbec in Argentina, and Tannat in Uruguay. Even in Japan, a minor wine-producing nation, there is a new respect being won for its very own *V. vinifera* grape, Koshu, and determined efforts to build consumer loyalty behind the indigenous *V. amurensis* (wild mountain grape).

A more recent phenomenon has been the willingness of consumers in traditional wine markets to see beyond a generic national picture in New World wine countries and to delve down into the regional detail where particular specialties or specializations can be found. In Australia, for example, AWBC, the industry's governing body, now formally recognizes 110 zones, regions, and subregions across the continent under its Geographic Indications System (Wine Diva, 2002).

As of January, 2004, the US government recognizes 170 American Viticultural Areas (AVA) or appellations (Professional Friends of Wine, 2004). California is itself an appellation that has 90 subappellations within it—all the way from the Central Coast appellation (the largest), with 5,463,269 acres, down to Cole Valley appellation (the smallest) with only 187 acres (Professional Friends of Wine, 2004).

The Key Players

Corporatization of the wine industry business model had its origins in California, with the application to wine of the same business logic that had earlier transformed food processing—including the development and application of new technologies, the exploitation of economies of scale, national marketing and promotion strategies, and brand building. The early models included Mondavi, Gallo, and Sebastiani, family businesses that grew and transformed into more conventional corporate entities. This was relatively recent; it began in the 1970s and gathered pace quickly through the 1980s and 1990s.

A similar pattern emerged in Australia in the early 1980s when nonindustry money first appeared, with the takeover of the renowned Penfold wine business by the Adelaide Steamship Company, later to become Southcorp. BRL Hardy was another example, created when the Hardy family business merged with the large bulk wine operation of the largely grower-owned Berri Renmano and then listed on the Australian Stock Exchange, the first wine company to do so. Another example was the management buy-out of the Orlando wine business and, subsequently, its acquisition by French multinational Pernod Ricard—looking for a preestablished distribution base in Australia for its range of beverages.

Each of these companies, following further expansion and consolidation, and aggressive international market growth, grew quickly to join the ranks of top wine producers globally. In turn, as global wine companies they have developed global brands. The top 20 brands account for almost 7% of the global market for bottled still wine. This trend is particularly important for the New World wine companies in the top 10 as they, alone, account for 6% of the total market (Shanken, 2003) (see Table 1.2).

The early successes of the Californian and Australian wine corporations inspired similar business ventures in other New World locations—most notably in South Af-

Table 1.2. Top Global Wine Brands (2002 Global Market Share)

Rank	Brand	Company	Origin	Millions of 9-L Case Depletions	Percentage
1	Gallo/E.& J. Wine Cellars	E.&J. Gallo Winery	US	24.4	1.07%
2	Franzia	The Wine Group	US	21.3	0.94%
3	Carlo Rossi	E.&J. Gallo Winery	US	12.4	0.55%
4	Tavernello	Eavior Societa Cooperativa arl	Italy	10.7	0.47%
5	Almaden	Canandaigua Wine Co. (Constellation)	US	10.1	0.44%
6	Sutter Home	Trinchero Family Estates	US	7.7	0.34%
7	Woodbridge	The Robert Mondavi Corp.	US	7.4	0.33%
8	Beringer	Beringer Blass Wine Estates (Foster's)	US	6.7	0.30%
9	JP Chenet	Les Grands Chais de France	France	6.3	0.28%
10	Riunite	Cantine Cooperative Riunite Scrl	Italy	6.1	0.27%
11	Jacob's Creek	Pernod Ricard	Australia	5.9	0.26%
12	Concha y Toro	Vina Concha y Toro SA	Chile	5.2	0.23%
13	Lindemanns	Southcorp Wines	Australia	4.9	0.22%
14	Inglenook	Canandaigua Wine Co. (Constellation)	US	4.8	0.21%
15	Rosemount Estate	Southcorp Wines	Australia	4.3	0.19%
16	Vendange	Turner Road Vintners	US	4.3	0.19%
17	Peter Vella	E.&J. Gallo Winery	US	4	0.18%
18	Kendall-Jackson	Kendall-Jackson	US	3.8	0.17%
19	Fetzer	Brown-Forman Beverages Worldwide	US	3.6	0.16%
20	Corbett Canyon	The Wine Group	US	3.1	0.14%
			Total	156.7	6.91%

Source: Shanken (2003).

rica, following the progressive deregulation of the industry and the removal of the special status that had protected the national industry marketing monopoly (KWV), but also in Chile, Argentina, and New Zealand.

Table 1.3 shows that a significant proportion of world wine trade and worldwide wine production is accounted for by New World wine producers. In fact, almost 30% of the wine produced by the top 10 wine-producing countries is from the New World. However, only about 19% of the volume and value of their total exports originate in the New World. The table also shows that some New World countries, individually, export large portions of their production. Among the New World wine countries, both Australia and Chile have significant export volumes as a percentage of production.

The Old World Responds

As in any competitive business situation, the Old World of wine hasn't been watching the success of the New World wines without responding. In order to preserve the traditional ways, regulatory, trade, marketplace, and advertising steps have been initiated to combat the intrusion of the New World ways. These have served to moderate, but not prevent, the spread of the New World influence.

Through diplomatic negotiations and in international forums such as the World Trade Organization, the European Union (EU) has attempted to limit imports of New World wines produced with new techniques that challenge traditions in Europe. There have also been attempts to require labeling for wines sold in Europe that would restrict the use of certain geographical indicators on wine, the use of certain nomenclature on labels and in marketing, and a further attempt to restrict the use of certain bottle shapes claimed to be the right of various traditional locations. These efforts have been strongly challenged by most countries outside the EU and the battle may continue for many years.

Table 1.3. Top Wine-Producing Countries (2001 Data)

Country	Wine Production		Wine Exports		Wine Exports	
	Sequence	000 hl	Sequence	000 hl	Sequence	US $ (millions)
France	1	58243	2	17484	1	5800.6
Italy	2	51300	1	17983	2	2439.7
Spain	3	31127	3	11662	3	1346.1
US	4	23800	6	2839	6	511.2
Argentina	5	15796	12	1041	10	155.5
South Africa	6	10983	10	1653	9	230.4
Germany	7	9662	7	2488	8	368.1
Australia	8	9080	4	3750	4	901
Portugal	9	7015	9	1692	7	468.9
Chile	10	6000	5	3008	5	652.3
New World as % of top 10		29.4%		19.3%		19.0%

Source: Anderson and Norman (2003).

In contrast, some EU winemakers have actually embraced New World labeling standards and viticultural and winemaking innovations. There are now French wines being exported, for example, that feature the grape variety more prominently than the regional appellation. Italy is protecting its market position by strongly promoting the linkages between the food dishes of specific regions and the wines that have been traditionally associated with those foods. Interestingly, Italy is trying to win back some of its traditional heritage by labeling some of their Primitivo wines as Zinfandel. Finally, in an attempt to replicate many New World practices, some European wineries (and many new wineries in Asia and Eastern Europe) have employed New World winemakers and technical staff from Australia and the US. Today there are around 500 Australian-trained wine industry professionals working in Europe.

Opportunities and Challenges

The past two decades have seen rapid and substantial transformation of the wine industry globally, and the emergence of a whole new phalanx of industry leaders. The future will undoubtedly bring further changes. Some of the more significant opportunities and challenges are outlined below.

Production and Consumption Equilibrium

One of the major challenges for the industry in this period has been to achieve growth while maintaining demand and supply equilibrium. The output growth pattern is cyclical but, because of the considerable elapse of time between vineyard development and eventual wine release, each incremental supply response to a demand signal can extend into the medium term.

For white wines the supply response may be as short as 3 or maybe 4 years, but for red wines it could be as much as 8 years. As a result it is difficult to forecast and accurately match production growth and consumer demand. Accordingly, the industry is characterized by periods of over- and undersupply, with the attendant impact on prices and profitability.

Overall, consumption is growing slowly over the long term. This trend is more pronounced in the traditional markets, making the emerging markets, such as the more developed markets in Asia, of particular value to the industry. In the short term, wine consumption (and industry profitability) can also be impacted by one-off events such as New York City terrorist attacks of 2001 and the marked slowdown in travel and eating out that followed, as well as by the prevailing macroeconomic climate.

Continued Corporatization of the Global Wine Industry

Consolidation trends by major wine companies have slowly begun to show up in the industry, but the top 10 producers still only hold a 12.8% market share. This is in major contrast to the rest of the beverage industry. The wine industry is still one where passionate newcomers and small producers rule. New winery startups continue and new countries are entering the marketplace.

Success requires long-term commitment and financing. Many large wine businesses are still family owned and face succession challenges. Tax laws, inheritance laws, and general family business issues make this difficult. Also, as family companies get larger they tend to inherit corporate character.

Antialcohol Groups and "Sin Tax" Advocates

In some parts of the world the demand for wine—and, indeed, industry profitability—is impacted by community tolerance or even advocacy for regulatory, legal, and taxation hurdles to limit growth of the wine industry. This is particularly pronounced in the US, where existing controls on interstate trade and campaigns for further restrictions by neo-prohibitionists pose threats to the industry.

Elsewhere, alcohol is often viewed as a luxury or at least a nonessential purchase by many governments, thus making it an easy target for taxation. Prices are artificially driven upward, impacting on demand and, in some cases, industry profits.

Continued Globalization of the Wine Industry

There is a substantial and growing global market in bulk wine, allowing inexpensive wines to be bottled in many locales (J. O'Neill, 2004) The largest wine companies have moved to global operational models where marketing decisions may be centralized and wine production is localized. Global wine corporations, such as Torres, Mondavi, Beringer Blass, Gallo, Kendall Jackson, Constellation/Hardy, and Southcorp, all operate in this way. A relatively recent trend has seen many of the larger global players committing to indigenous wine production (either as new businesses or through acquisition) in a range of countries as a means of more effectively expanding global market share and global presence.

New Wine Producers in Asia

The market for wine in Asia and, indeed, domestic production to meet this demand is growing at a rapid pace, though from a small base. Wine emulating contemporary Western styles is now made using modern winemaking facilities in 10 countries in Asia. There are now at least 700 wineries throughout Asia, many of them making wine at the higher end of quality expectations (Gastin, forthcoming). Half of them are in China, in 26 provinces, and over a quarter in Japan. The remainders are spread sparsely over the continent, from India to Indonesia—including Thailand, Korea, and Vietnam. Fledgling operations can even be found in Taiwan, Sri Lanka, and Bhutan.

As in so many other arenas, China has rapidly emerged as a global wine giant in its own right. It now has the eighth largest viticultural area in the world, with almost 300,000 hectares of vines, of which at least 50,000 hectares are conventional wine grapes, and is the world's 11th largest wine producer (Office International de la Vigne et du Vin [OIV], 1995–2000; Stevenson, 2004). Strong domestic consumption growth is the primary driver but, increasingly, export opportunities are opening up for the better and larger Asian producers.

Conclusion

The foregoing is a chapter in the history of the industry, but time does not stand still. There are already new trends emerging in the industry that will write future chapters. One of these is the likely extinction of the sharp boundaries between "old" and "new" that have been a feature of the past three decades. In the fifth edition of *The World Atlas of Wine* Hugh Johnson writes: "It was I, I confess, who coined this now much-maligned wine world split. Times have changed. Much of the 'Old World' has become 'New'; a little of the 'New' is deemed to be 'old' " (Johnson & Robinson, 2001, p. 6).

The creation of this new book should add to the body of knowledge of a recent business phenomenon and, in so doing, contribute to the mobility of good business practice for the benefit of those in the world of wine wherever they may be now.

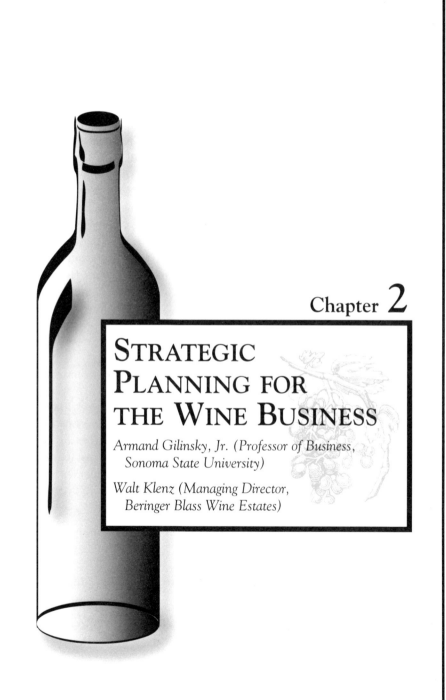

Chapter 2

STRATEGIC PLANNING FOR THE WINE BUSINESS

Armand Gilinsky, Jr. *(Professor of Business, Sonoma State University)*

Walt Klenz *(Managing Director, Beringer Blass Wine Estates)*

Case Vignette

How did Foster's Brewing Group, Australia's biggest brewer, come to make a name for itself in the wine industry? The answer: via acquisitions.

While during the 1990s beer consumption around the world was declining by 1–2% a year, consumption of premium wines (those costing over $5 a bottle) had been rising steadily—by over 7% a year in Britain and America. In 1996, Foster's purchased its first wine company, Mildara Blass of Australia. In August 2000, Foster's announced that it would buy 125-year-old California's Beringer Wine Estates for $1.5 billion. Beringer Wine Estates was subsequently merged with Foster's existing wine business, Mildara Blass, and renamed, in April 2001, Beringer Blass Wine Estates ("Beringer Blass"). In 2001, Foster's bought Napa Valley producer Etude Wines and 51% of New Zealand's Matua Valley Wines. In 2002, Foster's acquired Carmenet from Chalone Wine Group. Wine grew steadily to a current 40% of Foster's profits.

Beringer Blass sought to create new centers of excellence by segmenting its wine businesses into Trade, Services, and Clubs divisions. "The integration of the Beringer and Blass international operations is progressing well with initial synergies expected to be realized in 2002," according to the Foster's *Annual Report*. However, Beringer Blass remained behind such industry giants as Gallo and Constellation brands for market share leadership. Moreover, increasingly difficult trading conditions and imbalances of wine grape supply and demand impacted the wine business in 2002. Recent trends signaled accelerating worldwide consolidation, slowing growth, and market maturation in the premium wine industry.

Was Beringer Blass on the right track to becoming the first global wine business?

The overriding objective of this chapter is to provide the *questions* you need to ask to make the right decisions about the future of your wine business. Strategic management entails generating choices to be made among competing alternatives to produce a competitive advantage and earn above-average returns. Rapid technological change, mergers and acquisitions, increasing pressures for globalization, and changing local environments for wine businesses have heightened the urgency to ask the right *questions* about the future, such as:

- Which distinctive competencies should we be developing for our businesses?
- Where should we compete?
- How do we communicate our strategy to our stakeholders?

The central issue for strategic planning is the question of under what conditions does it make sense to attempt to transform a small business into a larger business, particularly in a maturing industry like the wine industry. That is, does size matter?

Positioning for Success

Much of the practice of strategic management is concerned with the relative performance of rival firms and the sustainability of the differences in performance over time. After all, industries vary greatly in the similarity of their firms in terms of strategies pursued. Some industries, such as the forest products and agricultural com-modity-producing industries, are very homogeneous in terms of marketing efforts, R&D expenses, or capital intensity (as measured by the ratio of assets to sales). Other industries tend to be very heterogeneous, comprising multiple strategic groups, such as insurance, pharmaceuticals, and automobile parts. Differences in performance can also be explained by the ability to adapt to or lead change amidst uncontrollable external forces (e.g., social/demographic, economic, political/regulatory, industry/competition, and technology).

While normally one thinks of a growth strategy in the context of emerging or growth stages in the industry life cycle (because these phases are where the most highly publicized start-ups occur), entry can take place in the mature phase of the life cycle as well. Maturing industries are characterized by slowing growth, diminish-ing innovation, more product and process improvements, more sophisticated cus-tomers, and increasing concentration of producers. In a maturing industry, growth niches for firms that are successful in differentiating a commodity product or sup-port service still exist. Famous examples of this strategy in consumer products in-dustries include Perdue Chicken and Orville Redenbacher Popcorn. These firms suc-ceeded in branding commodity products and achieving leading positions in their respective markets. They hold differentiated positions, and both enjoy the higher margins derived from the premium prices that they are able to charge. One outcome of a maturing industry is asset concentration and pursuit of *economies of scale*. Other firms have considered *innovation and focus* strategies as keys to their success.

The same holds true for the wine industry. The California wine industry, for ex-ample, is a regionally visible and important industry that is experiencing strong glo-bal competition in the face of a stable to declining customer base. Two important trends in the California wine industry are worth noting here: 1) a tendency toward consolidation and asset concentration among some industry participants, and 2) the emergence of niche players with specific product/customer targets.

The industry has moved towards higher industry concentration via consolidation and experiencing, in the aggregate, slowing growth, though certain premium wine segments appear attractive. As Allan Hemphill, formerly of Associated Vintage Group, noted, "Grapes have become a commodity—to be identified with the ground is no longer important. With so many competing uses of capital, many wineries have be-gun outsourcing as a conscious strategy . . . the future of the industry will be domi-nated by those who think differently. Those products that will succeed are those that taste good and are priced right" (Gilinsky & Campbell, 2000, p. 132). Absent a cost leadership advantage, differentiation of what has become a commodity product is indeed the key to success in the wine industry.

Competitive Forces

Porter's (1985) "Five Forces" analysis assesses industry attractiveness and factors influencing competitor power. These forces include: 1) intensity of competitive ri-valry among sellers; 2) threat of entry of new competitors; 3) threat of substitute products; 4) supplier bargaining power; and 5) buyer bargaining power. The follow-ing sections describe how each of these forces is played out in the wine industry.

Rivalry Among Competing Sellers: Moderately High

Rivalry in the premium wine industry is increasing because of the proliferation of domestic and international wine brands available for purchase at both on-premises (hotels, airlines, restaurants) and off-premises (specialty wine shops, supermarkets and hypermarkets, grocery stores, and direct sales via tasting rooms and the Internet) points-of-sale. The cost to switch brands for trade intermediates and consumers is low. Customers have a wide spectrum of appellations of origin, varietals, and brand choices. The US wine industry is composed of approximately 1500 wineries and the top 10 wineries account for 70% of US production. Imports from New World wine producers such as Australia increase competition. The US wine industry is highly regulated, prohibiting direct sales to consumers in all but 13 states. Outside the US, import restrictions to protect domestic producers and tariffs deter US producers' entry into export markets. Building knowledge of export markets' legal, distribution, and trade channels takes time and is costly. Conglomerate corporations increase rivalry by purchasing brands and leveraging their access to distribution channels to make them viable market contenders. On the other hand, smaller wineries can create a surge in demand through quality control and limited release of high-end, high-priced labels.

Threat of Entry of New Competitors: Moderate to Low

There is a moderate-to-low entry threat of new competitors due to increasing barriers to entry: capital intensity and government regulation. In addition, access to distribution is restricted (via the "three-tier" distribution system). In this environment, the only way for companies to grow market share is to take it away from a competitor, which intensifies rivalry. Mobility and exit barriers are also increasing due to the high multiples paid for acquiring wineries, the limited reusability of winemaking equipment for other purposes, and in some cases, a long family history of involvement with a particular brand.

Threat of Substitute Products: Moderate to High

Numerous substitute products compete with wine for the "dinner table segment" of beverages. Direct substitutes include alcoholic beverages from numerous varieties of beers to spirits. Indirect substitutes include nonalcoholic beverages that compete with wine such as carbonated drinks, water, juices, flavored noncarbonated drinks, teas, and coffees. Direct and indirect beverage substitutes create high competitive pressure because both trade intermediates and end-consumers have so many available choices. For the serious wine lover (enophile), however, there is, of course, no substitute for wine.

Supplier Bargaining Power and Supplier–Seller Collaboration: Moderate

The competitive pressures are moderate from suppliers (grape growers) because although they have the ability to give larger customers a competitive advantage, grape supply is abundant relative to demand. Large conglomerates that have a portfolio of many brands in the wine industry as well as large volumes of case production are able to leverage their buying power of raw materials: grapes and grape juice. This is accomplished via: 1) vertical integration into ownership of vineyards, 2) volume purchases from growers, and 3) capability to balance long-term contracts with growers with purchases on the spot market as growing conditions and harvest yields change. This, in turn, lowers their cost of goods, increases economies of scale, and places smaller competitors at a relative disadvantage.

Buyer Bargaining Power and Seller–Buyer Collaboration: Trade—High; Consumer—High

In the wine industry, trade intermediates have increasing clout due to consolidation of distribution channels. Consolidation among distribution and retail channels has augured dramatic changes in the wine industry. Today, six major distributors control more than half of the market for wine in the US. That more and more wine is now sold through supermarkets has also worked in favor of branded wines. Large wine conglomerates such as Beringer Blass can now promise to supply a range of branded wines—alongside other beverages from Foster's—in sufficient quantities to supply entire supermarket chains. US retail consolidation is being led by discount retailers such as Costco, Wal-Mart, and Trader Joe's. Because the majority of wine sales are in supermarkets (41%), these intermediates have the ability to choose brands to sell with extreme selectivity. The intermediates' goals are to have quick turnover, generate the highest possible margin, and not to necessarily carry the most prestigious brands. Specialty store intermediates (that hold 23% of all wine sales) tend to have more influence on selecting higher-margin, prestige brands because their customers are more educated and wine oriented. Switching costs are very low, prompting trade buyers to seek the most profitable and fastest selling brands.

The increasing role of drinks conglomerates in the wine industry signals that:

- The wine industry has evolved into a two-tier industry: few producers (highly concentrated) at the low end, and many producers (highly fragmented) at the premium end.
- The game for premium wineries is beginning to change, from protecting a niche in a highly fragmented growth market to capturing greater share of a rapidly consolidating and maturing market.

Driving Forces: Is the Wine Industry Attractive?

The wine industry has become a two-tier market: premium and low end. Relative to the low-end segment, the premium segment of the wine industry remains attractive due to above-average growth rates and fragmentation. The "five forces" analysis above indicates that on the whole, attractiveness of the premium wine segment remains high, although costs of entry are increasing. Concomitant needs for brand power and brand differentiation also restrict access. The low-end segment is unattractive due to flat sales and intense competition for market share from the major low-price producers, such as E.&J. Gallo, JFJ Bronco, Constellation, and The Wine Group. Figure 2.1 illustrates the mapping of industry attractiveness.

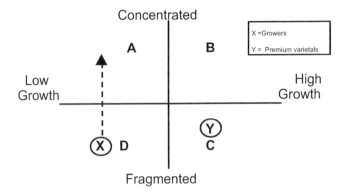

Figure 2.1. Mapping attractiveness of the wine industry. (A) Competition is stable, market characterized by few dominant large players. Barriers to entry often regulatory and financial. Success sustained by raising barriers to entry. (B) Competition is intense, aggressive. Limited number of players due to regulatory or financial barriers. Rapid growth presents opportunities for niche players to thrive. (C) Competition is intense due to chaotic market conditions and jockeying for position. Niche players have greatest opportunities for success if they can defend their niche(s). (D) Companies are highly vulnerable to market fluctuations and competitive forces. Not a long-term viable segment. **Reasons:** The industry is fragmented. Everyone is fighting for market share. There are high barriers to entry. There is a long period of development—approximately 6 years.

What Are Some of the Driving Forces?

- The scope of the wine industry is changing from domestic to international. This has been driven primarily by Australian exporters (such as BRL Hardy, Beringer Blass, and Southcorp).
- Retail/wholesale channels are undergoing consolidation. The increasing buyer power of trade intermediates drives scale.
- Industry leadership is being contested in both low-end and premium wine market segments. This drives increasing investment to build brand equity.
- Competitors are striving for critical mass to compete with larger players: 1) capital, 2) human talent, and 3) access to markets.
- Large drink companies are well placed to compete. Global distribution networks are already in place, providing: 1) access to wholesalers/retailers, 2) knowledge of customer/market dynamics, 3) portfolio efficiencies such as cost reduction through portfolio scale (in working with distributors and retailers), and 4) consumer understanding (depth of brand-building experience by large drink conglomerates).
- Global alcoholic beverage companies (such as Allied Domecq, Brown-Forman, Diageo, and Foster's) compete in "flat" markets for their "legacy" beer and/or spirits product lines. Each seeks higher growth markets for premium wines to diversify their portfolios. Yet, is bigger necessarily better? The next section takes up this question.

The Pros and Cons of Diversification

Michael Porter (1985) offers three tests for successful diversification based on the likelihood of increasing shareholder value. These tests are for: 1) industry attractiveness, 2) cost-of-entry, and 3) the "better off" or synergy test. Each of these is described for the wine industry in Table 2.1.

The premium wine segment is attractive. Although entry costs are high (and give no indications of abating), any planned acquisition needs to offer immediate profits as well as prospective double-digit growth. The major question mark is whether or not a business will be, indeed, "better off." That is, when will the sum of the acquired parts exceed the whole (synergy)? The short answer to this question is: "not immediately."

Potential advantages have been identified as economies of scale in distribution, learning curve effects, and increased capacity utilization. However, sharing resources transnationally will not come without attendant incremental costs. The potential incremental costs include coordination costs (such as scheduling the shared resource or transferring an item of know-how) and compromise costs (the fact that a resource currently employed exclusively by one unit will be compromised somewhat as its use is extended to another). The basic challenges for a diversifying wine business, then, are fourfold:

Table 2.1. Pros and Cons of Wine Industry Diversification

Porter's Test	Pro	Con
Industry attractiveness?	•Double-digit growth of premium segment •High fragmentation in 1990s	•Growth is slowing •Consolidation is increasing
Cost of entry?	•US$1.7 billion is relatively small price to pay for potential to become largest wine company in the world •Immediate sales growth and profit potential	•Highly uncertain future ROIs of wine segment versus beer segments •Future profit potential: likely to be constrained by costs of exporting wine; downward pricing pressures due to lackluster US and world economy; looming overcapacity in premium segment
Better off?	•Potential synergies in marketing •Clout in distribution channels	•Increased debt service costs and financial risk •High mobility barriers due to increasing costs of land and capital equipment •Wineries command high multiples for acquisition •High exit barriers

1. *Determine the areas of synergy* (i.e., leveraging wine-growing and winemaking technology and innovation across brands, brand marketing experience, access to distributors, or knowledge of export markets).

2. *Identify advantages that can be gained* from those synergies (i.e., ability to offset seasonal gluts or shortages in grape supply, product innovation and new brand development, or cultivation of new customer segments from marginal or non-wine drinkers).

3. *Quantify costs associated with leveraging synergies* across those activities or resources (i.e., identifying new staff requirements to manage an increasingly diverse portfolio of brands across continents, determining where duplication of effort can be minimized, or evaluating potential erosion of specialization and market focus as smaller acquired brands become integrated into the portfolio).

4. *Determine whether the advantages sufficiently outweigh the costs* to attain and sustain cost or differentiation advantages (i.e., the true appeal of a wine business portfolio that has brands in multiple segments to distributors and retailers; the capability to manufacture increasingly higher quality wines while simultaneously satisfying the needs and palates of a larger, more diverse customer base; the potential to cross-sell wine clubs and tasting rooms to wine consumers, etc.).

What are the hallmarks of a successful diversification? It is widely agreed that long-term stock appreciation is one. An enhanced reputation is another good indicator. Other positive signs include growing customer rolls, rising customer satisfaction and employee retention, and, of course, better earnings, though merger charges frequently depress earnings in the short term. Bottom line: the markets want a merger to make money, for the company *and* for shareholders.

Jeffrey Marshall (2001), writing in the *Financial Executive*, noted:

[In] large corporations, especially, it takes virtually Solomonic wisdom to create a structure that gives both parties equal say in how the combined entity is run. Many "mergers of equals" are perceived, in fact, as defensive mergers accentuating size rather than skill, and quite a few CEOs and CFOs have refused to do them. Indeed, many mega-mergers suffer from sagging employee morale as workers fret about job cuts and business realignments. At upper management levels, especially, things get very dicey—how many companies need two CFOs? When big deals are announced, a lot of worry translates into less work getting done, poorer customer service and a stock that drops, even if analysts and regulators bless the deal, which they often do. (p. 28)

According to Stephen J. Wall (2001), in acquisitions that do fulfill their promise—that really make two and two equal five—leaders paid a great deal of attention to the integration process and, not surprisingly, involved people at all levels of the process. When studying successful acquirers—the most prominent among them Cisco Systems Inc.—a number of best practices emerge. These primarily focus on involving all key stakeholders and taking the time to do the deal correctly. It is also important to develop a systematic, flexible integration process, and get people talking so that the issue of "what will happen to me" is addressed early. This helps people to commit to the merger process.

Globalization Alternatives

A wine business contemplating globalization must make decisions regarding: 1) the need to balance cost and the multibrands/multipositioning sides of its business model; 2) the need to be responsive to local market versus global market characteristics; 3) which overseas markets to enter; 4) when to enter those markets; and 5) on what scale to enter those markets.

The advantages and disadvantages of various strategies (international, multidomestic, global, and transnational) for competing globally should be weighed (see Table 2.2). The appropriateness of the strategies varies given the extent of pressures for cost reductions and local responsiveness. International and global strategies tend to be least appropriate in markets where local responsiveness to consumer tastes is important (e.g., in consumer food and beverage products industries, with the possible exception of sodas, beer, and spirits). At the same time, in the wine industry, competitive conditions are so intense that, to survive, companies must essentially do all they can to respond to pressures for cost reductions and local responsiveness. Table 2.2 illustrates some of the advantages and disadvantages of different strategies for competing globally. Yet changing a company's business model to build an organization capable of supporting a transnational strategy is a complex and challenging task: implementation problems associated with creating the requisite organizational structure and control systems are well documented.

The strength of the local business environment and the dynamism of a particular location together combine to provide opportunity for creating a multinational wine business. For example, Foster's country–level strategy (which is a hybrid of global and transnational) has led to economies of scope—supply chain and marketing intelligence—as well as financial structure, production, and distribution synergies within Australia. In addition, they were able to attain market power in the popular premium and ultra-premium wine market segments. This is due to four major factors:

1. *Factors of production*—Wine is a unique commodity. Wine production involves art and science, a blend of individual creativity and innovative technology. Wine is marketed by the geographical location of production and quality is associated with designated wine-growing regions (appellations) and designated grape types (varietals). Consumers expect wine from a particular region to possess unique qualities that differentiate it from other wines of the same varietal grown in different regions. Thus, the factors of production are highly determined by geographical location and environmental conditions.

2. *Demand conditions*—There is growing demand in wine consumption in certain regions due to the following factors: wine is considered a complement to food consumption; demographic trends leading to an overall increase in the wine-consuming population (aging baby boomers with increasing disposable income); the ever-growing introduction of wine to popu-

Table 2.2. Strategic Alternatives for Globalizing Wine Ventures

Strategy	Advantages	Disadvantages	Does My Strategy...
International	•Transfer of distinctive competencies to foreign markets	•Lack of local responsiveness •Inability to realize location economies •Failure to exploit experience-curve effects	•respond to needs for cost reductions? •respond to pressures for local responsiveness in the wine segment?
Multidomestic	•Ability to customize product offerings and marketing in accordance with local responsiveness	•Inability to realize location economies •Failure to exploit experience-curve effects •Failure to transfer distinctive competencies to foreign markets	•meet needs for localization in wine segment but does not address needs for cost reductions?
Global	•Ability to exploit experience-curve effects •Ability to realize location economies	•Lack of local responsiveness	•make sense for my segment but not (yet) for future segments? •meet pressures for cost reductions?
Transnational	•Ability to exploit experience-curve effects •Ability to exploit location economies •Ability to customize product offerings and marketing in accordance with local responsiveness •Ability to reap benefits of local learning	•Difficulties in implementation because of organizational problems	•meet pressures for cost reductions and local responsiveness?

lous Asian countries; and a general flattening of prices due to a glut in grape supply.

3. *Related and supporting industries*—The wine industry is closely related to the spirits and beer industries. They can share the same or similar distri-

bution channels and be segmented based on market demand into economy, subpremium, popular premium, and superpremium brands. As spirits, beer and wine are all alcoholic beverage products; they can be considered close substitutes for one another.

4. *Firm strategy, structure, and rivalry*—The wine industry has a high intensity of rivalry due to the proliferation of small and large wineries all over the world. The medium size winery is thus threatened by consolidation of larger wineries and their inability to compete with large wineries on the basis of low cost or with smaller wineries on the basis of quality or other differentiation attributes. Moreover, the wine industry relies heavily on backward integration to support a differentiation strategy; most premium wineries grow their own grapes and carefully control quality.

The above country-level stimuli and resources can be illustrated by the dynamics of competition among countries competing for global domination of the wine industry. Not all nations are created equal in terms of growing conditions for grapes, and not all cultures are attractive markets for wine made from those grapes (e.g., Asian markets have been particularly slow to change their cultural habits to include wine at the dinner table). The "Old World" wine-growing (and high-consumption) countries of Europe have held a historic competitive advantage in terms of perceived quality, which may or may not still hold true, at least, according to several leading wine trade magazines mentioned in the case. The "New World" wine producers in the US, Australia, New Zealand, South America, and South Africa would certainly argue that they are catching up to (and in some instances overtaking) the European producers in wine quality. In terms of consumption, Europe clearly remains the largest market for wine. Yet the New World wine producers (with the sole exception of the US) have vastly smaller domestic markets for wine. Naturally, the New World producers are eager to leverage their learning into global markets, in particular using favorable (until the end of 2000, at least) conditions in the public equities markets to finance growth.

How Does My Wine Business Stack Up?

With regards to analyzing the current situation and selecting future strategies, a business will want to use a SWOT (Strengths, Weaknesses, Opportunities, and Threats) Matrix, which is developed in many leading strategic management and entrepreneurship texts. Table 2.3 shows the SWOT analysis for Beringer Blass Wine Estates as of late 2002.

If there indeed is a race to become the first global wine company, it can be argued that Beringer is now in a much stronger position to succeed than it was before the merger with Foster's. Given the current uncertain trading environment for the wine industry and inevitable decline of incremental growth rates (from double digit) in the premium segment, Beringer's best route to leadership is likely to be found via continued portfolio additions. It is therefore likely that Foster's will continue to be a buyer or could itself be bought out by the likes of a larger conglomerate such as Diageo.

Table 2.3. Sample SWOT Analysis for Beringer Blass Wine Estates

Strengths	Weaknesses
•Long history in wine business •Recognized, award-winning brands •Foster's "deep pockets" and marketing capabilities •Established multicountry organization and management team •Low-cost leadership	•Capital intensity •Inability to develop core "global" brand(s) •Expansion strains management information systems for control and coordination •No global brand yet •Margin erosion in premium segment
Opportunities	**Threats**
•Glut of grape supply lowers raw materials prices •Educating a new generation of wine consumers •Continued market share growth via acquisition of well-established wine brands •Diversification into complementary "lifestyle" branded products •Higher margins from direct sales via tasting rooms and Internet	•Aging base and heterogeneous tastes of wine consumers •Economic downturns, declining tourism and on-premise sales •Intense price competition for off-premise (retail) sales •Consolidation of distribution channels, trade barriers •Government restrictions on direct sales •Industry entering slower growth phase of life cycle

Yet rival firms also have global intentions and strategies, and will also seek part-ners to preempt other competitors from achieving leadership first. It seems reason-able to expect that Beringer Blass will not be alone in the hunt. Allied Domecq, Brown-Forman, Constellation, Diageo, and E.&J. Gallo will likely pursue continued diversifi-cation via acquisition of other premium wineries. Potential acquisition candidates include Kendall-Jackson, Robert Mondavi, and Southcorp, any of which would ben-efit from a cross-border partner to leverage products into distribution channels. Be-ing first to globalization will not necessarily imply that a business has become the largest or the best. Indeed, it is unlikely that the "winner," if there ever is one, will arrive at the finish line alone.

In any event, the true winners of globalization will be wine consumers, who will enjoy access to increasingly high-quality wines at lower prices.

Is Bigger Really Better?

Though globalization is a reality in the wine industry, thousands of small family wineries still thrive in the New and Old World, and are highly successful in selling their wine locally or only within one country. This is possible because they are imple-menting a "niche" wine business strategy, which focuses on small case production of specialized grape varietals, appellations, customized brands, or other differentiation strategies utilized by small wineries. Traveling throughout Canada, the US, Chile, Argentina, Australia, New Zealand, and South Africa, a visitor will happen upon dozens of these small, thriving boutique wineries. The visitor is delighted to "discover such a jewel of a winery," and will buy the wine and proudly share it with friends. This direct marketing strategy, focusing on networking, memorable experiences with the customer, and capitalizing on local wine tourism, will always be a viable strategy, as long as the winery remains a "niche strategy" player. A good example of this is Jordan Winery in Sonoma County, which produces premium Cabernet Sauvignon in a small case production. Though encouraged many times to expand, Jordan has remained adamant in its specialized niche strategy. Figure 2.2 illustrates this concept of the strategy grid.

A second position on the wine strategy grid is the "mid-player." This strategy involves focusing on specific grape varietals and appellations, but producing larger quantities—200,000 to 500,000 cases—and selling in multiple markets (usually within at least two or more countries). This is a complex strategy to implement, which calls for much balancing of growth against assets. Companies utilizing this strategy must have strong and distinctive brands, efficient operating models, and a relentless focus on quality. There are fewer players in this area, because it is difficult to achieve economies of scale and high-quality levels at mid-size production rates. Successful examples of this strategy in the US include Sebastiani and Bonnie Doon, among others. Both wineries are well established with old, successful vineyards. More importantly, however, is the strength of their brand—Sebastiani on its quality, and Bonnie Doon on its creative and appealing marketing strategy, matched to tasteful wines.

The third major strategy is that of global player or "mogul," which is the choice of Beringer Blass and its competitors. Obviously, a characteristic of this strategy is to

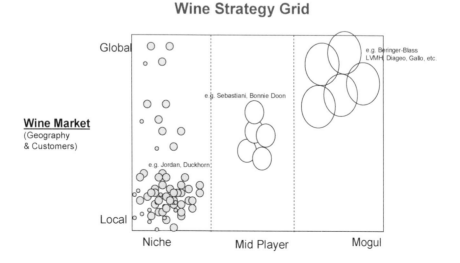

Figure 2.2. Wine strategy grid.

constantly be seeking successful brands from the niche and mid-player ranks. This suggests a fourth strategy for wine businesses—that of building a strong and prestigious brand, in order to sell it to a global player in an attempt to be global and gain economies of scope. Etude, one of the most recent acquisitions of Beringer Blass, is a good example of this. A small, luxury winery producing exquisite Pinot Noir and Merlot, Etude didn't have the resources to distribute globally. After being acquired by Beringer Blass, the Etude brand is now available in more than 20 countries. Another highly successful model is Cloudy Bay in New Zealand. Though they only produce a small number of cases of wine, they are distributed globally by their parent, LVMH.

The wine strategy grid illustrates the three general strategies wineries may pursue, but there are always some exceptions or hybrids. One of the most compelling questions this grid elicits is "when do you cross the *invisible line* of moving from one strategy to another?" Unfortunately, this is a case production and brand number that is always changing. The best advice is to utilize clear financial models to ensure that debt levels do not overshadow potential revenue streams in a mad pursuit for growth. In the end, bigger is not always better. It just depends on your wine business strategy.

Conclusion

Globalization, rapid technology, and product/service life cycle changes and industry consolidation greatly impact wine businesses. Such external forces dictate that wine businesses develop growth strategies with the highest potential for value creation and associated risk, or be eventually forced to exit from the market. These dynamics are particularly important for the emerging "New World" wine industry. The New World wine industry was founded and has been dominated for over a century by family-owned and family-run businesses. However, that domination has recently been challenged by the purchase of family wineries by alcohol beverage conglomerates that not only provide "liquidity events" for the family owners, but also seek to professionalize the industry in the wake of the external environmental challenges. How to compete successfully in the wake of industry consolidation, globalization, and hiring of professional management will become of increasingly significant importance to the wine business. The time to prepare is now.

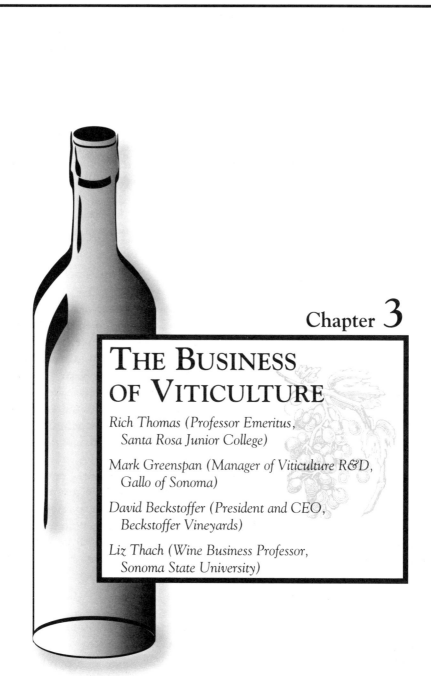

Chapter 3

THE BUSINESS
OF VITICULTURE

*Rich Thomas (Professor Emeritus,
Santa Rosa Junior College)*

*Mark Greenspan (Manager of Viticulture R&D,
Gallo of Sonoma)*

*David Beckstoffer (President and CEO,
Beckstoffer Vineyards)*

*Liz Thach (Wine Business Professor,
Sonoma State University)*

The sight of a vineyard stretching green and verdant along a hillside during harvest is uplifting to behold, especially one that is heavy with fruit and has the potential of creating good wine and a healthy financial reward for the vineyard owner. However, the green of the vineyard doesn't always translate to positive cash flow, as multiple variables come into play regarding the business of viticulture.

This chapter describes some of the basic viticulture issues from a business perspective. It begins with an overview of vineyard selection considerations, including information on appellations, the major types of grape varietals, regulations, and zoning. From there a discussion of the planting issues is presented, including prepping the vineyard, installing irrigation and trellising, and planting the vines. Next, an overview of the annual vineyard management process is provided, with a description of the seasonal growth cycle of the vine as well as farming processes to support it. Finally, some of the current issues facing viticulture in the New World, as well as future issues, are presented. The chapter concludes with an example of how a world-class vineyard is managed at Beckstoffer Vineyards.

Vineyard Selection

In selecting a vineyard location, the most important considerations are *climate and soil*. Though wine grapes can be grown in many parts of the world, there are certain locations that are considered to be ideal. These are referred to as the five Mediterranean regions of the world, namely: 1) the European Mediterranean region (Italy, France, and Spain); 2) the North Coast of California (near Napa, Sonoma, Lake, and Mendocino counties); 3) the South Coast of Australia (near Adelaide); 4) the Central Coast of Chile (between Santiago and Talca); and 5) the central coast of South Africa. These regions all have warm dry summers and cool wet winters, which are excellent climates for growing grapes. Obviously, four of these five regions are found in what are considered to be New World wine countries.

Soil is also important, in that grapes thrive best in slightly rocky soils with a certain balance of acid and nitrogen. For example, soils that have too much clay are more difficult for vines to grow. On the other hand, soils that are too rich in nutrients do not stress the vine enough, so the quality of the fruit is not as intense. Therefore, consideration of soil is very important in vineyard selection. However, in certain cases, it is possible to augment the soil with appropriate nutrients and additional soil amendments to make it more palatable for wine grapes.

The Issue of Appellation

An obvious business consideration regarding vineyard selection is the cost of the land. Vineyard real estate costs are usually dictated by *appellation*. An appellation is a designated wine grape growing region of the world that is defined by soil, mountain ranges, bodies of water, and weather. In the US appellation is often referred to as an AVA, or American Viticultural Area, and must be approved by the government. For example, in Sonoma County, there are currently 13 approved AVAs, ranging from Rockpile, Dry Creek, and Alexander Valley in the north, to Russian River near the coast, and Sonoma Valley and Carneros in the southern part of the county. Grapes from vineyards in these specific appellations can usually demand more money, because the appellation has been verified as an ideal place to grow a specific type of grape varietal. For example, Pinot Noir grapes from the Russian River can usually demand more money per ton than Pinot Noir grapes from other AVAs in different parts of California.

Famous appellations in other parts of the New World include some of the following: 1) Australia is well known for the Barossa Valley, McLaren Vale, and the Adelaide Hills; 2) New Zealand is famous for the Marlborough region; 3) Chile is well known for its Maipo, Rapel, and Maule valleys; 4) Argentina is best known for the Mendoza region, where more than 90% of its grapes are grown; 5) South Africa is famous for the Cape region; and 6) Canada for the Okanagan Valley in British Columbia and its Ontario region for excellent ice wines.

Obviously the more famous an appellation, such as the Rutherford in the Napa Valley, the more expensive the price of land. For example, recent prices for Napa vineyard land range from $50,000 to $200,000 per acre. In the Barossa Valley of Australia undeveloped vineyard land ranges from $20,000 to $60,000 per hectare (1 hectare equals 2.47 acres), but that doesn't include the cost of water, which would amount to another $5,000 to $7,000 per hectare. In Bordeaux, France, vineyard land has been sold at ranges of $200,000 to $600,000 per hectare. Though vineyard land fluctuates based on the location and the amount of grapes on the market, land in famous appellations will always be sold at a premium.

Which Grape Varietal to Grow?

Appellation also dictates, to some extent, the type of grape varietals to grow. This is because the climate and soil in a specific appellation are usually appropriate for growing certain varieties of grapes. For example, the Napa Valley is famous for its Cabernet Sauvignon grapes; and Dry Creek Valley in Sonoma County is famous for its Zinfandel grapes. This is because each of these appellations has the perfect mixture of soil, sun, and moisture to nurture these specific types of grapes to a state of high perfection. Indeed, appellation is so important that in some countries, such as France, the government actually dictates the varieties of grapes that can be grown in each appellation.

Though it is possible to grow other types of grapes in an appellation that is known for only one or two varieties of grapes—by modifying the soil and other scientific methods—"Mother Nature" still dictates, for the most part, where specific grapes should be grown. Table 3.1 illustrates some of the specific grape varietals that are famous in New World countries.

Therefore, when selecting a vineyard site, it is important to be aware of what type of grape variety one wants to grow, because the variety can dictate where to buy land. The choices in varieties are also complex, as there are more than 1000 different types of grapes in the world. The most famous ones, however, descend from *Vitis vinfera*, a Mediterranean vine used for most of the famous vineyards and wines in the world. Of these, the most well-known white is Chardonnay, the Queen of Grapes; and the most well-known red is Cabernet Sauvignon, the King of Grapes. Other famous white grapes include: Sauvignon Blanc, Johannisberg Riesling, Viognier, Chenin Blanc, Pinot Gris (or Grigio), Gewürztraminer, Sémillon, and Muscat. Other famous red grapes include: Pinot Noir, Merlot, Malbec, Syrah (or Shiraz), Cabernet Franc, Zinfandel, Sangiovese, Tempranillo, Barbera, and Petite Syrah.

Table 3.1. Famous Grape Varietals in
New World Countries

Country	Grape Varietal
Argentina	Malbec
Australia	Shiraz
Canada	Vidal Blanc
Chile	Carmenère
New Zealand	Sauvignon Blanc
South Africa	Pinotage
US—Napa	Cabernet Sauvignon
US—Sonoma	Zinfandel

Grape Regulations

In the New World, wines are usually listed by their varietal name on the front of the bottle. However, the percentage of grape variety that goes into the bottle is usually determined by government regulation within the country. In many New World countries, at least 85% of the grapes must be of the variety listed on the label; however, this varies by country. For example, in the US at least 75% of the grapes must be of the variety listed on the bottle. If the bottle says "Chardonnay," then at least 75% of the grapes must be Chardonnay grapes, but the other 25% may be Chenin Blanc, Sémillon, or another variety. However, if the bottle also states that the grapes are estate grown and bottled, then 100% of the grapes must be grown on the estate. Another grape regulation that is becoming more common is when a wine bottle lists a "vineyard designate" of the name of the vineyard in which the grapes were grown. If this is listed on the bottle, then at least 95% of the grapes must come from that vineyard.

This system is different from the original system established in the Old World wine countries. In most of these countries, the grapes that go into the bottle are labeled based on the appellation from which they originate. In this case, it is expected that the consumer is familiar with the type of grapes and the style of the wine from that region. For example, in France if someone buys a bottle of Bordeaux, they know that if the wine is red, it will contain a primary blend of the five red grapes that are grown in Bordeaux, namely: Cabernet Sauvignon, Merlot, Malbec, Petite Verdot, and Cabernet Franc. If the wine is white, it will contain a primary blend of Sauvignon Blanc and Sémillon grapes.

Zoning Regulations

A final issue with vineyard selection has to do with the land zoning regulations in the area in which the vineyard will be established. Most New World countries require that permits must be obtained to establish a new vineyard, and that the land must be zoned for agricultural use. In addition, there are environmental issues to consider, such as the amount of water needed for the vineyard, how the water will be recycled and cleaned if chemicals are used in the vineyard and the water drains into other areas, as well as erosion issues. For example, in many parts of California, there are hillside vineyard ordinances that require new vineyards with a slope of more than 30% to complete an engineering evaluation and implement a plan for erosion control.

Other zoning issues have to do with obtaining permission to cut down trees, and/ or replant trees if taken down due to vineyard establishment. For example, in South Australia, many of the native Eucalyptus trees were chopped down years ago when agriculture first came to the McLaren Vale. Now the government has implemented a program to replant many of the native trees near the vineyards and old orchards. Related to this is the impact on wildlife. Special fencing may be required to keep deer and kangaroos outside of vineyards so that they cannot eat the leaves. In addition, gophers, which may attack roots, and certain species of birds, which may eat the grapes, must be considered.

A final vineyard zoning issue has to do with neighbors, who may have houses near the vineyard. In California, land must be zoned for agriculture use, and neighbors living next to a vineyard are often concerned about the noise of tractors or other equipment, as well as drifting sulfur dust or other chemicals that may be used for pest control within the vineyard.

In conclusion, based on all of the issues that must be considered when selecting a vineyard, it is important to obtain a vineyard real estate agent and other expert advisors to assist in the selection and permitting processes.

Planting the Vineyard

Once a vineyard site has been selected, and clearance on appropriate permitting has been verified, the land can be purchased. Many vineyard owners need to obtain a loan to purchase and develop the land. Banks and other financial institutions will require a soil sample report, a cost–benefit analysis, and a marketing plan—ideally a signed contract from a buyer to purchase the grapes upon maturity.

The Soil Sample Report

It is important to analyze the soil in the vineyard by taking samples of soil from various parts of the vineyard site, as well as conducting a visual appraisal of soil structure and texture. The sample is then sent to a lab for analysis. The resulting report will describe the type of soil (e.g., clay, sand, loam), the pH level of the soil, calcium, magnesium levels, water holding capacity, and other important information. In addition, it will suggest the type of grape variety and rootstock that will perform best in the particular soil and appellation, as well as any additional nutrients that should be added to the soil, such as lime. Finally, it will provide information on the amount of water the vines will need. This information is used to help calculate the cost of establishing the vineyard.

Cost–Benefit Analysis

Developing a cost–benefit analysis for a loan on a vineyard usually requires an expert in finance and accounting, and is covered in later chapters in this book. However, the basic elements of this on the *cost side* include: cost of the land, cost to prepare the soil, cost of the grape vines, trellising, irrigation system, fencing, other equipment, installation, and vineyard maintenance. The *benefit side* of the equation is the "potential yield and price of the grapes over the years." In general for yield, most grape varieties start producing a 10% yield at 3 years of age; 30% yield at 4 years of age; 70% yield at 5 years of age; and then 100% from age 6 to approximately age 30. From age 30 on, most grape vines produce less fruit, but at usually the same or higher level of quality. For this reason, most tables illustrating net returns begin at year 4 and extend for 30 years.

Regarding the price side of the equation, most New World wine countries measure this as price per ton or tonne (1000 kilograms or 2200 pounds in US: 1 kilogram = 2.2 pounds) or gross dollar per acre or hectare (2.47 acres = 1 hectare). The price fluctuates based on the supply within an appellation as well as global supply of a specific grape; however, it is possible to calculate an estimate of the price per ton range based on historical prices within a region. This is usually what is provided as part of a cost–benefit analysis as part of a loan process to purchase vineyard land, and is calculated in best, average, and worst case scenarios.

The Marketing Contract

Because grapes are an agricultural product, and are dependent on the good will of nature, as well as the cyclical nature of grape supply (see Figure 3.1), it is important for growers to secure a long-term contract with a winery before planting a vineyard. This negotiated and written contract establishes the price the winery will pay for the grapes over a period of time, usually 3 to 5 years. It also describes how the vineyard must be managed, including amount and type of irrigation, fertilizer, thinning, and harvest specification. Any deviations from the contract may result in a reduction of the agreed upon price, or even cancellation of the contract. Most financial institutions will not provide a vineyard development loan without a written contract.

If a grower doesn't have a long-term contract, he or she may choose to sell their grapes on the spot market, which may fluctuate quite broadly, depending on the global grape supply. There are some years when growers actually make more money selling their grapes on the spot market, but if they are bound to a written contract this is not possible. The trend, however, is for growers and wineries to establish long-term buying relationships that are of a win–win nature for both parties.

Preparing the Land

Once the vineyard has been purchased and any needed financing has been secured, the land can be prepared. This includes some type of "ripping" or "slip-plowing" of the soil so that the grape vine roots can penetrate the various layers within the soil. In addition, all of the old roots and large rocks are removed from the field. A special type of tractor is usually required to do this type of work. Prepping of the land in this manner usually occurs in late summer, and then a thin layer of straw or hay is placed over the soil so that it can rest and erosion is prevented until planting of the vines in early spring.

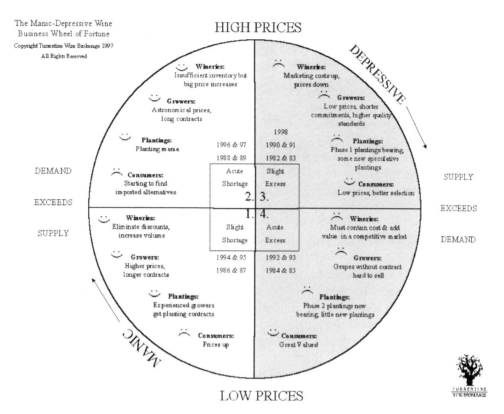

Figure 3.1. Cyclical nature of wine industry. Reprinted with permission of author, Bill Turrentine, Turrentine Wine Brokerage, LLC, 2003.

Laying Out the Vineyard

Determining the number of rows in a vineyard, as well as the spacing between rows, is part of the design, or laying out, of the vineyard. This is done differently based on the needs and philosophy of the grower. Traditional vineyard row spacing in the New World has been wide (12 × 8 feet in the US) so that tractors can travel between the rows. This is similar in Australia and New Zealand, as they perform much mechanical harvesting and pruning of their vineyards. However, current trends are towards narrower row spacing, such as 6 × 8, 6 × 9, 6 × 10 ft, or 1 × 1 meter (vine × row spacing).

In the Old World, most vineyards were traditionally designed with tighter spacing (3 × 3 feet), because many were established earlier and based on hand harvesting. Philosophies are also different, however; many New World countries believe they can achieve higher yields and higher quality by planting the vines further apart, but with higher trellising. On the other hand, many Europeans argue that even though each of their vines yields less because they are so stressed due to tight spacing, their quality is higher (vines need to be stressed to produce higher quality). They also argue that they produce just as much—because they have more vines per acre/hectare. Regardless of the choice, it comes down to the particular philosophy and needs of the grower, and now many different types of spacing are found around the world.

Planting the Vines

Once the vineyard layout has been determined, and the grape variety to be planted has been selected (e.g., Zinfandel), there are two other important decisions to make regarding the type of rootstock and the age of the vine to be planted. Regarding *rootstock*, this is "the root of a grape variety to which a fruiting vine is grafted." Some grape vines are planted on their original roots, but a large majority are grafted to a heartier rootstock that is resistant to soil-borne diseases or pests, and/or because they will grow well in certain types of soil. Some of the more common rootstocks are St. George, 110-R, 1103 Paulsen, 101-14, and 5C.

Many of the rootstocks are from vines that are native to North America, which have been grafted with the *Vitis vinifera* grapes from Europe. This combination creates a hearty vine, and was used to replant many of the vineyards of France in the late 1800s after they were ravaged by phylloxera, a root insect related to aphids. Interestingly enough, one of the few countries in the world that is still planted to the original *Vitis vinifera* rootstock from centuries ago is Chile. This is because Chile is more isolated from the rest of the world, and the diseases and pests that have infiltrated the vineyards of other countries have not entered Chile. There is some concern on how long this may continue, however.

The second planting decision after choosing a rootstock is whether to use "green vines" or "dormant benchgraft vines." Green vines are newly grafted vines that are less than 1 year old. They were grown in a greenhouse from a piece of grafted rootstock and have green leaves on them. Dormant benchgrafts were also grown in a greenhouse as green vines, but then were planted in the ground for 1 year and then removed in the winter when they were dormant. They look like a stick and have no leaves—similar to any bare-rooted plants available at nurseries.

There are pros and cons to using either choice. The advantage of green vines is they are less expensive (US$2 to $3 per vine) and can be planted later in the season (as late as early summer). The disadvantage is they require more water, are less hardy, and require 1 more year before they produce grapes, in most cases. The advantage of dormant benchgrafts is they can be planted earlier in the season—late winter to late Spring (March–May in the Northern hemisphere; July–September in the Southern hemisphere); generally they take 1 year less to produce fruit, are hardier, and require less water. The disadvantage is they usually cost at least US$1 to $2 more per vine than green vines.

The holes in which to plant the vines usually must be dug to at least 2 feet in depth. In large vineyards, special equipment is used to do this. However, in smaller, steep, or rocky vineyards, this is still often done by hand using a pick-axe and shovel. Once the holes are dug, any additional soil or nutrients may be added, and then the vine is placed in the hole and the soil is filled in around it. Often grow tubes, which look like plastic tubes, are placed over the young vines to protect them from the elements and pests (deer, rabbits, etc.). In this way, they begin growing safely within the tubes, which are removed when the vine is older and has climbed out of the tube. Obviously the cost of digging the holes, planting the vines, and installing the growth tubes is part of the business and cost issues regarding vineyard installation.

Installing Trellising and Irrigation

Another important viticultural business issue is installation of a trellising and irrigation system. Both of these are costly items but, once installed, will last for years. There are many different types of trellis systems in various price ranges that can be used. The most common in New World countries, and often the least expensive, is the traditional vertical shoot positioned (VPS) trellis. With this system, the vine grows up a central iron pole, and then is trained "to the cordon"—that is, the strongest shoots from the vine are tied horizontally to wire (either on one or two levels). From the cordons tied to the horizontal wire, additional shoots grow upward, leaving the fruit clusters (grapes) to hang down below the cordon.

Selection of the most appropriate trellising system often depends on the appellation and the amount of sun exposure to the canopy each day. Canopy management—using trellising systems to manage how much sunlight the grapes receive, thus impacting fruit quality—is one of the important areas of viticulture. This is why visitors will see many different types of trellising systems in the New World countries.

It is worth noting that the historical method for trellising was to leave the vine alone. In this case, it naturally grows in the form of a short "tree or bush." In Australia, these old vines are referred to as "bush vines." In the US they are called "head-pruned vines," in reference to the method in which they must be pruned. In ancient times, the most popular trellising systems were to let the vine grow up a wall or a tree.

Irrigation systems also differ by vineyard and country. Most modern vineyards use automatic timers to water the vineyard through "drip" irrigation lines, which are hung along the bottom wire of the trellis system. These irrigation systems often serve a dual purpose of watering and delivering a liquid fertilizer as needed. Historic vineyards relied upon the rain and fog for moisture, or used flood irrigation methods that usually involved diverting a local river to flood the vineyards at certain times of the year. This method is still used in parts of Chile and Argentina. In many appellations of France, it is against government regulation to irrigate vineyards, so growers there rely totally on "Mother Nature." This has led to the practice of a "vintage" year, meaning "the year in which the grapes got ripe," due to the correct amount of natural moisture and sun.

Vineyard Management

Once a vineyard has been planted, it must be managed on a yearly cycle. This involves hiring workers to manage the process, as well as purchasing or leasing the appropriate equipment and supplies. Because the vineyard is governed by nature, its schedule is also adjusted to the seasons. Following is a high-level outline of the annual vineyard management process.

Spring: Bloom (Northern Hemisphere: March–June; Southern Hemisphere: September–November)

In the spring, the dormant vine (no leaves) goes through bud break, in which the first green leaves shoot from the wood. There is very rapid growth of the leaves and multiple shoots streaming from the main cordons at this time. The vine can actually grow up to 1 inch in length per day. Each of these shoots will form two clusters of small flowers (similar to a lilac flower). These will "bloom" when the individual flower "throws the petals" and some tiny green balls are left on the vine. These will later grow into the grape cluster. During this time of year, the major concern is both frost and rain, which can damage both the leaves and fruit cluster. Therefore, various types of technology, such as heaters, large wind machines, and sprinklers are available for use in the vineyard to combat this threat. In addition, there is potential danger from insects and disease, which may call for pesticide management. Finally it is important to "sucker" the vine during the spring, or cut off any new shoots that grow near the roots or trunk. This allows all of the energy within the vine to focus on the upper cordons and fruit clusters.

Summer: Veraison (Northern Hemisphere: June–September; Southern Hemisphere: December–February)

During the summer, the vine will pour all of its energy into the fruit cluster in an attempt to ripen it. As the sun continues to shine on the vine, the fruit cluster will go through a process called *veraison*, in which each small grape will become larger, change to its mature color, and begin the ripening process. (All grapes are green when first formed.) Depending on the grape variety, there is a range of mature colors: pale yellow; light green; red; purple; and an inky blue-black. During this season, it is important to thin the leaves as part of canopy management to insure the fruit cluster receives enough sun and that too many vines don't drain energy from the grapes. In addition, it is often necessary to "thin" the clusters by cutting off the excess fruit clusters, so that more energy can be directed to the larger and healthier ones. This also helps to insure the quality of the grapes for intensity of flavor. Finally, continued pest management is necessary, as well as watching for "powdery mildew," which results from too much moisture. It is for this reason that higher levels of sulfur dusting are conducted in the summer.

Autumn: Harvest (Northern Hemisphere: September–November; Southern Hemisphere: March–May)

In autumn, the grape clusters become ripe enough to be harvested. For this to occur, the *brix* (sugar level within the grapes) must reach a certain level. This is usually between 22 and 26 degree brix (percent sugar), but also depends on the grape variety and region. For example, in the Marlborough region of New Zealand, it usually doesn't get hot enough for the grapes to reach this level of brix. Therefore, they often harvest their famous Sauvignon Blanc at levels ranging between 17 and 21 brix. Another consideration is the acid level of the grapes. All of this calls for much measuring of the grapes, which is usually done by hiring workers to pick small samples of the grapes and analyze them in a laboratory. Once it is determined that the correct level of sugar (brix) and acid is reached, then the harvest begins.

Harvest is an incredibly busy time of year in a vineyard and winery. Workers often work very long hours to ensure that all of the grapes are picked at the perfect time. Most of this work occurs early in the morning, when the grapes are firm and the sun hasn't warmed them to a higher temperature. The grapes are either hand-picked by workers or harvested by machine, and then rushed to the winery in large trucks. The concern is to get the grapes to the winery to be crushed while they are still fresh.

In Australia, where they don't have a large agricultural labor force, they use machines to harvest over 90% of their vineyards. This is actually more economical, and allows them to produce good wine for a lower price than some other countries. In some of their vineyards, they actually crush the grapes into must in the vineyard by machine, and then freeze it—before transporting it thousands of miles by truck to the winery. Crushing in the field and keeping the grapes cold with dry ice (CO_2 cap) allows them to maintain the quality level of the grapes, yet also produce an economical wine.

A final concern during harvest is the weather. Rain is about the worst thing that can happen during harvest, because it causes the grapes to become water logged and lose flavor. This is bad for quality. On the other hand, weather that is too hot or too cold can also cause problems during harvest, as the grapes either become too ripe too fast or do not ripen in time. It is for this reason that growers around the world watch the weather reports anxiously during harvest. It is also the reason that Mediterranean regions, with their hot dry summers, are so ideal for grape growing.

Winter: Dormancy (Northern Hemisphere: December–February; Southern Hemisphere: June–August)

After harvest, the vines slowly begin to "go to sleep." First their leaves begin to change colors, into golds, yellows, oranges, and reds. Then the leaves fall to the ground, and the vine is left as a black skeleton of itself. It rests and lets the winter rains soak into its roots. The grower finally gets to rest also for a month of two after harvest, but then must begin the pruning season. In many parts of the New World, this is done by hand, so workers again must go to the fields and individually prune each vine so it can grow again in the spring. Pruning a vine correctly takes special skill, and is also dictated by the type of trellis. Again, in certain countries, and especially Australia, most vines are pruned by machine, where "hedge or box pruning" of vines is very popular. Finally, fertilizer is applied to the vines during the winter so that they can begin their growth cycle in the spring, strong and vibrant.

The Issue of the Maturing Vineyard and Regrafting

Some growers and winemakers prize grapes from old vineyards. Indeed, in many parts of the world there are vineyards that are well over 100 years in age still producing grapes. However, because yield decreases as the vine ages (though many say quality increases), growers concerned with higher financial returns will often tear out an old vineyard (30+ years) and replant. Though it will take them approximately another 3 to 5 years before the vine production reaches an acceptable level, many believe this is preferable to harvesting smaller yields.

Another issue has to do with regrafting of a vineyard that is producing a grape variety that is not as popular or is oversupplied. For example, when there was a surplus of Chardonnay on the market several years ago, many vineyards grafted their vines over to Sauvignon Blanc or Pinot Gris. Though this can be costly in terms of labor—each vine has to be regrafted by hand with a graft from the new variety—it is a faster way to convert a vineyard than tearing out vines and replanting. Both of these are business decisions that need to be analyzed carefully in terms of cost-benefit, as well as forecasting future market needs.

How Many Bottles of Wine Does Each Vine Produce?

A mature grape vine will produce approximately 10 to 12 pounds of grapes (22–26 kilograms). This translates into five bottles of wine at 750 milliliters each, or 1 gallon (3.7 liters). Another way to view this is approximately 589.5 grapes are needed to produce one bottle of wine. This varies, however, because different grape varietals have different sizes of grapes.

If analyzed from the per ton perspective, 1 ton of grapes equals approximately 160 gallons of wine. Since there are five bottles of wine in each gallon, then 1 ton yields approximately 800 bottles of wine. This is a useful equation when determining production for a total vineyard. For example, if a small 2-acre vineyard generally yields 4 tons per acre, then the total bottle production of the vineyard would be 6400 bottles (2 acres × 4 tons × 800 bottles). As a case has 12 bottles, the approximate case production for the vineyard would be 533 (6400/12).

Important Issues in Viticultural Business

In examining the business of viticulture today and in the future, several important issues arise. Each of these can impact the profitability of vineyards in various New World countries, depending on the scenarios that continue to occur now and in the future.

New Technology in the Vineyard

The advances made in technological equipment for the vineyard over the last few years have been prolific, and have resulted in increased product quality and cost savings for those companies that use them. The majority of the technologies enable vineyard managers to collect data that can be stored and analyzed in a database, and facilitate more efficient, information-based farming decisions. The acquisition, evaluation, and application of diverse agricultural data types over time and space is often referred to as "precision farming," and is already in use in other agricultural industries. Currently, major groups of vineyard technology can be grouped into three categories: 1) automated weather monitoring equipment, 2) global positioning system (GPS), and 3) sensor technology.

Weather Monitoring Equipment is used to monitor humidity, temperature, wind, and solar radiation in the vineyard. The equipment is usually set up on large poles at various locations within the vineyard, and collects information 24 hours a day. The stations transmit weather data frequently using radio signals to a computer base station. The base station has software that determines critical information regarding the progress of disease and insect pest populations (which develop according to weather patterns) and regarding how much water is being used by the vineyard.

Employing the vineyard pest and disease information, the vineyard manager can then examine the data to determine the appropriate amount and timing of pesticides and fungicides that are needed. This is an improvement from traditional practices where large vineyards were sprayed on a set schedule, because there were no data available indicating the need for these inputs. This can result in large cost savings, because those materials need only be applied when necessary and not on a constant interval, as was done conventionally. Savings are realized in material costs, labor costs, and equipment maintenance costs. Vineyard sustainability is improved by the judicious use of such vineyard protectants.

Vineyard water use information from the weather stations allows growers to irrigate according to the needs of the vineyard, and not simply by a set schedule or a gut feeling. The information provided is a quantity of water that is evaporated from the vineyard, for which the grower can replace all or a portion of through his irrigation system. Scheduling irrigation using this information results in cost savings from reduced water costs, pumping costs, labor costs, and system maintenance costs. When combined with drip irrigation technology (where water is applied in controlled amounts to each vine) the water status of the vineyard can be manipulated to provide the best quality of wine from each location. Excessive irrigation degrades fruit and wine quality and overstimulates vine growth while, on the other hand, insufficient irrigation leads to vine stress, reduced productivity, and poor fruit maturation.

The weather stations have other benefits as well, including alerting vineyard managers to frost danger in the spring, so that immediate action can be taken to protect the crop (e.g., use of heaters, sprinklers, wind machines, etc.). Many a vineyard manager has been awoken in the middle of the night by a phone call generated automatically by a weather station alerting him that temperatures are approaching levels that can destroy their crop if not protected. Additionally, the weather data are stored in a computerized database and can be analyzed from a historical perspective, which allows vineyard management to track local climate and microclimate characteristics and make more informed decisions about how to farm the vineyard in the future.

Global positioning systems (GPS) are small satellite receivers that can be handheld, placed on the roof of a harvester or tractor, or used from an airplane. The receiver collects data from satellites rotating around the earth. The data report the exact coordinates of where the receiver is located on the earth to within 3 to 4 feet (higher accuracy devices are also available). These detailed geographical data are very useful in several ways. For example, a handheld device is useful when a vineyard scout, or technician, is monitoring a vineyard for disease or pest damage. Pest and/or disease severity may be assessed throughout a vineyard and entered into the device at any number of locations. The severity indices are mapped to each pinpoint location using the GPS signal. When the scout returns to the office, the information can be downloaded to a computer and a severity map can be generated using the set of observations just collected. The vineyard manager can use this map to generate an application map of, for example, a fungicide to control bunch rot. Rather than spraying the entire block with the material, only the portions of the vineyard having significant levels of bunch rot need be treated, thus saving time, labor, and material costs. Taking it one step further, an application map can be generated and uploaded to a unit mounted to the sprayer or tractor that is also equipped with a GPS unit. The application map can be used to automatically control the amount of material being sprayed based on the tractor's location in the vineyard.

On a harvester, a GPS can be useful in tracking the location in the vineyard where the highest and lowest grape yields are harvested. For example, mechanical harvesting machines can be outfitted with sensors that automatically weigh the fruit being harvested in each part of the vineyard. These data are combined with the GPS location to identify which locations in the vineyard produce the highest and lowest yield, as well as to identify patterns of yield variability within the vineyard. Finally, GPS technology is often used on airplanes when taking aerial photographs of vineyards. The aerial images provide an assessment of vine size throughout the vineyard and are geographically referenced to the same locations as the yield information and can be overlaid onto one another. Using special geographic software, the vine size and yield information can be analyzed to identify areas of the vineyard that are overcropped and/or undercropped. Vineyard managers can then assess what might be causing this variability and take actions to balance the vineyard yield, such as pruning styles, bunch thinning, fertilizer, or irrigation—depending on the situation.

Sensor technology is used to measure the characteristics of a grape. Newer sensors use reflected light in visible and near infrared light bands to measure grape composition. Grape samples are taken in locations throughout the vineyard during the ripening phase of the vineyard season. These samples are analyzed using special equipment that immediately determines not only the brix and acid level of the grapes, but many other characteristics that are important to producing the best wine from each vineyard. These data allow both the vineyard manager and the winemaker to make adjustments to their "farm plan" regarding irrigation and fertilizer amounts, as well as canopy management techniques, to ensure that the mature grape is of the highest quality. Most importantly, though, the data provide real-time information as to when the grapes should be harvested. Harvesting at optimal ripeness for flavor and texture of the wine is the single most important decision of the season. With the rapidity of measurement made possible by advanced sensor technology in combination with GPS technology, the assessment of grape maturity may be done rapidly throughout a block to determine regions of a block having different levels of ripeness. Harvest of portions of blocks can then be performed to capture fruit at optimum ripeness while awaiting harvest of less ripe sections of the vineyard.

In conclusion, all of this new technology in the vineyard not only helps to increase the quality of the grape harvest, but also results in cost savings due to savings in material and labor. Large vineyards around the world are already using most of these technologies, and expect to apply newer technologies as they are created. Eventually, it may be possible to gather specific data from an individual vine in a 500-acre vineyard across the globe and act upon it accordingly. All of this begs the question, however, of what will happen to the small family vineyard still farmed in a traditional manner without the luxury of expensive technology. It is possible that many of these smaller vineyards will be acquired by the larger vineyard corporations. However, it is also feasible that some of them will continue to farm in a traditional manner, in which the human eye and hand will nurture the vine instead of a machine. As the cost of technology decreases, some of the technology will be adopted even by smaller growers.

Labor Versus Mechanization Issues

The increase in technology use within the vineyard raises the question of the fate of the vineyard worker, who has traditionally managed, pruned, suckered, and picked grapes by hand. Now, in the larger vineyards, much of this work is done by a machine that can both prune and harvest the vines. In addition, new trellising is being used not only to facilitate the machine harvester, but also to reduce the amount of time spent on leaf pulling, so workers are no longer needed to do this either. It is only in the small, prestigious vineyards, or those planted on hillsides, that traditional vineyard workers are still needed. Even though it has been proven several times over that mechanically harvested wines are of the same quality as hand-harvested wine, many winemakers still retain a bias for hand-harvested grapes in high-end wines.

Interestingly enough, many of the vineyard workers in the US and Chile are reporting that they would rather do other types of work anyway. Working in the vineyards was something their parents and grandparents had to do, and it is no longer fashionable for many of them to work the vines. This trend, which is resulting in a shortage of vineyard workers in the US, is also driving a need to adopt more mechanization in the vineyards. Those workers who do remain must become "knowledge workers" and learn to use the new computer and satellite technologies that are infiltrating the vineyards.

Organic and Biodynamic Vineyards

Another trend that is receiving more attention in viticulture is that of organic and/or biodynamic farming. Originating in Europe, many consumers there are demanding products that are grown without pesticides. Organic farming is usually defined by a government body, and if food products are grown and produced according to their regulations, they can be labeled "organic." In the wine industry, *organic viticulture* is basically growing grapes without the use of synthetic pesticides or fertilizers. The only exception to this is sulfur, which is used to combat powdery mildew, and is considered organic because it is a natural substance. Organic viticulture has been adopted by both small and large vineyards in several areas of the world. It is also being used as a consumer marketing tactic to appeal to those customers who will only purchase organic products.

Biodynamic farming is more extreme than organic farming, and is more philosophical in nature. Based on the work of Rudolf Steiner, it is defined as "a science of life-forces, a recognition of the basic principles at work in nature, and an approach to agriculture which takes these principles into account to bring about balance and healing" (Wildfleuer, 1995). Biodynamic farming usually doesn't allow for the use of sulfur, but it does promote use of organic fertilizer and farming based on the cosmic rhythms of the earth. Currently biodynamic viticulture has only been adopted by a few small vineyards in Europe, the US, and New Zealand.

ISO Certified Vineyards

Related to the trend of organic viticulture is another trend that is starting to be driven by consumers in Europe and New Zealand. This is ISO certification for vineyards. ISO, which stands for the International Standards Organization, certifies business processes that have been documented and proven to result in consistent product manufacturing practices, as well as continuous improvement. Within a vineyard, the certification is called *ISO14001* and can be described as an environmental management system that requires vineyards to document inputs and outputs, and analyze the effects these have on the environment. It also supports sustainable agricultural practices. To date, several vineyards in Europe, as well as seven in New Zealand (Sileni Estates, Ata Rangi, Palliser Estate, Martinborough Vineyard, C.J. Pask, Vidal Estate, and Mission Estate Winery) have been certified. The growth of this trend will most likely depend on how important it is to consumers.

Growth of Vineyards Around the Globe

A final trend to consider for viticulture is the growth of vineyards around the world. Many vineyards in Eastern Europe are coming into full production. In addition, India and China are planting large vineyards. For example, in the last 10 years, China has invested much money into developing large vineyards in the northern area of their country, near Mongolia. They have received much consulting support from the French and Australians, and appear to be able to produce and harvest grapes at a very economical price, due to their low labor costs. Currently it is not clear that the wine quality is sufficient to be exported globally, but the rate of wine consumption is climbing steadily within the country.

The question of what will happen to grape and wine prices, with so many vineyards being developed throughout the world, is one that needs to be asked. With wine consumption still at a small growth rate in most parts of the world (or decreasing in France and Italy), what changes and new trends will this increase in wine grapes have in the future?

Vineyard Management at Beckstoffer Vineyards

Beckstoffer Vineyards was started in Napa Valley, California, in the 1970s by Andy Beckstoffer. Uniting a passion for wine and a keen knowledge of business, Andy began purchasing prime vineyard land in the Rutherford Bench appellation of Napa. As his reputation for growing high-quality wine grapes grew, many of the top wineries approached him to purchase grapes. Today Beckstoffer Vineyards has become the largest independent vineyard owner in the North Coast of California, owning and operating approximately 3000 acres of vineyards in the Napa Valley, as well as Mendocino and Lake Counties.

Viticultural practices at Beckstoffer Vineyards are driven by a clear mission and strategy. The stated mission is "To be the highest quality grape grower of Northern California coastal premium winegrapes through the advancement of modern business and viticultural technologies—doing it our way! To realize exceptional returns from farming and grape sales while building an 'estate' in vineyard properties." The company has grown steadily since its inception, frequently taking advantage of opportunities to expand its operations in the North Coast. Each of its three regions is managed under a clear strategy. In the Napa Valley, the emphasis is on producing the highest quality grapes using the best processes, people, and technology. The emphasis here is not to be the low-cost producer, but to be the best and produce the highest quality grapes. The strategy in Mendocino and Lake Counties is also to produce high-quality grapes, but with an emphasis on the cost side of the equation as well, because these regions currently do not command the high prices seen in Napa appellations.

Much of the success of Beckstoffer Vineyards lies in its sustainable farming practices and use of advanced farming techniques. The company has a strong commitment to sustainable farming and has successfully integrated practices including cover crops, biological pest controls, optimized water management, habitat preservation, and erosion control practices into their farming plans. They also own several organically certified vineyards in Mendocino County.

Beckstoffer uses some of the newest vineyard technologies to monitor and analyze their vines, including weather monitoring stations, GPS-based mapping, geographic information systems (GIS), and plant moisture sensing tools. The data are collected, analyzed, and used as a tool to make viticultural and farming decisions on matters such as irrigation scheduling, pest control, nutrient applications, and other vineyard management issues. They also employ modern farming technologies such as automated irrigation systems, pulsating sprinklers for frost control, and handheld computers to increase farming efficiency in the vineyard. Mechanical harvesters are used in parts of Mendocino and Lake Counties to help reduce costs, but all of their Napa Valley vineyards are hand-harvested at the request of their winery customers.

Much emphasis is placed on progressive management practices and employee relations at Beckstoffer Vineyards. Decisions involving vineyard investments and redevelopments are assessed using computer financial models and discounted cash flow analyses to calculate returns. Custom-built agricultural accounting software enables managers to receive monthly reports that compare actual costs, labor productivity, and equipment use to budget. Additionally, much importance is placed on positive employee relations, with strong efforts to ensure that employees are well trained on viticulture and safety practices, as well as how to operate vineyard equipment. Employee surveys and performance reviews are scheduled on a regular basis to provide opportunities for constructive feedback from employees on working conditions, and frequent employee events promote the family atmosphere that is important at Beckstoffer Vineyards. Furthermore, all employee communication is provided in both English and Spanish to support the hundreds of Spanish-speaking field workers. Three separate office locations are established for the more than 200 full-time workers, and competitive pay and benefits are provided for all employees. Finally, Beckstoffer employees take a lead in participating in community activities and in supporting local associations, such as the Farm Bureau, Napa Valley Grape Grower's Association, and California Association of Winegrape Growers.

Beckstoffer Vineyards operates with a viewpoint of "partnership with the customer." Beckstoffer will create a "farm plan" for each vineyard block, and then discuss the plan with winery clients so it can be customized to fit their specific winemaking needs. The quality and history of certain Beckstoffer vineyards have become so well known that several wineries designate the specific Beckstoffer vineyard of origin on the wine label.

Indeed, "keeping the customer in mind first" is one of the success philosophies of Beckstoffer, and is used in much of their decision making. They look at their winery clients as partners rather than merely buyers and see themselves as an integral part of the final product, not just a materials supplier. Prices of many of Beckstoffer Vineyards' grapes are, in fact, indexed to the final price of the bottle of wine that they go into, thereby sharing the risks and rewards with their winery partners.

At Beckstoffer Vineyards, vineyard acquisitions and redevelopments are, to a great extent, based on "knowing the market." Knowing when to buy, when to plant, and what to plant can be the difference between success and failure in a business where there can be several years between the time you purchase a vineyard and the time you produce your first grape.

In conclusion, Beckstoffer Vineyards is an excellent example of a vineyard operation that is focused on the triple bottom line. It operates with practices that are economically viable, environmentally friendly, and with a clear focus on customers, employees, and community.

Chapter **4**

THE BUSINESS OF ENOLOGY

Linda Bisson (Professor of Viticulture & Enology, University of California, Davis)

Roy Thornton (Professor of Enology, California State University-Fresno)

Peter Gago (Winemaker, Penfolds)

Winemaking is a complex process. Not only is it formed from a marriage of science and art, but it is also shaped by the whims of "Mother Nature" and the financial dictates of business practices. This can create both opportunities and challenges for the winemaker, and potential clashes with the winery CFO, as the business of winemaking unfolds to create the glories of a fine wine that can generate a positive financial return for the winery.

This chapter provides an overview of the major business issues regarding enology (the study of winemaking). It includes a review of the basic winemaking process and associated cost issues. In addition, it explores the decision-making process regarding first, second, and multiple labels. Finally, this chapter provides an overview of some of the new technologies and methods being explored in winemaking, as well as future issues impacting enology. The chapter ends with a description of the role of the winemaker, with special emphasis on the tension between the "art" and "business" of winemaking.

Business Decisions in the Winemaking Process

From a business perspective, the basic winemaking process can be broken down into six major steps. These are: 1) harvest and crush; 2) fermentation; 3) aging; 4) blending, stabilization, and finishing; 5) bottling and labeling; and 6) storage. The decisions and methods used in each of these steps can vastly impact the total price of production, as well as the final qualities of the wine. It is for this reason that a winery needs to be very clear on the type of wine they want to produce and the market segment to which it is directed. Are they in business to produce high-end luxury or artisan wines at very high price points; do they want to produce midprice wines the "fighting varietals"; or are they in the jug, or high-value wine business? Table 4.1 describes some of these price categories (Perdue, 1999). Another option is to produce wine at two or more of these price points and create second or multiple labels to distinguish the wines.

A newer trend is to identify the preferred flavor profiles of specific consumer segments and craft a wine designed to please the palate of the consumer. Australia has invested much money in this type of research, and has been successful at producing fruit-forward, less-oaked wines that are very popular with consumers around the world. Now a few other wine countries are beginning to follow this trend, which is different from making wines that please the palate of the winemaker or wine critics or adhere to a strict regional definition of "terroir." Clarity on strategic direction, however, is critical in making business decisions about the winemaking process. Wine style strategy drives everything from where the grapes are sourced, to the types of fermentation tanks, barrels, and packaging used. However, once a decision has been made, a wine business can move forward in the winemaking process with clarity of costs, rates of return, and other business issues

Step 1: Harvest and Crush

The process of negotiating and contracting for grapes was described in Chapter 3, but because the price of the grapes can be the most expensive component in a bottle of wine, it is important to reiterate this point. In a luxury wine, the winemaker

Table 4.1. Standard Wine Price Categories

Jug	up to $3
Popular premium	$3–7
Fighting varietals	$7–10
Classics	$10–14
Premium	$15–25
Ultra-premium	$25 and up

will want the highest quality of grape possible, and will dictate farming and harvesting requirements to the vineyard. This may include how much water, fertilizer, thinning, etc., is used, as well as at what brix and acid levels the grapes should be harvested. All of this impacts the total cost of the grapes, and dictates the cost of a bottle of wine. However, it is important that the costs of each step of the wine production process be known and calculated on a per bottle basis to guide winemaking practices and keep per bottle costs in the desired range.

There is an old adage in the American wine industry that states if you divide the price per ton of the grapes by 100, then you will know the minimum you need to charge for the bottle of wine. For example, if you paid $2800 per ton, then you need to charge at least $28 per bottle. Costs per ton generally reflect costs of farming, and many of the practices employed for the production of grapes destined for luxury wines increase the cost of viticultural input. Obviously this doesn't hold true in every case, or every country, but it illustrates the impact of the price of grapes on a bottle of wine. An alternative to per ton pricing is per acre pricing. In this case the costs of farming are covered directly by the purchaser. This allows the winery to fully understand the cost of vineyard operations and to decide if they are really warranted. It is also linked to payment on quality, rather than tonnage.

There are also business issues associated with the crush process. This is mainly tied up in the cost of the crush equipment and labor. A small winery may choose to outsource the winemaking process to a "custom crush facility," or third party, that will crush, ferment, age, and bottle the wine for them. This is a common strategy for beginning wineries that may not have the capital to invest in crush equipment, or may not have the proper permits to establish a bonded winery.

However, there is a point when it becomes more economical to invest in crush equipment. This usually includes a grape drop bin, sorting table, destemmer, crusher, press (can be one piece of equipment), hoses, cleaning equipment, pumps, and other associated items. The type of available equipment varies. For example, batch or continuous presses can be purchased, and each contributes different attributes to the juices produced. Oftentimes for a new winery only one type of item can be purchased. The winemaking management team will have to decide on what equipment will be meet their wine business strategy. Chapter 12 of this volume provides more detail on some of the pros and cons for the decision points on this topic.

The crush process is different, depending on the type of wine. White grapes are crushed and immediately pressed to yield juice. Red grapes are crushed, but fermentation proceeds in the presence of the skins and seeds. Juice containing skins and seeds is called "must." In some cases, red wine fermentations contain intact berries or clusters. Table 4.2 illustrates some of the basic differences.

Step 2: Fermentation

The fermentation process is critical to producing a good-quality wine. Fermentation is the process wherein *the sugar in the grapes is converted to alcohol and carbon dioxide*. For this to occur, yeasts must be present. There are yeasts naturally occurring on the grape surface or found on the surfaces of the winery that can grow in juice or must and conduct the alcoholic fermentation, which is then called a "native flora fermentation," but many winemakers will also inoculate a wine with a *cultured yeast* strain. The main reason is that cultured yeasts give the winemaker more control over the fermentation process. This is because some native yeasts are unpredictable and may get "stuck," and the wine will not complete fermentation on time. This leads to loss of tank space, requires manipulation of the arrested fermentation to get it to complete, and more careful monitoring of the fermentation, all of which can increase the final cost of the wine. Not only can it be costly to get the wine "unstuck," but off-characters may form, resulting in an inferior wine that must be discarded, treated, or blended out. Therefore, a sound management process may be to "take out an insurance policy," by using native yeasts on 90% of the juice or must, but inoculating 10% of it in a different tank with a good cultured yeast strain. This way, if fermentation starts to slow or develops an off-character, the winemaker can add yeast from the "insurance tanks." This is a good safety value that can keep costs in check and allows for the development of a good-quality wine.

Other obvious cost issues with fermentation are the types of tanks or barrels used. Most wineries ferment in stainless steel tanks with temperature controls. This way they also have the option to conduct a "cold soak" pre-ferment if they choose, and ensure that the wine does not rise above 85 degrees (the point at which delicate flavors begin to burn off). However, some wineries prefer to ferment in large vats/foudres. This was the traditional method from the Old World, and is still used in some countries today. For example, some of the smaller wineries in Chile still use large oak

Table 4.2. The Crush Process

White Wine	Red Wine	Blush Wine
1) Grapes are sorted	1) Grapes are sorted	1) Grapes are sorted
2) Grapes are destemmed & crushed (usually)	2) Grapes are destemmed (usually)	2) Grapes are destemmed and crushed
3) Juice is drained from the grapes and skins are removed	3) Whole grapes and/or whole clusters, or crushed grapes with skins, are put in fermentation tank	3) Red grapes with skins are fermented for a short period to create "pink" color, then juice is pressed and skins are removed
4) Juice is put in the fermentation tank	*Juice is pressed from grapes later	4) "Pink" juice is put in fermentation tank

fermenting barrels, and the Mondavi Winery in Napa recently switched to using specially designed large oak fermenting barrels for its high-end red wines. Though the barrels were quite expensive, Mondavi believes that they produce a higher quality wine based on their cost–benefit analysis.

During the fermentation process, most red wines will produce a "cap" of grape skins that float to the top of the tank. This cap contains a lot of the tannins, flavor, and color or *anthocyanins* that create the unique quality of the red wine. These components must be extracted from the skins in the cap during the winemaking process. Therefore, winemakers usually "break the cap" several times a day to mix with the rest of the wine. This allows the ethanol produced during fermentation to serve as a solvent removing important components from the cap. It also allows the heat of the fermentation to be used for extraction of cap components. This process, called "punching down," can be done manually with large paddles or with special equipment that is either built into the fermentation tank or lowered over the tank. In one variation of this technique, the entire cap is submerged in the tank. If a more temperate approach is needed, one can more gently irrigate the surface of the cap to extract components without risk of mechanical rupture of cap components. This can be done with a pump by pumping fermenting juice from the bottom of the tank, the racking valve, over the top of the cap. This process is called "pumping over." It is also possible to take all of the juice to another tank, allowing the cap to settle to the bottom, then return the juice to the original tank. This is called "rack and return." Which process is used depends upon the varietal, the level of extraction achieved, and the style of wine being produced.

The fermentation process can last from a couple of days to several weeks, depending on the type of wine being made. The process is finished when most of the sugar has become alcohol, which causes the yeast to die. The resulting alcohol level usually ranges from 8% to 16% (MacNeil, 2001). Obviously, the length of the fermentation impacts the cost of the wine, as does the need for refrigeration. In addition to ethanol and carbon dioxide, fermentation also produces heat. If too much heat is produced by the yeast, the wine can lose volatile characters and take on a "cooked" character. Fruity white wines and blush wines take less time to ferment, but may require more cooling. They generally cost less to produce than red wines because they are typically not aged as long. Some wines will go through a second fermentation, which is called *malolactic fermentation*, and is described in more detail in the aging section.

When the wine is finished fermenting, it is drained from the tanks (with red wine it is also drained off the skins) and pumped into either another tank or oak barrel for aging. This is called "free run" wine. The remaining skins and wine are usually gently pressed again to get additional wine, which may be mixed with the free run wine or used for a different label. The remaining material—bits of grape debris, skins, stalks, seeds—is now called pomace and is usually used as mulch and placed back in the vineyards, though some enterprising wineries will sell it to other companies.

Following is a quote from Simon Blacket at Wolf Blass Winery in the Barossa Valley of Australia (L. Thach, personal interview, July 2003). He describes some of the sophisticated winemaking techniques regarding fermentation, as well as cost-savings measures they use in the winemaking process:

We've upgraded the new Wolf Blass winery with the newest and best wine-making technology in the world. For example, each of controls on these stainless steel fermentation tanks is linked to a computer network. A winemaker who is traveling in Asia can log onto his or her laptop to check the progress of the fermentation in this very tank, and make adjustments to the temperature from thousands of miles away.

When it is finished, this facility will have the capacity to handle the equivalent of 80,000 tons of grapes. . . . Every thing that goes into the wine making process here is recycled in some form, and if possible, used to gain revenue. For example, we actually sell our treated waste water to the local golf club. Everything here is operated with the utmost efficiency for both quality of product and cost-savings, which helps drive revenue.

Step 3: Aging

Aging of wine is done to allow the flavors to more fully develop; sometimes to permit the wine to take on some "oak" flavor (when newer oak barrels are used); to allow polymerization reactions and softening and stabilization of the flavor and to encourage all of the elements to balance out. It can last from a few weeks to several years, and can greatly impact the cost of a wine. The costs are associated with the amount of time a wine is "tied up in the aging process," as well as the cellar space and overhead costs for storing it. In addition, wine can be aged in less expensive stainless steel tanks, or oak barrels that range in price from US$300 to $2000. The price is dependent on where the oak is from (which can range from Romania to the Nevers Forests of France), as well as the cooperage and process used to make it.

Cooperages, which craft the oak barrels, use a variety of methods. In addition to determining the type of wood from which the barrel will be made, they also "toast" the inside of the barrel with fire and smoke. The old-fashioned and more expensive method is to place the barrel over a real fire. A less expensive method is to use a torch gun. The level of "toasting" determines what type of flavor will be imparted to the wine—ranging from a light toast to a heavy, spicy toasted flavor. Some barrels are produced using hot water or steam rather than a flame to shape the staves.

To complicate matters further, an oak aging barrel will impart oak flavors for only about 3 years. After that, there is less flavor imparted and the barrel is usually used for storage, for aging where oak extractives are not desired, or is sent to the flower garden. Luxury wines are usually made in very expensive barrels, which are often used for 1 to 2 years only. Some winemakers will blend wines made from new and older barrels; and some will blend wines made from barrels from different countries. The type and age of the oak barrel can make a big difference on the final taste, quality, and cost of the wine.

A less expensive method for imparting "oak flavors" is to use oak *"tea bags"* or chips or *oak staves*. They can be put inside a stainless steel tank or added to an older barrel that has lost its flavor. These methods are often used for less expensive wines.

The issue of how much oak flavor to add to a wine is one that has received much attention in the international wine press. Some countries, such as Italy, have traditionally used very little oak in their popular Chiantis and Sangioveses, whereas others, such as Spain, often age their high-end Tempranillos for 5 years or more in oak.

Americans have been accused of "adding two-by-fours" to some of their California Chardonnays, whereas the Australians have countered this trend by using absolutely no oak in a number of their Chardonnays and labeling the wines as "unwooded." The issue of how much oak consumers like in their wine is one that is being researched in more detail through the use of flavor profiling.

Two other components of aging are *malolactic fermentation* and *racking*. Malolactic fermentation usually occurs naturally with red wines and some whites when they are barrel aged. It occurs when malolactic bacteria in the wine convert the "malic" (tart) acids to "lactic" (milk) acids. It often creates a creamer taste to the wine and softens the acidity, which is usually considered desirable.

Racking is allowing the particles within the wine to settle to the bottom of the barrel or tank, and then drawing off the clear wine into another tank or container. Wine may be "racked" several times during the aging process. It not only helps clear particles from the wine, but also adds some air, which may enhance the mature flavor of the wine. The amount and timing of oxygen exposure during aging can be important to the softening and development of mature flavors. This exposure to air can occur naturally during movement of the wine between tanks or barrels or can be done deliberately via the process of "microoxygenation." In this case, air is deliberately bubbled through the wine to increase the exposure of wine components to oxygen.

All of the components of the aging process impact the price and taste of a wine, and are also perceived as part of the "artistry" of winemaking. Creating the perfect flavor and balance of a wine depends, in part, on the aging process.

Step 4: Blending, Stabilization, and Finishing

Many would argue that step 4 in the winemaking process, especially the blending component, is where the true artistry of the winemaking process begins. In the blending phase, the winemaker blends together wine from various tanks or barrels to create a perfect harmony of taste and structure. France has always been lauded as the birthplace of blending, as anyone who tastes a great Bordeaux can attest. These wines are usually blended from five grapes: Cabernet Sauvignon, Merlot, Petite Verdot, Malbec, and Cabernet Franc. However, the blend is never the same from year to year, as the weather and other factors impact the composition of the grapes. Therefore, the winemaker must taste and blend different amounts of wine from each varietal to achieve the harmony of the whole "Bordeaux." Only a master winemaker can perfect this blending process.

However, in many New World countries, single varietals may be bottled, with 100% of the wine coming from the same variety. This is not always common, but it does occur. The type and percentage of wine that can be blended is also dictated by country regulations. For example, in most countries, if a wine is advertised as a single varietal on the label, at least 85% of the wine in the bottle must be of that grape varietal. However, it can come from different barrels or tanks, and be made from different types of oaks and yeasts. Therefore, there are endless permutations in the making of a fine bottle of wine, and every year it may be slightly different. Thus, many people refer to the blending process as the artistic heart of the winemaking.

Once the blending process has been completed to the satisfaction of the winemaker, many wines will also need further stabilization or flavor adjustment before going to the bottle. The processes of fining and filtering may be employed. This is not always necessary and depends upon the clarity of the wine post-aging and blending. The purpose of *filtering* is to clear up any small particles floating in the wine. Some settling will occur naturally so not all wines will need to be filtered, but if cloudiness remains suspended in the wine filters can be used that will remove the particles either via a mechanism of exclusion of the particles from the wine due to the small pore sizes of the filter or due to adsorption of the particles to the filter matrix.

Fining refers to the addition of agents to the wine. Some fining agents may be used to help particles agglutinate so that they can be removed more easily by filtration. Other fining agents are used to remove undesired components from the wine. Clays will bind to proteins and remove them. Some of the protein fining agents, like egg whites, will remove phenolic compounds and can make the wine less bitter or astringent. Fining agents can also be used to adjust the color of the wine. Fining is controversial, because, if overdone, it can strip the wine of flavor. Filtering has less of an impact on wine as it does not remove flavor or aroma components, but if ultrafiltration is used the macromolecular structure of the wine may be impacted. Both fining and filtering are focused on improving both the visual clarity of the wine and microbiological stability.

The wine must also be stabilized against unwanted reactions occurring postbottling. Protein removal discussed above is done to make sure a protein haze does not form in the bottle. It may also be important to prevent tartrate crystallization in the bottle. To do this, the wine is supercooled, which catalyzes the crystallization of the tartrate so that it can be easily removed from the wine. This way the crystals, which are mistaken for ground glass by many consumers, will not be present in the wine at the point of sale. It may also be necessary to make sure the wine is microbially stable. If there are residual nutrients it may not be possible to control microbial growth in the bottle with only an addition of sulfur dioxide. In this case, it may be necessary for the wine to undergo a sterile filtration as it is being bottled. This is especially true if there is any residual sugar in the wine. The "sight" of the wine in a glass is one of the five phases of wine appreciation, as described in Table 4.3.

A final and very critical part of the four major winemaking steps described above is sterilizing and cleaning all of the equipment each time wine is moved from one container to another. If this is not done correctly, then certain yeasts and bacteria can grow in the equipment and taint the wine. The most common of these is "Brett character" caused by growth of the yeast *Brettanomyces*. Brett character is the subject of

Table 4.3. The Five "Ss" of Wine Appreciation

1st S = Sight	to view color & clarity
2nd S = Swirl	to volatilize the esters
3rd S = Sniff	to smell the aroma
4th S = Sip	to taste; gargle in mouth
5th S = Swallow	or Spit; enjoy the finish

much study currently; some claim that a little of it enhances the wine and gives it more "interest." Virtually everyone agrees that any of the "barnyard, horsey" Brett character results in spoiled wine.

Acetic acid bacteria can also grow on the surface of wine, producing acetic acid and ethyl acetate, giving wine a vinegar flavor. The wine must be protected against oxygen to prevent this from occurring. *TCA taint* is produced by mold growing on wood and wood products and interacting with chlorine-containing compounds. TCA is a volatile compound that can infect wine by spreading through the air. It causes a dank, musty smell in the wine that can be detected by consumers in very low concentrations. If this invades a winery, it is very costly and time consuming to get rid of. That's why the best wineries are very clean, and require much labor to maintain.

Step 5: Bottling and Labeling

Many small wineries will outsource the bottling and labeling process, because it is an expensive process that is only conducted a couple months out of the year. Investing in a complete bottling line doesn't always make sense for a new winery, when they can hire someone else to do it. One of the more popular methods is hiring a "mobile bottling line," which arrives on a large truck and is set up outside the winery.

However, most larger wineries will have their own bottling line on premise, and may even offer bottling services to other wineries for a fee. Business issues regarding bottle and label type and design are often regulated to the marketing division of a winery, but it must be done with consideration of wine production costs. A standard bottle size and design are usually less expensive to process in terms of overall material and processing costs than a specially designed bottle that requires hand-labeling and perhaps etching. Again these are all decisions that must be considered as part of the overall wine strategy. Table 4.4 lists the major components for a wine bottle, and a range of costs (Perdue, 1999). Obviously the use of half-bottles, magnums, and other odd-sized bottles would have different prices ranges.

The bottling process is usually a very noisy one, as the bottles clank down an assembly line with workers who guide them through the filling, labeling, and corking/closure process. Workers must use hearing protection and be properly trained on the operation of the equipment as a safety precaution.

Step 6: Storage

The last major winemaking process that has business implications is that of storage. Most wines, once bottled, are stored for a time so that the wine may "marry" or

Table 4.4. Sample Bottling Costs for Standard 750-Milliliter Bottle

Bottle	20–75 cents per bottle
Cork	8–35 cents per bottle
Foil	0–25 cents per bottle
Label	3–35 cents per bottle
Bottling, corking process	18–35 cents per bottle

harmonize within the bottle. This is called *reductive aging* or *postbottling matura-tion* (MacNeil, 2001). The cost issues obviously have to do with the storage space, as well as the delay in getting the wine to market. Many wineries will rent storage space at special warehousing facilities designed to store wine at appropriate temperatures, as well as ship it to distributors and customers, whereas others maintain in-house storage. New World wine countries often differ on their philosophy regarding bottle aging of wine. Chile, for example, tends to bottle age the majority of its high-end red wine for 1 to 3 years before release. Some of the older wineries in Chile, such as Santa Rita, have large underground caves and cellars with stacks of unlabeled bottles filled with wine, which, once aged, are dusted and labeled for shipping. Australia and the US bottle age some wines in shorter time segments, usually 6 months to 1 year. There are some exceptions, however, such as the famous Penfolds Grange, which is first aged in oak for up to 2 years, and then bottle aged for another 3 years before release.

The Use of Multiple Labels in Winemaking

Many beverage industries will produce more than one type of beverage and use different labels or brands to differentiate types. Coca-Cola, for example, sells regular Coke, as well as Diet Coke, Caffeine Free Coke, and other brands. It even alters the taste of its regular Coke for different countries and cultures around the world, based on the preferred taste profile of its major customer segments.

The wine industry also uses multiple labels, but usually to distinguish its high-end, more expensive wines from the less expensive ones. This is particularly useful for a winemaker, who may discover that the quality level of a grape crop from a specific block is not good enough for the high-end label, so it is rerouted to their second-tier label. A good example of this is Opus One in Napa, California. They produce a very high-end "Bordeaux" style red wine, which retails for approximately US$135. How-ever, they also sell a second label called "Overture," which retails for US$40 and is only available for sale at the winery. Many other wineries around the world follow this tradition; however, what they do not always advertise to the customer that they produce the secondary label. It may be sold through different channels and not be associated with the winery.

The use of secondary or multiple labels is a business decision made by the man-agement team and winemaker. Many small wineries will begin with only one label, but later on see an opportunity to procure grapes or bulk wine at a good price, and therefore will expand into a "second" product line. The advantages of doing this are the flexibility of cashing in on a good opportunity, as well as maintaining the high quality of the first label and not diluting the brand. The disadvantage is potentially flooding the market with a wine that is difficult to sell.

A growing trend in the use of second labels is that of "private labeling," in which a grocery store, restaurant, airline, or cruise ship wants to sell a wine with their own label. They contract with a winemaker to produce a wine that matches their image and price range, and then sell it at their establishment under a different label. In most cases, the name of the winery and winemaker who made it is never divulged. Large grocery stores in the UK, such as Tesco, and Safeway in the US are currently using this process. This is an excellent method for wineries to sell more wine and potentially enhance revenues.

The Role of the Winemaker at Penfolds

The role of the winemaker at Penfolds is threefold: 1) to ensure the grapes are picked at the optimal time to maximize the fruit quality, 2) to preserve those fruit characters by ensuring the length of time in barrels and the temperatures at which the wine is stored is optimized, and 3) to blend the right grapes and varietals to achieve the style in which the winemaker pursues. It is easy to make great wine if the grapes coming from the vines are of superior quality.

Winemaking has evolved over the last few years in that while there are still many differences within regions and states amongst winemaking techniques, there are fewer differences around the world than perhaps 10 years ago. For example, many of the regions around the world are using Italian filtration systems, German presses, and Australian rotary fermenters. The Old World, as defined in the wine industry, has adopted this new technology as well as the New World of wine. The technology does not replace the "art" of winemaking, but rather just allows fine winemakers around the world do what needs to be done on a much larger scale. This willingness to use new technologies has allowed great wines to be produced on a much larger scale than before. Advancements such as air-conditioned warehousing, filtration methods, computer-controlled fermenting, stainless steel crushers, and microoxygenation have all contributed to the ability to produce fabulous wines on a commercial scale.

Metaphorically, it is like a manufacturing a stereo. Once a person could buy a stereo in which all of components were produced by one manufacturer. Now the best quality stereo manufacturers purchase components from around the world from the suppliers who build the best components. When these are combined together in the final stereo system, the resulting sound quality is far superior to that produced by the old stereo manufacturers who made all of their own components. This is similar to winemaking when looking at all the technological components now used in producing fine wine.

Some of the future trends in winemaking may include the usage of enzymes, the prevalence of adding acids, increasing flavor by increasing alcohol to up to 15%, and, of course, the one that nobody wants to mention—genetically modified grapes. All of these future possibilities are under exploration today and some are utilized to different degrees. However, it would be premature to say they are the norm or standard in winemaking.

At Penfolds, the role of the winemaker involves a number of major objectives. First, it is the responsibility of the Penfolds winemaker to maintain the style differentiation of the various Penfolds wine ranges, while optimizing the quality of any given vintage. Penfolds traditional strength is its ability to blend across variety and area to maintain a "house style" for many of its wines (e.g., Grange, Bin389, Koonunga Hill). That said, it also makes many wines from single regions (e.g., RWT Barossa Valley Shiraz, Coonawarra Bin 128 Shiraz) and it also creates single vineyard wines (e.g., Magill Estate Shiraz, Clare Valley organics). To optimize the quality within each style, more time is spent in the vineyards batching grapes and keeping parcels separate. This leads to enhanced grower relationships—paying by the hectare instead of by the ton—and resulting in smaller yields, but higher grape quality. In other words, it is the responsibility of the winemaker to make the best possible wine within the style that the brand has delivered over time. Thirdly, and perhaps most importantly, as a Penfolds winemaker, one of the key responsibilities is to look ahead 5 to 10 years by trialing and experimenting with new styles and varieties. This keeps the brand innovative and fresh while respecting its history. Finally, as all winemakers will attest, there is a need to minimize mistakes and wine faults. While it takes fabulous grapes to make great wine, there is still an obligation to overdeliver at all price points and optimize grape resources accordingly.

New Technologies in Winemaking

The study of winemaking is a fascinating one, as there are ongoing attempts to identify new methods and technologies to enhance the taste of the wine. This has resulted in increased quality and consistency of winemaking around the world. Some of the new technologies that are being emphasized today are described.

Microoxygenation

With this process tiny bubbles of oxygen are released into the bottom of the fermentation tanks. This creates reactions that modify tannins, remove green characters, and stabilize color. The more mature taste of the wine is considered desirable. What is exciting about the process is that it softens the wine by reducing astringency/phenolics and shortens the time the wine must age in barrels. For example, a wine that may have been barrel aged for 18 months in the past may now only need to age for 12 months. Therefore, microoxygenation can save a winery money and increase quality. There are a few downsides to the process, however, and winemakers must be careful not to overdo it. This can cause some backlash effects in the taste of wine and result in increased costs in the long run.

Co-pigmentation

Another exciting new discovery is called co-pigmentation. The color of wine is often not just due to the concentration of the pigment molecules or anthocyanins but to the types of compounds these compounds physically interact with in the wine. This complex color is called a co-pigment. Co-pigmentation of a wine can be manipulated by manipulating the concentration of the noncolored species that form co-pigments. This involves blending different types of wine to achieve more stable and interesting colors, as well as unique tastes. For example, some winemakers are experimenting with a blend of the Viognier grape and adding it to red wines to help stabilize the color of the wine. By doing this, they have discovered that Viognier creates a more interesting color and taste. The process of co-pigmentation is expanding, and winemakers are becoming more creative and thinking outside of the box as they blend new and exciting wines.

Flavor Profiling

A third process that is receiving much attention of late is called flavor profiling. In flavor profiling enologists first determine the characters most attractive to consumers for a specific varietal. Enologists are spending more time identifying specific impact flavors or characters for a given varietal and determining how those characters can be enhanced or modified. This helps to determine the optimal time to harvest to ensure the best flavors will stay in the wine and not disappear during the winemaking process. Flavor profiling links the impact characters of a varietal to the palate preferences of specific consumer segments. For example, in California, there is ongoing research on the preferred wine flavor profile of the Hispanic market. Currently this market segment does not consume much wine, but is the dominant consumer group in the state. Therefore, wine researchers are attempting to discover what wine flavors they prefer and link that data to the grape data. From this information, they can craft a wine that will be popular with this customer segment.

Another exciting feature of the flavor profiling research is that it will not only allow winemakers to produce wine that specific consumer segment like, but will also result in data about the grape varietal, vineyard, and harvest that will increase consistency and quality. No longer will it be a gamble regarding when to pick the grapes, because the winemaker and vineyard manager will have the ideal flavor data for the grape and know when it forms, stabilizes, and disappears. This type of information may also allow winemakers to eliminate certain steps in the winemaking process, such as extended or cold maturation. This in turn can reduce costs and maintain or increase quality.

Current and Future Issues in Enology

There are several current and future issues that impact the business of enology. One of the most controversial is the development of a *global wine brand*. There have been rumors in the global wine industry for several years that one of the major wine players will eventually be able to achieve this—though it has not occurred to date. If a true global wine brand were to develop, it would be similar to the Nike model, in which a tennis shoe is designed, but the material and labor to make it are sourced from around the globe. The consumer doesn't necessarily know from where the rubber, cloth, shoelaces, design, etc., originated from; instead, they focus on the final branded product, for which they are willing to pay a premium.

If this model were to play out in the wine world, someone would create a wine that had a consistent taste year after year. They could source the grapes from any location in the world that met their quality and price requirements. They could produce it in any country that had low production costs, but produced at a high-quality level. Their only concern would be the consistent taste, quality, and price.

This is very counter to the current method of making wine, which relies on the concept of terrior: the soil, weather, tradition, terrain, method, and people who make the wine. Wine has always been a "local" craft, even though it is sold globally. The conventional thinking is that the consumer should be able to "taste the place in the glass." Therefore, the development of a global brand would break all tradition. However, there are some intriguing benefits with the concept. The winery that developed such a brand could achieve excellent return on investments, because they would have the flexibility of sourcing their grapes from any place in the world that fit their brand flavor profile. Furthermore, if they could deliver a strong brand with consistent taste, with good advertising they could develop a loyal following similar to Coke. Whether or not this will come to pass is still to be determined.

Another issue or trend in the business of enology is that of *customer focus and sustainability*. For many years winemakers have been accused of making wine they like versus what the average customer prefers. This is changing, and wineries need to be on top of what consumers like and want. They need to explore consumer preferences, experiment with new varietals, and help develop the novice wine consumer, rather than making fun of them because they prefer sweet, nontannic wines. Australia is already doing an excellent job of this.

Related to this is the need to focus on sustainable winegrowing practices that are environmentally and socially friendly, as well as economically viable (see Chapter 15 for more information on this trend). More and more, consumers want to know that their wineries are using "green and clean" practices to sustain the environment, such as recycling waste water, using natural fertilizers and pesticides, reducing energy use, and supporting wildlife and vegetation habitat.

Related to this issue is the one of making *organic wine*. The number of organic and biodynamic wines that have come on the market in the last several years has increased dramatically. Many of these are in the European markets, as consumers there want to know that their wines have been grown and made using organic standards. This is an issue that some New World countries have already addressed (e.g., New Zealand) but that others may need to pay more attention to in the future.

A fourth issue or trend is the *quality/value equation and consumer profiling*. Many consumers believe that wine is overpriced. This is why many drink other alcoholic beverages. The great success of Charles Shaw wine in the US, and similar brands in other New World countries, attests to the fact that consumers will drink wine, but they want to believe they are getting a good price for the quality. Much of the research suggests that the novice consumer starts at low-end wine and trades up, yet many wineries still set their prices beyond the average consumer target. Wineries need to do a better job at profiling their customers at the different market segments and then producing products that meet their needs.

A final issue, which has been mentioned in other chapters, is that of *ISO certification*. This is a process whereby wineries document all of their production processes and confirm that they follow them exactly to ensure quality results. To achieve ISO certification, external auditors visit the winery to evaluate whether or not everything has been documented and is accurate. The benefit of doing this is that, in the future, some retailers and consumers may demand this type of certification. Therefore, wineries that get a jump start on documenting practices may come out ahead in the future.

Interestingly enough, in California, state regulations are so strict that most wineries are already documenting processes to conform with these requirements. In addition, those countries that are encouraging wineries and vineyards to adopt sustainable wine-growing practices are also facilitating the process towards ISO certification, because of the rigorous review and documentation of existing management practices.

Conclusion

In conclusion, the business of enology is a fascinating but complex matter. There are multiple decisions that must be made regarding customer needs, company strategy, costs, and revenue generation. In addition, there is always the variable of "Mother Nature," who may bless the vineyards one year with abundance and quality grapes, and then either rain, hail, or not warm them with sun the next. The winemaker's job is never stagnant. Circumstances are always changing, but there is a satisfaction in the profession, because, like a fine wine, a winemaker does grow better with age. With each season, with each vintage, the winemaker learns new ways to adapt, and this continually growing knowledge and experience is critical to the bottom line of a wine business.

Chapter 5

GLOBAL MARKETING

Tony Spawton (Associate Professor of Wine Marketing, University of South Australia)

Larry Lockshin (Professor of Wine Marketing, University of South Australia)

The term globalization is familiar to all working in the modern business world. No longer are markets mainly domestic and local; businesses of all types are competing with others from around the world. The wine sector, too, is now part of this globalization process. In some respects wine has been one of the most localized of products. Until the middle of the 20th century, much of the world's wine was purchased and consumed within 50 kilometers of its production. At the same time wine has been one of the first agricultural goods widely traded between countries and regions. Records as far back as ancient Egypt identified superior wine-growing regions, and by Roman times, individual vineyards had reputations for quality and were in high demand.

Nearer to the modern day, wines from Bordeaux have been highly demanded in England, as have been ports from Portugal and sherries from Spain. Over the same period of the last 150 years or so, new wine-producing countries, called the New World, have developed production and some level of exports to their Old World parents. This was part of the colonial mentality of creating agricultural sectors to export back to the home country. Historically, this trade was often at the mercy of political struggles in the Old World. For example, Britain affected wine growing and exporting from Australia both positively and negatively as they raised and lowered tariffs depending on whether they were at war or peace with France, Spain, and Portugal. The decision for Britain to join the EEC, as it was then, meant that wine exports ceased for almost two decades.

This chapter provides an overview of the key trends in global wine marketing that drive the rationale for globalization in the wine trade. Then some of the success strategies for entering the global market are discussed. From the strategies, direct and indirect exporting are defined, and examples of how some of the best companies are organized for marketing outside their domestic sphere are provided. The chapter continues with a detailed list of specific tactics for exporting, including some views on organizing for export, an export readiness checklist, market choice considerations, distribution systems, competitor analysis, advertising and promotion, and pricing. The chapter concludes with sections on branding for export, communication and promotion issues, and the export value chain and logistics.

Key Trends in the Global Wine Sector

Why is the wine industry becoming more international? First, trade liberalization and the mutual recognition of enological practice have *reduced tariff and nontariff barriers to wine marketing*. The European Union agreements with bilateral partners, like Australia and South Africa, have reduced the various technical nontariff barriers, such as fill level monitoring in bottles, nonacceptance of certain wine production practices, and the like. Nevertheless, the marketing nontariff barriers of differential labeling requirements, limitations on entry into the distribution systems of markets, curtailment of advertising and promotional tactics, restrictions on the usage of regional names and traditional winemaking expressions still operate to frustrate the global trade in wine, which has grown in volume terms at less than 1% per annum over the last 20 years. China's entry into the World Trade Organization (WTO) has resulted in the reduction of import duties on wine, which not only will allow the prices for imported wine to drop, but also will make domestic producers more competitive as they now have less of a price advantage. This could eventually result in China exporting wine into the global marketplace.

Another major trend has been the *economic development* of the world. Higher standards of living are associated with higher wine consumption. Although the relationship is not a direct one, as living standards and wages rise, so too does the demand for bottled wine. Wine sold in bulk, as in "fill your own containers," is typical in traditional wine-drinking countries; bottled wine is the main import and export in the New World and the newly developed countries, such as in Asia. The growth of food safety regulations and the drive for "product integrity" by importing markets with the increasing strategy of "Mis on Boutelle" (i.e., bottled at source) will accelerate the trend to packaged wine globally.

Economic development and the heuristic and hedonic lifestyle associated with wine have fostered tourism and multicultural interests. A generation ago, people were happy to consume the traditional foods and beverages of their parents. If their parents migrated to a new country, such as the US or Australia, often their traditional foods were looked down upon and their children craved the "normal" foods and beverages of their new country. Now people are much more interested in preserving their traditional foods and beverages. Italian, Thai, Indian, Malaysian, Greek, Spanish, French, and Chilean foods are all available in restaurants and even in many supermarkets. Tourism and television have opened the eyes and the mouths of consumers in developed countries, and wine has been part of that awakening. Wine consumption has markedly increased in places like the UK, Scandinavia, Canada, Australia, Holland, and now Asia and even India and China as a result.

At the same time, *wine production has spread widely*. Wines are available from over 70 countries in the world, although only a few constitute the major wine-exporting countries. France still leads the world in total wine exports (Table 5.1), followed by the major Old World countries. But the New World has emerged as a major competitor, especially in key export markets, like the UK and the US, and in new markets, like Asia.

Table 5.1. World Wine Exports

Country	2001 (million hl)	Share (%)
Italy	18.3	26.54
France	15.8	22.91
Spain	9.9	14.42
Australia	3.8	5.74
Chile	3.1	4.48
US	3.0	4.29
Germany	2.4	3.44
Portugal	2.0	2.90
South Africa	1.8	2.55
Moldovia	1.6	2.32
World total	68.97	100

The next global trend has been the well-documented *decreases in consumption* in the Franco-Latin countries and the accompanying *increases* in the Anglo-Saxon and Asian ones. Overall global consumption has not increased very much in the past 10–15 years, only about 2% overall, but regrettably is expected to fall over the next decade unless the decline in consumption in the Franco-Latin countries is arrested and new markets are opened up in Northeast Asia and elsewhere. Although better quality wine is being made around the world (a higher percentage is being sold at the premium, $US5.00 and above price range), total global consumption has hardly changed. There are very recent hints from the US that substantial consumption increases are beginning, but the ability for wine marketers to convert these potential increases to sales has been slow due to a lack of commitment to wine marketing; as a result there is an increasing surplus of premium and ultra-premium wines in most New World- and Old World-producing countries.

Another global trend has been the very fast increase in the percentage of *wine sold through supermarkets and discount stores*. Across the world, even in such traditional places like Italy, over 50% or more of total wine sales are now ending up as fast moving consumer goods (FMCG or packaged goods). The positive side to this is that it increases the availability of wine to more people, who would not normally go into a wine specialty store to shop. Oversupply has produced good-quality bargain wines, although recent statistics show that people already drinking wine are buying most of these, but some are using these inexpensive wines to extend the number of drinking occasions. The downside, and a very large one, is that the packaged good system favors larger companies with consistent quality, strong logistics, brand management, and enough capital to engage in regular high/low supermarket promotions. As even the specialty stores become corporate chains, the number of SKUs (units on the shelf) has shrunk from 1500 or so to 800 in the specialty chains, and to 350–500 in the supermarkets. This again reduces the chance for smaller producers to be on the shelf.

The other side to this trend is that availability should *create more wine drinkers*. Some of these drinkers will develop into wine-involved or interested consumers, who want to experience the diversity of the global wine offer. These consumers and the existing involved buyers will make sure that independent specialty stores remain and the better managed ones will prosper. Even in supermarkets, where there is high demand, specialty wine shops within the supermarket are being developed and trialed. As long as there is demand for interesting and unique wines, the market will respond and smaller wineries will have outlets, though only the better managed ones will survive.

The final trend is that HORECA (hotel, restaurant, café) is still strong in many traditional wine-drinking countries and it is growing in many New World ones as well. Sales have been lost to the overall social trend of quicker eating and eating at home in some Old World countries. But the major change has been the disappearance of the generation of café-based wine drinkers. This has reduced overall consumption, but these people mainly drank the lowest quality level of wine and are being replaced by choosier drinkers. One of the big issues here is the lack of good data, due to the large number of small privately owned firms in this sector. New World countries seem to be embracing the café society and, as noted above, international cuisine. This opens the door for smaller wineries to find sales outlets in the HORECA channel in the faster growing wine markets.

One of the key differences between the wine trade and other consumer products is the relative fragmentation of production. Even with alcoholic beverage companies buying into the wine trade (Diageo, Pernod Ricard, Allied Domecq, for example), the sector is much more fragmented than comparable beer, spirits, and other consumer beverages (Figure 5.1). This has two major implications for wine producers. First, there is a lot more consolidation that is likely to occur. As the retail channels consolidate in major wine-consuming countries, there is a greater impetus for suppliers to become larger in order to deal with them. Second, on the other side of the ledger is the opportunity for smaller wineries to stake a claim in the global market. The next section looks at some successful strategies for global marketing among large and small wineries.

Success Strategies for Global Marketing

Technically, there are no global wine companies as there are global soft drink companies. Wine is still produced and labeled by the country of origin. Some of the largest wine companies are multinational, in that they make and sell wine from more than one country. However, they do not use the same brand name for wines from different countries, in contrast to the strategies of Coca-Cola or Pepsi-Cola. Most wine companies are exporters: making wine in a single country and exporting that product to other markets. Developing a strategy for exporting marketing depends mainly on the size of the wine company.

The larger wine companies have more options for developing international markets. Direct exporting is the main one, and it will be covered below, because it suits

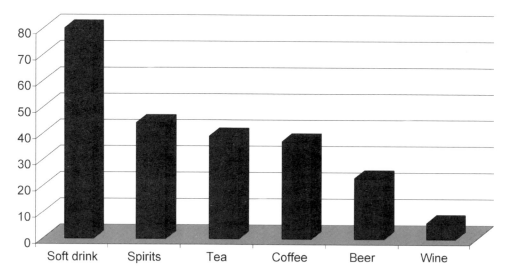

Figure 5.1. Global market shares of the major beverage categories (Rabobank, 1999; reprinted with permission).

all sizes of wineries. Large companies can invest directly in other countries and produce wine there for either the domestic market or to export. BRL Hardy, now owned by Constellation Brands of the US, bought an estate in southern France, La Baume, and then expanded production by buying grapes from around the region. The resulting wines are sold in France and exported to the UK and back to Australia.

Another method of internationalization is to buy an existing winery in another country. The Constellation Brands purchase of BRL Hardy in Australia, The Foster's Brewery purchase of Beringer in the US to merge with its Mildara Blass wine business, and the Pernod Ricard (France) purchase of Orlando Wynham in Australia are all examples of this strategy. It is usually driven by gaining immediate access to a producing winery and the accompanying economies of scale in distribution and selling and the circumvention of nontariff barriers designed to discourage exporters entering a market. The other issue for exporters such as Australia or any country for that matter with a currency value less than that of the import market (Euro or US dollar) is the "in-market cost" (the cost of distribution incentives and advertised promotions) and retention from margins earned in that market are paramount, rather than using a "repatriation and pay" method from the home market. This has driven (where possible) distributor and agent ownership of joint venture arrangements to facilitate this. Contract production and marketing joint ventures are growing in importance, with BRL Hardy/Stellenbosch Wines an example. BRL Hardy has similar ventures with wineries in Sicily; in a similar manner Mondavi and Antoniori have joint ventures in Chile.

All of these strategies focus on the need to gain sufficient critical mass to support distribution volume expectations and the maintenance of hard-won retail selling space. The Beringer buyout by Foster's, for example, allowed an immediate increase in distribution for Australian wines into Beringer's home market by the existing sales force, while at the same time the Beringer wines could take advantage of Mildara Blass's larger market position in the UK. Retail consolidation means that large supermarket and discount buyers are aiming to reduce the costs by purchasing the widest range of wine needed from the fewest suppliers, thus reducing the purchasing and logistics costs. These multinational producers can bring a sales book (the list of wines available from a single sales person) listing wines from multiple countries, with multiple brands at a range of price points. The joint ventures use the same strategy but also have the strategic choice of whether to use the well-known existing brand name or to develop a new one. Often a new brand name is chosen, because the existing name has such a close tie to a different country, but the company name may include the joint partners as a kind of subbrand to identify and build on existing brand equity, such as the brand "Yellow Tail" developed specifically for the US market through a joint venture agreement.

Smaller wine companies, typically of less than 1 million cases and most often much smaller than that, are forced to use direct or indirect exporting methods to targeted countries as their main means of internationalization, as they do not have the critical mass of volume and capital required to undertake the globalization strategies of the larger corporations and are therefore committed to export as their prime market entry strategy. The larger companies choose this route as a stage of their market development to gain early market share and to establish themselves as a part of a new category within wine. As the required efficiencies of competing in the FMGC market intensify, the alternative strategies detailed above have become more necessary and more attractive to maintain market share once it has been established and to provide the logistics and service such as just-in-time (JIT) deliveries and stocking requirements the supermarkets demand from all suppliers.

Definitions and Examples of Exporting

The rest of this chapter will focus on direct exporting, but first a short paragraph on *indirect export*. This was the favored method of export when negotiants, merchants, and brokers bought wine at the winery and undertook the total export process on behalf of the producer. These indirect facilitators are usually country of production focused, but have the advantage of both expertise and resources to provide effective export support and logistics consolidation to gain the better full container (FCL) shipping rates than the premium lesser (LCL) rate. The advantage to the winery is that their product is bought under the trading terms of a local market transaction and paid in the local currency. The main disadvantage is that the wine could be sold in any market or any segment of that market without any reference to the exporting winery. This method is still a recommended method for very small wineries to enter the market that have neither export experience nor the skilled staff to deal with the complex export marketing process and the maze of nontrade barriers that need to be taken into consideration along the way.

The first ingredient to successful *wine exporting* is a strong management desire and commitment to the process. Without this, most export strategies fail. Exporting requires a large commitment in resources and time to be successful. Potential wine exporters should ask themselves what they have to gain by exporting, given that every part of the process is more expensive than the same thing in the domestic market. Gaining market information, travel, packaging, shipping, warehousing, insurance, managing the sales force, and reacting to competitors all cost more when it is done at a great distance. Typically wineries choose to export because they believe there is little room for expansion in their domestic market or that prices and margins will be higher overseas. These assumptions should be tested before the final decision is made. Some wineries make the decision to export based on some desire for prestige or for travel to distant markets, rather than on more objective criteria of sales and profit growth. Countries with either small or shrinking domestic markets are the home of most of the larger exporting wineries in the world; Australia, New Zealand, Chile, and South Africa are countries with limited domestic markets; France, Italy, Spain, Portugal, and Argentina are countries with large, but shrinking, domestic bases.

Once the decision to export is made, the key next step is to decide the target country for exporting. Wineries new to exporting are advised to focus on a single market at first to learn how to do it and to have the requisite management time available. The easiest markets to export to are typically those that have already been targeted by other wine companies in your region or country or already have a well-developed wine-consuming culture. This means there is already some market recognition for your country or region of origin; distributors and retailers are aware of the styles and need less cajoling and information to make a decision. Of course, long-standing export markets may have less opportunity than some newer ones, but this must be balanced against the cost of informing a new market not only about your brand, but also about your country or region, which is a long and expensive process.

Examples of Three Australian Exporters

Here are three brief examples of Australian companies that successfully took this path. The first is the very large BRL Hardy and their brand, *Banrock Station*. This was a new brand in 1995 developed from a large planting of grapes in Australia's Riverland region, the warm and dry inland area responsible for the majority of Australia's commercial wines. Initially Banrock Station was developed for the Australian market as a slightly higher priced commercial (sold in bag-in-box or casks) wine with an environmental positioning. The old station (large farm) was completely rejuvenated by opening up the original wetlands, which had been drained, changing irrigation practices to limit water usage, integrated pest control, and building environmentally aware buildings. The wine was sold in brown labeled bottles and casks, the same wine in each format. Initially seeds to plant trees were attached to each package to reinforce the environmental message.

The venture was so successful in Australia that it was taken almost in its entirety to the UK market. The same positioning was used, which, just like in Australia, was unique for a large and relatively inexpensive wine. As sales grew, the company invested in a state-of-the-art environmental cellar door, with passive heating and cooling, water recycling, and fantastic views over the rejuvenated lagoons and wetlands surrounding the vineyards along the Murray River. Even though the cellar door is more than a 2-hour drive from Adelaide, it is one of the most visited cellar doors in Australia, with many international visitors choosing to camp in the parkland developed out of the old sheep station. Here, the export strategy was almost exactly the same as the domestic one, because the positioning was relevant to both countries. The size of the vineyards meant that the domestic Australian market was not large enough to absorb all the sales, so export to Australia's (and BRL Hardy's) largest overseas market was the best way to expand sales. BRL Hardy took advantage of the fact that they already had a sales force and good distribution in the UK to launch this brand with good promotion and shelf space. Now, 8 years after its Australian launch, the brand sells over 3 million cases, mainly in Australia and the UK, but also in the US and other export markets.

Peter A. Smith, a retired Australian aerospace engineer, developed a different type of export strategy for a brand new small winery called *Bartonvale*. He started the vineyards with the idea of growing a top-level Shiraz in Barossa Valley and exporting it at very high prices to the lucrative US market. He had no plans to sell the wines into the domestic Australian markets, where high levels of competition would limit his chance of gaining cult status and high prices. He chose vineyard sites that were near existing high value locations and used cuttings from vineyards already supplying cult-level wines, like Penfolds Grange and Peter Lehman's Stonewell Vineyards. He hired Rolf Binder of Veritas Winery to make his wines, because Rolf already had several of his own cult wines selling in Australia and the US. The idea was to make exclusively Shiraz and Shiraz blends in a style that critics like Robert Parker would rate highly.

He looked for an importer distributor that had experience selling these types of wines to high-end specialty wine stores and exclusive restaurants. Peter Smith had a four-page list of questions to ask prospective distributors about their existing portfolios, how much time and effort they spent marketing new wines, how much he would have to bear of the promotion costs, how they developed an executed marketing plans with other small wineries, etc. His chosen distributor, Dan Philips of the Grateful Palate in California, already had a portfolio of Barossa Valley Shiraz, including some cult wines, like Torbreck and Three Rivers. He was able to go into small exclusive retailers with a shelf of these cult wines and had access to many top restaurants. Once the wines were made and the quality fit the plan, small amounts (all that was available) were sent over to the US at retail prices of about $20 to $30. These were the lower end wines of the range, though still with relatively high prices. This helped establish awareness and prepare the market for the more expensive offerings. Within 2 more years, the higher priced wines showed their potential by receiving Robert Parker scores from 92 to 97 points, and the strategy was moving exactly to plan.

Wineries often think that they need to have a premium product image to export. Take the case of *Kingston Estate* in the Riverland of South Australia. Located in a traditional "bulk wine" and therefore perceived low-quality region, Kingston Estate decided to build its reputation in the commercial and commercial premium export markets. Using bulk wine sales as leverage it gained access to the BOB (Buyers own Brand) of the Scandinavian monopolies, the growing "by the glass" dispensing of the café market in the UK, and the commercial wine segment in New Zealand, by leveraging its own branded product as the "house wine" in the process. This successful marketing strategy was so effective that this became the basis for the launch of the Kingston Estate brand into the domestic market in Australia. This dual marketing strategy of using export as leverage for domestic marketing success has made Kingston Estate one of the leading wineries in Australia.

Each of these cases, though different, illustrates key parts of a successful marketing strategy. First, a particular market and set of distribution channels should be chosen that match the company's ability to produce and market the wine. Next, the wine must be of the quality that fits its intended price and position, whether this is a low-priced commercial wine or a high-priced cult wine. With the strategy and wine in place, the company must execute it properly. All aspects of the product and packaging must fit its intended profile; the distributor should have access to the intended outlets and be able to deliver the marketing strategy developed with the winery, whether this is mass distribution through supermarkets or exclusive distribution in selected shops and restaurants. Finally, good follow through over time is necessary to maintain the momentum in the market by managing the sales force or distributor, reacting to competitors, and enhancing the brand's reputation and awareness. We now discuss the organizational structures and the basics of branding necessary for successful exporting.

Tactics for Exporting

As noted above, successful exporters first must commit to the long-term process of investing and maintaining their export activities. Whether the company is large or small, someone must be responsible for the export activities. In a large company, an export manager- or vice president-level position is usually dedicated to these activities. Smaller companies may just add to the duties of the marketing manager or general business manager and, as exports grow, the companies usually will hire an assistant to deal with the paperwork and logistics of exporting, while the manager deals with the actual marketing and selling. In one sense, exporting is no different than selling on the domestic market. You must manage all the same activities, but now at a greater distance, with a few extra difficulties thrown in, such as language differences, regulation differences that may affect packaging and even the wine processing, and cultural differences in how wine is sold.

Organizing for Export

In organizing for export, it is important that responsibilities be clearly defined. Someone must take overall responsibility for the activity, but in most cases there is too much to do for a single person, who also has domestic marketing responsibilities. In this case, it is useful for a second person to take charge of information collection about the potential target market and begin investigating potential distribution partners. Often there is an export advisory service maintained by the government or even the trade association. These entities help provide information about target markets, regulations, and sometimes even potential partners. They can help arrange meetings in the chosen market with key informants and advice of upcoming trade events where more information and meetings with prospective distributors can occur. Some countries provide this service for free or at a low charge, while others add "user pay" fees depending on the amount of service or information required. These services are usually very cost-effective for smaller wineries, with little information or experience in the potential target country. There are often consulting companies that offer similar services, but charge more and advertise a more customized product. Wineries should ask for references and investigate whether these customized services are worthwhile before jumping in.

Larger companies can have a quite complex organizational structure for multinational marketing. Typically, there is an overall marketing manager or vice president who is responsible for all marketing and selling activities in all markets. When a large domestic market is involved, there can be a national sales manager, who may or may not report to the marketing manager. Many companies choose to have a matrix-type organization, with some crossover responsibilities for different aspects of the export market. For example, larger companies usually appoint specific market or regional managers, such as the European marketing manager, or the Asia-Pacific marketing manager. These people may have single country or even subcountry regional managers in place for large brands. Each of these managers is responsible for overseeing the distribution system, setting targets for different channels or even specific retail chains, providing sales promotional support for the sales team, setting prices or price ranges, managing advertising, and working with the brand managers.

The matrix comes into effect when companies also have specific brand managers responsible for their large brands. The brand manager works with the regional managers, both domestic and export, to maintain specific brand positioning in all markets. They often have responsibility for the overall packaging, advertising, and pro-

motions to make sure all fits within the brand's positioning strategy. They must ensure reliable supply to all markets and adjudicate when production does not meet
demand, or develop strategies with the individual market managers to increase sales,
when production increases.

Orlando Wyndham has global marketing managers for its Jacob's Creek and
Wyndham Estate brands. They also have regional managers for Europe, North America,
Asia-Pacific, and Africa-Middle East. Within each of these regions there are country
managers for the largest markets, like the UK, the US, Canada or for regions, like
Scandinavia. There are also specific country brand managers, like the brand manager
for Jacob's Creek in the UK. This brand manager would report directly to his or her
country manager, but the brand manager would also be working with the Jacob's
Creek global brand manager to make sure that all activities fit within the overall
positioning of Jacob's Creek. For example, one of the major retailers may ask for a
price reduction in Jacob's Creek and be willing to place a very large order. The proposed price might be outside the range that the local brand manager has authority to
provide. The global brand manager for Jacob's Creek would be involved in the decision as to whether this low price is approved or a different bargaining strategy is
proposed to the retailer. The country manager would be involved, but would not
have authority to reduce prices beyond a certain set point. Their role would be to
provide advice on negotiation to keep the price within the expected range and then
to oversee any logistics necessary to import and warehouse an unplanned for increase in Jacob's Creek for this promotion. At the same time they would be providing
the same services to the other brand managers in the UK.

A smaller company must make similar decisions, but with fewer brands and fewer
outlets these decisions might be handled through discussions between the overall
marketing manager or business manager in the home country and his or her agent in
the export market. The same planning must occur, but with usually one brand it is
not necessary to have a complex management structure.

The next steps in organizing the company for export involve a set of activities
summarized below in an "export checklist." It is important that individuals within
the company or those acting as part of the distribution channel are aware of their
roles and responsibilities. They should have definite timelines established for comple-
tion of their tasks, so that all necessary activities are performed in the right sequence.
It is no use having a label ready and printed if the wine is not ready for bottling, or
having a distributor actively seeking placements when the wine has not been approved legally for import into the country.

An Export Readiness Checklist

Wineries should have a process for export market operations, almost a checklist of
activities to ensure that nothing is missed or can go awry. The export market for
wine is highly regulated by virtue of wine being an alcohol and therefore subject to
alcohol-based regulation as well as that of food safety and product liability. The salability of wine has always been in question as wine is a perishable, fragile, low-value,
high-transportation-risk product.

To enter the export market wineries should have detailed knowledge of the following factors.

1. The *external capabilities of your winery*: the quantities of wine and the styles of wine you have available for sale and whether they match the expectations of the market segment you intend to export to. Be thorough and assess these not just for a single shipment but for a strategy of long-term development.

2. What are *cash resources and credit line facilities*? In direct export payment terms tend to be long, 120 days plus. Market development costs are high to negotiate contractual arrangements and establish a logistics network to ensure you can get your product to market in a saleable form.

3. Ensure you are acquainted with *tariff and nontariff barriers* and their operation and requirements. Mutual acceptance of enological practice may be becoming common, but be very aware of exemptions of various processes or additives by various markets. Your winemaker association should keep a register of these market requirements that you as the exporter need to be conversant with.

4. Labeling is used as a nontariff barrier. *Label approval* is often mandatory. Ensure the claims you make are acceptable and that the label layout complies with the mandatory requirements of the importing country. Ensure you do not breach copyright and intellectual property law, and brand law. Some markets require health warnings, standard drinks statements, ingredient details, winemaking process information, and traceability coding as the basis for possible product withdrawal.

5. Understand the *styles of wine* that are selling in your proposed market. This will require some market research as most markets and cultures have differing taste expectations. Taste is the key determinant to product choice in all markets.

6. Have a system to help you systematically *choose your export market of choice* and whether you are able to both compete in and service that market. Remember that export marketing is much more difficult and competitive than just selling in your home market. If you are unsuccessful in selling wine in New York or Houston, then perhaps you should be not be considering export anyway.

Market Choice Considerations

If you are then ready to proceed, consider the following for market choice. Level of consumption is very important. Be very careful of using just per capita consumption. It is deceptive as it includes the total population not just the alcohol-consuming population. You need access to consumption studies that specifically tell you:

- who is drinking wine (gender, age, and income profiles);
- when do they drink it (as an aperitif or as an accessory to food);
- where is the main location of consumption (home or outside the home);
- frequency of consumption;
- the occasion of consumption for less frequent consumers;
- where do they buy their wine (supermarket or specialist outlet);

- what purchase cues do they use and their relative importance (country of origin, variety, region, brand name);
- price paid based on usage occasion (everyday vs. special occasion pricing).

This information should form the basis of both the strategy and positioning you take in the export market, and how you design your marketing mix to be a part of the consumers' repertoire of wine brands.

Distribution Systems

The key issue is that you are aware of the permitted levels of marketing and market access available to exporters. The choice of agent/distributor is critical in this context. The company should be accredited and respected to be able to deal with the resellers in the market. The greatest challenge for any exporter is to gain a compatible match of agent/distributor. All arrangements with resellers or agent distributors should be by *contract to supply arrangements*, be performance based, and have *termination and dispute clauses* and their jurisdiction nominated. Distribution systems can be classified as follows:

1. *Regulated open market* (e.g., UK). The characteristics of these markets are those of FMGC marketing, direct negotiation with the retailer, freedom to market directly to the consumer, multiple outlet selling and availability, societal control on consumption and abuse (drink-drive, underage drinking, curtailment of advertising). Resellers are concerned with margin and stock turn.
2. *Central/state government controlled* (Canada and Scandinavia). Controlled distribution, curtailed availability, central purchasing and on-selling to resellers, limited direct sales to the consumer (Canada only), products need to win a "listing to be sold," advertising and merchandising regulated in government-owned stores, price promotions common, product trial and tastings on-premise only.
3. Mixed systems of the above.

Advertising and Promotion Opportunities

Advertising and promotion opportunities should be made available to you from your winemakers' associations, such as:

- which wine shows and expos;
- the role of the wine press;
- the ability to advertise and the media available to capture the target market attention;
- tastings and tasting promotional opportunities.

Competitor Analysis

Portions of your competitor analysis should also be made available to you from your winemakers' associations. Questions to consider are as follows:

- Is there a domestic industry and how strong is it and what defensive strategies are being adopted to limit imports?

- How parochial are the consumers and are they prepared to switch preferences?
- How many other wineries from your country are in the market and what is the status of these wines in meeting consumer category requirements (expressed as share of category)?
- What is the market positioning and availability of wines from your country across the "usage" spectrum?
- What are competitor and local marketing expenditures on promotion and brand building?
- What are relative cost efficiencies and margin generation for resellers?

Pricing Levels

The price levels operating in the market are an essential analysis. The cost escalation of export is a significant factor in determining where wineries compete. You need to go into export to make a profit in the longer term, but you also need to price your products to recover your additional cost of exporting. These costs will include additional packaging costs, compliance certification, label modifications and special print runs, reinforced shippers, containerization, shipping, insurance, duties, and/or excise. The first consideration is the general price range in the export market, as the greater the price range in each category the better the opportunity for cost recovery. For example, the price range of £3.99 to £9.99 for commercial premium wines in the UK market allows a range of positions where profit can be generated, whereas in the ultra-premium price range of £9.99 to £15.99 there is price congestion resulting in brand limitation at reseller level. From a winemaking point of view, the winemaker needs to aim at *overdelivery of intrinsic quality* to justify the imported wine cost-derived price premium. Failure to deliver the intrinsic value proposition will lead to market failure or the need for loss-making price discounting in order to drive sales.

Branding for Export

The simplest thing, of course, is to maintain existing positioning and branding activities in all markets. This makes the job of the marketing or brand manager much easier. True global marketing companies strive to maintain a single brand image in all their markets. This is easier said than done. A pair of Levi jeans, for example, has different positioning in its home US market than it does in many international markets, where it is seen as more exclusive and at a higher relative price position than at home. This is not a bad strategy, and some wine companies specifically pursue higher prices and positions in export markets than in their home markets. Marketers should be aware, however, that as price rises sales generally decrease, so a large selling brand in the home market may not achieve equivalent export sales if it is positioned at too high a price point. This goes back to the initial reasons for export, and the overall brand positioning must fit within these parameters. The initial branding decision, therefore, is whether to maintain the existing brand position, allowing for country differences, or develop a new brand or brand extension for the export market(s).

Most companies decide it is easier and better to maintain their existing brand and make adjustments for different export markets. We will discuss this branding strategy first, and then briefly discuss developing a new brand for export, because many of the same processes are used, but larger changes are made.

Product or Wine Style

The first decision is whether the wine style itself is acceptable in the target market. This can be done by taking samples and tasting them with knowledgeable wine channel members in the target market: importers, retailers, or restaurateurs, who sell wines of the same type and price point. Sometimes it is necessary or advisable to change the blends or style for a specific market, especially if the market has large enough potential to warrant separate blends. Many large multimarket Australian wines, for example, have slightly fruiter blends for the UK market and slightly more oak in their US wines. Smaller wineries do not make any adjustments in wine styles for export markets. The cost in tank space, materials, and inventory does not warrant this investment. Sometimes, wineries will remove wine earlier from barrel or leave some in barrel longer as a reserve wine for a specific market, because these activities are not as costly as having separate blends for each market. Obviously making any changes to wine styles must be driven by strong knowledge of the tastes of the target market.

Packaging

Certainly the packaging is often changed for different markets. There are often specific label requirements for information to appear in certain font sizes and positions (front or back label), which are different from the home market. Care should be taken in making too extensive or unnecessary changes. If possible the front label should be the same for all markets. This may mean changing the domestic label slightly, but the overall cost of having only one front label may be much less than having different ones for each market, which can not only affect label costs, but bottling and inventory costs as well. Back labels usually must be changed for export markets. Again, the fewer different labels the better, because of the reduced inventory costs and increased flexibility in allocating or reallocating wines to different markets. Sometimes a split back label is most cost-effective, with a generic top back label and a different label with required information below. The rest of the package should be as much the same as possible for the above-mentioned reasons.

There are no specific recipes for a good or attractive label. Label designers often speak of designing above the price point, so that a $10 bottle of wine has a $15 to $20 look to it. Wine producers are advised to use well-recommended label designers with experience in wine label design. When considering a design that will be used for domestic and export, it is important to maintain simplicity. Cultural differences between countries can make very complex labels unattractive in some places. Even brand or company names (if it is the brand) should be considered in the light of multiple languages. What may be a well-known landmark or place name domestically can be nearly impossible to remember or pronounce in another country. Most successful brand names are simple one or two relatively short words. The label design and the brand name should clearly link to the brand position. For example, the Banrock Station label proclaims, "Good earth, Good wine," clearly communicating its sound environmental position along with the focus on the value of the product. Initially the label was made in a recycled style brown. Now after 8 years on the market, the label has been brightened, because the positioning is more towards the wine quality, but still a drawing of the river and trees is visible to connect the brand's position. As recommended above, it is very useful and inexpensive to test label concepts with key distributors, retailers, and restaurateurs in the export market before launching.

Product Line Considerations

One of the key questions in branding for export is the size and composition of the product line: How many different varieties? Different price points? Package sizes? These decisions mainly focus on the company's strategy for the overall size of the brand and where it is to be sold. The decision will be quite different for a brand aiming for 1 million cases or more than for one attempting to sell 10,000 cases. Too often wineries with relatively small brands develop and try to sell far too many product variants, which not only confuse the market, but this adds unnecessary expenses in production, packaging, inventory, and selling costs.

We will look at each of these decisions in turn. First, we discuss the range of wines by style or variety. Wineries should consider that knowledge of their country or region will be much less in export markets than in the home market. Consumers and even trade buyers may have only general associations of varieties and regions: Australian Shiraz, California Cabernet or Chardonnay, New Zealand Sauvignon Blanc. This makes the task of marketing a broad range of grape varieties more difficult, especially for the smaller producers. At the higher price points, buyers will have some knowledge of region and variety: Barossa Shiraz, Napa Cabernet, Marlborough Sauvignon Blanc. This actually makes it more difficult to sell other varieties from the same region, such as Cabernet from Barossa or Pinot Noir from Marlborough. The best strategy is usually to go into these higher price point markets with one or maybe two varietals and establish the brand name, especially among the trade and high involvement buyers. Then the line can be expanded as awareness of the quality of the brand grows. The winery may use different well-known regions for its varietals, but the key link here is to the variety–regional–quality association.

We do know from market research that consumers choose more by grape variety than by country or region of origin in the higher volume outlets. So, at lower price points, in supermarkets and discount outlets, selling by variety with a brand identification works well. Here the strategy is to gain shelf space and grow brand awareness. Successful wineries often go into the market with two to four varietals simultaneously to maximize shelf space and reduce overall logistics costs. Both the trade and the winery benefit from this strategy of multiple varieties of the same brand. As brand sales and awareness grow, more varietals can be added to the mix. Jacob's Creek is a good example of a wine that originally entered the UK market with its Shiraz Cabernet and a Chardonnay, while in its home Australian market it had a wider line of offerings. Now the line consists of a range of blends, such as Shiraz Cabernet, Cabernet Merlot, Shiraz Grenache, Chardonnay Sémillon, and a range of single varietals, such as Shiraz, Cabernet, Merlot, Chardonnay, Riesling, and the newly released and successful sparkling Pinot and Chardonnay. All of these wines are branded Jacob's Creek and sell within a relatively close price range, with the blends slightly cheaper than the single varietals. Growing the range like this allows the consumer more choice within the same brand and at the same time acts as a very positive promotion with the large amount of shelf space.

There is some debate as to whether a different brand name should be used in export markets than in the domestic market. We believe that there is more leverage from maintaining the single brand across markets than from trying to start a new one. Sometimes there are issues that make this strategy impossible and a new brand has to be developed for the export market. The local name may be prohibited in the export market or too difficult to spell or pronounce. In this case, the new brand should still make a connection to the home market through its name and positioning. Wine remains one of the few multinational products where the country and region of origin are highly important.

Pricing

Another decision is whether or not to extend the brand to different price points or to launch new brands in those price points. Larger wine companies usually have different brands for different price points. This is especially true for high-volume brands selling at the lower, $5 to $10 US price point. It is often difficult to convince the trade and consumer that the same brand that sells for $7 has a higher quality wine for $15. There are some exceptions to this rule, but generally it is easier to create a new brand at a higher price point than to try and extend the range upwards. This is due to two reasons. First, consumers wonder what the difference is if they taste the high priced wine and it is not to their liking (usually it will have more concentration and oak treatment). Second, the segment that buys wines at $7 is not the same segment that buys at $15, so the promotion of the higher priced wine to the existing consumers is not very effective. You have to promote to the higher price buying consumers anyway, so a new brand is not much more costly to launch.

One of the major issues in deciding price points for a line with different quality and price levels is the distance between the suggested prices. If the distance is too small, then when the upper line goes on promotion, it actually intrudes upon the price point of the lower line. This can quickly denigrate the consumer perception of the lower priced wines. Managers should keep in mind the ongoing retailer strategy of lowering price points for wine, both on and off promotion. A wine that starts with a list price, for example, at $15.99, may soon find itself selling on promotion for $13.99 or even less. Soon that becomes the new "regular" price and the wine is now within $2 to $3 of the next wine in the same line below it. When a new promotional price occurs, the wine may end up at the same price as the lower quality wine in the same line. Managers must first set suggested retail prices that allow for discounting and, second, strongly resist resetting the suggested price after long discounting periods.

This leads to the general discussion of pricing wines for export. As we state above, there usually is little difference in the overall positioning of wines for export versus the same wines in the domestic markets. However, the actual price points often do differ between markets. This is typically due to duties and taxes, which often differ substantially. These taxes and duties affect all wines equally, so the relative prices of wines are not affected. But also, wineries need to consider the extra channel members and their mark-ups, which affect the final retail price. Usually there is an importer, who assists in receiving the wine and clearing it through customs. This importer can also be a distributor, or may sell the wine to distributors for resale to retailers. We will discuss channel arrangements in the next section. Wineries should be aware that there often are extra margins in export and maintaining equivalent prices to the home market can take some planning. Sometimes wineries either have to accept a lower margin or consider moving into a slightly higher price point to maintain existing margins.

Wine companies should investigate each potential export market's price points before they make the final decision to enter that market. Depending on the market, there are various publicly available reports, often in local trade journals, that give an idea of the price points in the market. Again, wineries can easily discuss these issues with potential distributors or importers, who know the market well. It is also useful to visit the market and note the brands and regions, which you know from your home market and see where they position themselves as to price. Given the well-developed international wine market, a useful strategy is to decide whether to be above, below, or equal to an existing brand or brands in the chosen market. Of course, price has a direct relationship to the overall positioning of the wine and its potential volume of sales. New brands in the market looking for high-volume sales usually enter at a price point below that of wines with similar quality. Kumala from South Africa is a good example. The wine quality matches many of the mainstream Australian and American brands in the UK market, but it is priced below those from Jacob's Creek, Hardy, and Gallo. In only a few years, it has moved solidly into the top 10 wine brands in the UK.

Smaller wineries will not be looking to sell wine into these lower price points, but the lessons are applicable at any price point. Look for wines of similar quality and prestige and decide where you want to position relative to them. Palliser Estates, from Martinborough, New Zealand, one of the ultra-premium wines from that country, for years has used relative price as part of their marketing strategy. Their aim is to be at or very near the highest priced wine in their category, which is clearly part of their overall positioning. At the same time, wine quality, packaging, and communication must meet the same positioning objectives. As international markets become more sophisticated, there is little room left for wines that do not deliver the total package of quality, look, communication, and prestige at the appropriate price. The problem is that these developed markets have little room for new brands without pushing out another brand. Therefore, the new brand must bring something special to the market. Often this is easiest done with a slightly reduced price to existing wines. This of course reduces revenue and itself has a detrimental effect on the wine's position in the market.

Communication and Promotion

Price must be accompanied by relevant communication or promotion strategies appropriate for the market. Larger brands, selling hundreds of thousands or millions of cases, obviously have larger budgets and can afford more mass appeals. These can range from price promotions accompanied by cooperative advertising and shelf talkers to billboards to sponsorships. Very few wines have the budgets to use mass media, such as television, for promotion, although it can be argued that this medium reaches more consumers per dollar spent than any other. Mass media only works in countries that have a relatively high proportion of wine drinkers. Otherwise such broad exposure is wasted on many nondrinkers. Another issue with mass media is laws prohibiting or restricting the advertising of alcoholic beverages. France and many of the Scandinavian countries do not allow advertising for wine or other alcoholic beverages. Other restrictions exist in many countries. Wine exporters can usually get a guide to these laws from their home government's foreign trade office or the branch in the destination country.

The first rule of communication strategy follows on from pricing and positioning: it must be appropriate to the overall position of the wine. Like packaging, there are no hard and fast rules. In fact, a good communication strategy often breaks through consumer inattentiveness by being unique and creative. That said, we will first look at some of the standard practices and then move to some examples of more creative promotions, including sponsorships.

Retail stores often demand that wineries participate in various *price promotion campaigns*, especially for different holidays. The fact is that this is when many infrequent consumers come into the market and regular consumers buy more wine. So it is important to participate. The key issue with price promotions is to work to keep the discounts reasonable and within the image range of the brand. Sometimes it is possible to provide other, value-adding offers, without dropping the price of key wines, but the opportunity differs by country. Supermarkets in the UK, for example, still use price promotions almost entirely as their means of promoting wine for various holidays and rarely give wineries other opportunities to promote their wine. In other countries, wineries can promote and add value to their offer without reducing price by bundling their wines with another product, such as buy three bottles of this wine and receive a free set of wine glasses, corkscrew, apron, or even another type of wine made by the same winery. These value-adding, nonprice promotions are better for attracting attention without reducing the perceived price point of the wine.

The ultimate, though expensive, promotion is to *give tastes of the wine*. There is nothing better than experience to introduce and sell a consumer on your wine. These types of promotions should be managed carefully due to their expense. Whether it is in a specialty wine store or restaurant, be sure that as many as possible of those tasting your wine are potential buyers. There is no sense in offering tasting of a $30 bottle of wine in a venue that caters mainly to $5 buyers.

It is very positive to *work with restaurants* in export countries, where the foods might differ from the home country, to develop promotions matching food with the wine. This may be a free glass of wine with a specific dish, or a tasting of wines with multiple dishes for a fixed price, or just a wine by the glass promotion. Back labels that extol the virtues of the wine with roast lamb, for example, do not add much value in countries that hardly consume any lamb. Food-based promotions with local cuisine can overcome this and at the same time build brand recognition with the trade and consumers.

Another excellent promotional scheme is to *work with wineries from the home region or country as a group in specific export markets*. We noted above that consumers choose wines by variety at lower price points, but region becomes much more important at higher price points. Food-based promotions by a group of wineries, either at a single or at a group of restaurants, can help build awareness and understanding of specific regional characteristics, which is essential to gaining prestige and higher price points. Individual wineries are not often able to do this on their own. The argument can be made that smaller wineries will do much better developing events for their region than they will by spending the same amount of money on their own brand in export markets. At their ultimate, these regional promotions can include wines and wineries that may be unable to send representatives, and have to rely on their local distributors, but still can add value to the overall promotion and their own brands. The Australian wineries often work in this way. Wineries usually pay differential participation prices for these promotions based on their size. Wineries can choose to participate directly or pay a fee and provide wine for their local agent to pour. The wineries that participate directly obviously gain more, but even those that cannot afford to help round out the overall promotion and help develop the awareness of the whole region.

Press releases and *sponsorships* are standard means for wineries to gain awareness and increase sales. The rules and techniques really don't differ much from the ones used in domestic markets. It is just more difficult to source information as to whom to send the press releases to and how to focus them. It often pays to hire a local agency that can manage this for you. Be sure to choose one that is well established in the wine area and has a good reputation for press releases that create activity on behalf of the brand. In essence you are buying local knowledge, about whom to send to for different types of releases and how to write those releases in the proper language for the country and culture. It is very rare for a domestic company to understand and be able to promote a winery in a different country.

Sponsorships follow much the same rules. It is important to understand the kinds of consumers you are seeking to influence, before deciding or developing any sponsorships. The people drinking your wine may differ dramatically in different countries, even if the wine is sold at relatively the same price points. Again, it often pays to work closely with your distributor, if they have the expertise, or with a good PR company that understands the wine market. Sponsorships should deliver awareness and, in the best cases, tasting or purchasing opportunities with your target market.

The Export Value Chain and Logistics

The contraction of market opportunities in the future will mean a heightening of competition between wine industry organizations. This competition will be undertaken at all levels of the value chain: country versus country, region versus region, brand versus brand, and retailer versus retailer. Realizing this inevitability, there has been a series of acquisitions, mergers, joint ventures, and strategic alliances as the industry organizes itself to improve the efficiency of value delivery, and by doing so protect and/or gain market share.

The wine product is becoming more homogeneous with a *consistent quality now a common expectation* as a key performance indicator (KPI) of wine salability at all levels of the distributive chain, so the natural variability due to climate and grape vine disease are being negated by better techniques of vineyard management and the use of quality-enacting technologies in the winemaking process. On a global basis, there is a growing homogeneity of offer as the grape varieties used are concentrated into:

- White wines: Chardonnay, Sauvignon Blanc, Chenin Blanc, Gewürztraminer, Riesling, Sémillion
- Red wines: Cabernet Sauvignon, Pinot Noir, Syrah (or Shiraz), Merlot

New varieties are being trialed, but their consumer impact is not expected until the longer term.

The result is that the way that companies compete will change from a product focus to a service focus facilitated by *database marketing, relationship management*, and *networking cooperation* between the various members of the supply chain. Before going on to discuss these we need to spend some time on the transactional marketing activity of export marketing.

Wine is a product where there is still a "high salability risk" on the part of the distributor, retailer, and consumer. The practice of claiming climatic variations is no longer accepted and a general level of quality is now expected as the norm. In addition, poor practice such as secondary fermentation, wine "in bottle" variations, unbalanced wines, oxidation in young wines, and crumbling corks are no longer tolerated at any level. The failure of the winemaker to provide saleable product results in a penalty being charged for product returns and replacements by the retailers.

The improvement of packaging practice has been significant toward providing salable products, with "clean room" conditions in bottling halls or at least for the "filling heads" now common practice. Closure has become a key issue due to widespread product failure of the commonly used cork stopper, resulting in a switch to the "Stelvin closure" (screw cap) or to new high technology cork closure substitutes on many commercial and premium wines in some markets.

The salability integrity of the wine product is fundamental in a FMGC market as well as a superpremium market. The distributive and consumer salability expectations are the same irrespective of the positioning. Wine is a low-value, perishable, and fragile export. The protocols for shipment for export need to be thorough to ensure salability and to maintain market value. Precautions that need to be taken to ensure ship passage include:

1. Product damage can result due to heat/cold/vibration/excessive hydraulic movement in the bottle. Wine containers should be stored at 20°C, and below the waterline of the container ship.
2. Vibration causes a wine bottle to rotate 10 times per 600 miles of transit so special export shippers and dividers are necessary, or the use of "sleeves" for ultra-premium bottles. Without these precautions the risk of label, bottle rotation, and capsule scuffing is inevitable.
3. In transit condensation inside the container needs to be guarded against as collateral damage to shipping cartons can be substantial, causing collapse and resulting in breakage and other damage.
4. Breakages due to rough handling can also cause collateral damage to the remainder of the shipment.
5. The container needs to be secure from risk of pilferage.

Similar conditions apply for road and rail transport and interstate shipment. Remember the wine bottle is one of the only packaged products (with bottled water) where the product is displayed as a part of the dining or entertaining ritual on most usage occasions, so the maintenance of a high level of package presentation is essential.

Conclusion

In conclusion, global wine marketing is an exciting but complex business in which the wine management team not only needs to focus on the big picture, but be aware of the many details of operating in various countries. Clarity around the reason for exporting, targeting markets, and understanding the needs of the consumers in those markets is critical for success. In addition, investment in an exporting infrastructure, including designated personnel and financial resources, is very important. The future for global wine marketing is large, with the potential to tap into and grow new markets around the world. Savvy wine businesses recognize this opportunity and pursue strategies to capitalize on this growing trend.

Chapter **6**

WINE MEDIA AND PUBLIC RELATIONS

Tor Kenward (VP, Public Relations, Beringer Blass)

*Megghen Driscoll (Public Relations Director,
  Allied Domecq)*

*Tim Matz (President/Managing Director,
  Jackson Wine Estates International)*

The wine industry is remarkably fragmented, and with the thousands upon thousands of choices available to consumers today, making an educated choice can be extremely daunting. Research shows us that a consumer will actually trade from wine to another adult beverage if they become intimidated or overwhelmed by the choices available. To make this process easier and safer, today's consumer has come to rely upon third-party endorsements as a way of selecting their wines or validating their choice.

Most people wouldn't dream of purchasing a computer system without doing the proper research to find the best quality or the greatest value for money. However, when it comes to wine, consumers need not do any research because the wine critics already have.

This chapter describes the very important role of the wine media, as well as their relationship with the public relations staff of a wine business. It begins with a focus on wine media by describing the role of wine media, why it is so important, the role of the wine journalist, and the impact of wine scoring systems. The second half of the chapter describes the role of wine public relations, including definitions, relationships with wine media professionals, and the communications vehicles used for public relations. The chapter ends with a brief overview of some of the future issues for wine media and public relations.

Defining the Role of Wine Media

Wine media can be roughly defined as the group of writers, journalists, and reporters who evaluate and communicate the benefits of wine to the public. The role media plays in the wine industry is paramount to the current success and future growth of individual companies and brands. While it provides individual challenges and opportunities for wineries, brands, and journalists, it has been a critical contributor to the overall growth and expansion of wine consumption in all regions of the world. As with the influence of the press throughout our daily lives, media coverage of the wine industry has similar effects.

There are four major roles media plays within the wine industry:

1. As consumer advocate where the writers or journalists feel they have a core obligation to protect the consumer from overhype, misrepresentation, and too much irrelevant information.
2. As a third-party, unbiased endorser of brands where there is vested interest to be as objective as possible.
3. To introduce and educate consumers to new brands, styles, varietals.
4. To provide newsworthy interesting and fact-based information for the consumer to make a more informed purchase choice.

The role media plays is one of the most important parts of the marketing mix (when communicating brand information) within the wine industry, but it also extends beyond that as it is also the means to deliver and communicate messages about the industry, companies, and social responsibilities and issues relating to alcohol. The marketing side of the role of media mostly pertains to brands, products, and companies communicating messages of imagery, rational and emotive benefits.

The Importance of Wine Media

The media possesses a huge influence over the wine-consuming public, using magazines, journals, newsletters, radio, television, and the Internet to deliver messages about wineries, particular brands, varietals, and products. There are a handful of key influential writers and publications that have national influence, but there are also many markets where there is a particular following from a local writer or wine journalist. Additionally, almost every local paper has a weekly or monthly wine review, either by syndication or a food critic who happens to cover wine. Both the national media and the local critic are very important.

As this book is focused on New World wine regions, it is notable that the role of media is more relevant in the US than perhaps any other large wine-consuming country in the world. This perhaps is due to four reasons:

1. The US historically is not a wine-consuming nation so third-party endorsements are heavily relied on.
2. Due to the relative newness of our industry, the consuming palate is not as developed, and hence relies on knowledge gathered through the media.
3. It is the nature of the American consumer to seek guidance via critics and experts, no different than when evaluating movies to view or electronics to purchase.
4. The wine business is so fragmented and there are so many choices (which change slightly each year) that the overwhelmed consumer counts on recommendations of the "experts."

Role of the Wine Journalist

The role of the wine journalist is to act as a third-party critic evaluating wine from the objective characteristics as well as the subjective differences within each wine. They will give guidance, direction, facts, and opinions about different wines. While knowing the facts about wine is consistent amongst wine critics, it is important to understand wine critics are individuals with different opinions. Every wine critic has a unique palate; therefore, their preferences for wine styles will vary. Most wine journalists are somewhat or extensively trained in tasting wine and hence they know how to maximize their use of the senses. While they will likely agree on the facts, such as grape variety or residual sugar, it is not uncommon for wine critics to judge a specific wine completely differently. The subjectivity in tasting comes into play because each individual has unique, varying degrees of taste, just like DNA is different in everyone. For example, one person might adore sugar and pick that flavor up more readily than spice. Additionally, a person may have been exposed to more exotic-tasting foods in their younger years, and may have developed tastes much greater defined than someone with a more limited diet.

Many wine journalists, with their trained palates, tend to classify wines in a "box," such as Rhone style or Bordeaux style or Beaujolais style. After the taste profile is put into a box, subjectivity comes into play because varying taste buds will gravitate to the different flavors. An example of subjectivity would be when judging or tasting Syrah/Shiraz, wines from the same grape; each could taste very differently depending upon many factors, including country of origin, microclimate, vinification techniques, or oak maturation (the options and outcomes can be staggering). For example, an Australian Shiraz may have bold, fruit-driven characteristics with hints of white pepper whereas a classic Rhone style Syrah will likely be earthier. Both can be fabulous wines, just different.

Gatekeepers

A gatekeeper is a term used within the wine industry that defines a person or group of people who have extraordinary influence impressing their opinions within the wine community. For example, a gatekeeper in the retail segment would be a key buyer of a major chain. As it pertains to the media, a gatekeeper is someone whose opinions, views, and expertise are respected, accepted, and credible within the wine industry. A gatekeeper can be a respected wine writer, but the term is not limited to just journalists.

There are many experts out there who do not have a media outlet to express their views; however, they can be as influential and important as a local or national reporter. These "gatekeepers" are often called upon by the media to provide perspective, content, and personal recommendations. This group is made up of high-profile Master Sommeliers, Masters of Wine, key retailers, and restaurateurs. For example, having the Master Sommelier at the Ritz Carlton in New York promoting wine in his restaurant or on a panel discussion can add tremendous value to a brand's reputation and credibility.

Wine Scores and Rating Systems

While scores or ratings are perhaps one of the most controversial subjects within the media, it is also one of the most influential measures when promoting wine. Wine scores provide a quantifiable rating system for the industry to differentiate wines, therefore allowing the trade and consumer to make informed decisions. Due to the influx of so many types of media and the speed at which it is delivered to the reader or listener, wine messages have become like so many other messages, the latest or most memorable sound bite. For example, if a consumer sees that a specific wine has received a 90-point score or a 5-star rating, he/she will feel that wine is an acceptable or even preferable choice. Table 6.1 outlines the three major types of wine scoring systems used by the media.

Of course getting a good review in a national publication is sure to result in additional sales and brand recognition, but a very targeted message in a small market can do wonders in that specific city. For example, getting a "best buy" in *Consumer Reports* magazine is extremely powerful on a national level, just as getting a positive wine review from a respected critic in a local newspaper will have tremendous impact in that local market.

Defining Wine Public Relations

Wine public relations can be roughly defined as "developing and promoting positive winery news and brand information via advertising, journalism, and special events

Table 6.1. Three Major Wine Scoring Systems

System Name	Scoring Method	Examples
20-Point UC Davis System	Rates wines on a scale of 1 to 20, with 20 being highest (13–20 = average to outstanding quality).	Mostly judging at Wine shows
Star or X System	Rates wines on a scale of 1 to 5 stars or "X"s, with 5 stars being highest.	*Wine X Magazine,* *San Francisco Chronicle*
100-Point System	Rates wines on a scale of 50 to 100 points, with 100 being highest. Used most frequently.	*Wine Spectator,* *Wine & Spirits Magazine*

for the public."According to Posart and Fransen (2004), professionals in wine public relations are experts in the art of "spinning" a message within the media to promote a particular wine business.

Obviously, within the wine industry, one-on-one communication with consumers, distributors, and wine journalists is beneficial; however, this doesn't always have the scope of brand communication that is desired. Therefore, good wine public relations insures that the message reaches much larger audiences, via newspapers, magazines, journals, radio, television, and other media channels. By promoting winery news and information via a third party, it is often perceived that there is more credibility in the message (Academy of Wine Communication, 2003).

After consistent messaging from a wine public relations department, eventually it is possible that a reporter/critic or journalist will actually use the brand communication points within their articles. However, this is a very unpredictable process—it can happen overnight or it can take years. An example of this happening rather quickly is the Charles Shaw brand, also known affectionately as "Two Buck Chuck." This brand was released in early 2003 via a grocery outlet called Trader Joe's in the Western US. Through the endorsement of this trusted grocery store, thousands of consumers purchased the wine at a price of $1.99. With such a low price, and a decent taste, it immediately became an overnight success. Cases of the wine flew off the shelves, and the success of the brand was so phenomenal that it was covered in newspapers and magazines across the country, as well as on the national evening news on a major TV station.

An example of a second wine brand that took much longer to achieve fame, but perhaps has been more effective in the long term, is Penfolds from Australia. This brand was virtually unknown in the US, even though it had been sold in Australia for more than 150 years. When it received a *Wine of the Year Award* in the mid-1990s, demand for the wine was so great that stores had to allocate the amount they sold to customers because they couldn't keep it on the shelves. Both of these wine brands are good examples of excellent public relations campaigns promoting positive brand messages and stories.

Public Relations Role

The role of wine public relations is to work in partnership with top management, sales, and marketing to deliver consistent messages on company/corporate affairs and on the wine brands within the portfolio. Within an organization, wine public relations fulfills two key responsibilities:

Responsibility #1: The primary responsibility is to act as point of contact and communication liaison to anyone outside the organization, addressing issues in corporate affairs, government relations, and crisis management. Public relations personnel are responsible for delivering a consistent, clear, and concise message to all the appropriate parties to ensure that what should or needs to be said is accomplished. On occasion public relations professionals have to address very sensitive issues, problems, or challenges presented in the marketplace. Examples could include a specific wine quality issue that penetrates the public perception, or a highly allocated wine that has been recently written about and is in great demand. In these cases, as with any others, it is imperative that the public relations professional communicates the facts very accurately so the message is not misperceived in any way. Facing these types of issues is perhaps the most challenging responsibility within public relations, and can either make or break a company's reputation.

Responsibility #2: The second responsibility is to act as communication liaison for all the brands to the outside media, trade, and consumers. This involves expressing the attributes and imagery to best convey the message the brand wants to communicate. This is where public relations works closely with sales and marketing to ensure consistency on how the brand is marketed across all tiers.

Because public relations professionals have different roles and responsibilities, where this group reports varies: sometimes to marketing and sometimes to executive management. Either way, the sensitivity of the information requires that public relations staff be closely linked to senior management in an organization.

Relationship Between the Wine Reporter and the Public Relations Professional

Public relations professionals work very closely with wine writers, reporters, and journalists. These are perhaps the most important relationships a public relations person can have in the wine industry. The influence this core group can exert on brands and companies is tremendous and requires time, energy, and professionalism by all parties.

The wine reporter relies upon the public relations professional just as much as the public relations professional relies upon the reporter. There is always a fine balancing act between the two parties because each has individual goals but needs the other party to achieve those goals. If you can provide a credible and interesting hook or angle, the reporter will probably use it. The key is in establishing a relationship with the person and having first-hand knowledge of what they write about and who their audience is.

Communication Vehicles

There are five major vehicles that are used by wine public relations and media professionals, which are described below.

Consumer Publications

Consumer publications consist of any medium that is targeted at the ultimate wine purchaser. These include newspapers, magazines, newsletters, and the Internet/websites. Wine-specific publications provide a targeted forum to reach wine consumers. Some of the largest circulated magazines are *Wine Spectator*, *Wine Enthusiast*, and *Wine & Spirits*, which have tremendous influence with both the trade and the consumer.

Wine critics educate consumers by describing and promoting wines from specific wineries primarily through the use of consumer publications. Wine companies often use consumer publications to advertise their individual brands. Advertisements are most often used to promote brand attributes and educate consumers on the various differences of wines, regions, and grapes from around the world.

Newspapers are primarily used as a means to promote wines by individual wine companies (mostly through advertising) and provide a vehicle for wine writers to critique wines (mostly through editorials or columns). This is a consumer-driven medium that targets the wine purchaser in a given market. It is important to note that a third-party endorsement will always carry more weight in the eyes of the consumer than a paid advertisement.

Trade Publications

Trade publications are specifically targeted at suppliers, wineries, restaurateurs, retailers, and distributors. Examples of trade publications include *Santé, Impact, Market Watch*, and *Beverage Dynamics* to name just a few. Trade publications are a popular medium used by wineries to inform the trade about their brands and their company. They are also a means for wine writers to provide descriptions, knowledge, and opinions on various wines and wineries. Additionally, almost every state has a local beverage publication, such as the *Pennsylvania Beverage Journal, Massachusetts Beverage Journal*, or *California Beverage Journal*.

Radio

Radio is a medium that is less utilized in the wine industry relative to many other industries, perhaps due to cost and reach to the specific targeted audience. When used it is primarily a vehicle for wineries to advertise specific brands where it is paid advertising in the traditional sense. Radio can also be used sometimes to provide a platform for an interview between a show host and a wine expert (e.g., a wine critic or writer, a winery representative, or industry advocate). Local radio shows are a terrific way to generate publicity, although they are used much less often than traditional print publications.

Television

Television, while less used than written publications as well, is a medium used within the wine industry in two ways. It provides a platform for traditional advertising, although this is not a common practice for wineries, mostly due to cost, reach, and general societal pressures of limiting wine exposure to specific targeted age groups. Secondly, television is a medium used to educate and promote wines via specific wine-related shows. In order to get television coverage one must have a compelling story to tell. It must be noteworthy, informative, and/or entertaining. While it is not always easy to get television, the results can be exceptional.

Internet

Almost all wine companies (including individual brands) and publications now have websites, which are geared toward the consumer. The Internet has become a very effective medium to communicate information about the wine industry, especially in terms of cost efficiency and speed to market. Due to the sophisticated abilities to segment specific groups or individuals, messages on the Internet can be written and delivered in customized ways to ensure effective communication.

The Future of Wine Media and Public Relations

The media and public relations will always play critical roles in the wine industry. With the influx of new brands into the marketplace, living in a society where information overload exists, and consumers being more hurried now than ever before, the roles of public relations and the media will continue to be platforms that create brand awareness, communicate attributes to consumers, and provide the information necessary for the trade and consumers to make an informed choice.

In the overall marketing mix, public relations will continue to be one of the most cost-effective ways of obtaining and retaining brand recognition and brand loyalty. The media—whether it is via print, radio, television, or the Internet—will continue to be a critical vehicle used to communicate consistent, clear, and concise messages to the intended audience.

Chapter 7

THE IMPORTANCE OF WINE BRAND

Linda Nowak (Wine Marketing Professor, Sonoma State University)

Jean Arnold (President, Hanzell Vineyards)

Paul Wagner (Wine Marketing Professor, Napa Valley Junior College)

Branding has been around for centuries as a means to distinguish the goods of one producer from those of another. Technically speaking, whenever a person or organization creates a new name and puts it on a bottle of wine, they have created a new brand of wine. A brand can be a name, term, sign, symbol, or design; however, the US Treasury Department's Tax and Trade Bureau (TTB) requires that some kind of brand name be on the front label of the bottle.

This chapter describes the process of establishing a wine brand. It begins with an explanation of why branding is so critical, and then describes conditions for successful branding. Next it provides an overview of wine customer segmentation, and then describes how to position a brand. Information on how to ensure consistency of brand image, the characteristics of a good brand name, and customer loyalty techniques are also provided. A section on the special challenges of taking a national wine brand to international markets is also included. Finally, the chapter ends with a description of how two famous wine brands were developed.

The Importance of Branding

Why is branding so important? Well-recognized brands make shopping easier for the consumer. No one wants to evaluate the advantages and disadvantages of several thousand different wine brands every time they go to the store. Many wine drinkers are willing to try new wines, but having gambled and won, they like to buy a sure thing the next time. It saves time and reduces risk.

Promoting a wine brand has advantages for wineries as well as consumers. A good brand reduces the winery's selling time and effort. Sometimes a winery's brand name is the only element in its marketing mix that a competitor cannot copy. Also, good brands can improve the winery's image, speeding acceptance of new products marketed under the same name. In other words, if the winery has a good reputation for its Chardonnay, consumers may be more willing to take a gamble on the winery's Sauvignon Blanc.

In the very competitive wine industry, it is critical that the winery differentiate its wine in some way from other wines that are competing for the same market. These differences may be rational and tangible—related to the quality of the wine—or more symbolic, emotional, and intangible—related to what the wine brand represents in the minds of the consumers. The wine brand name and all of the quality, price, and symbolic images the consumer recalls about a specific wine brand are what distinguishes a wine brand from its unbranded bulk counterpart.

Some wineries create competitive advantage with value—through providing decent quality and a low price. Other wineries create competitive advantage through producing the highest quality wine they can. Other wineries do not stop at creating a great wine; they use nonproduct-related images and stories to make the wine memorable to the consumer. In the wine industry, these intangible image associations may be one of the most effective methods for distinguishing one brand from all of the others.

Creating a successful wine brand entails blending all elements about the wine together in a unique and memorable way that appeals to the target customer. The wine must be of good quality, the brand name must be appealing and in tune with the consumer's perceptions of the wine, and the packaging, promotion, pricing, and all other elements must meet the consumer's tests of appropriateness, appeal, and differentiation.

Conditions Favorable for Successful Branding

According to Perreault and McCarthy (2002), it takes time to establish a respected brand. The following conditions are favorable to successful branding:

- The product is easy to identify by brand or trademark.
- The product quality is the best value for the price and the quality is easy to maintain.
- Dependable and widespread availability is possible. When customers start using a brand, they want to be able to continue using it.
- Demand is strong enough that the market price can be high enough to make the branding effort profitable.
- There are economies of scale. If the branding is really successful, costs should drop and profits should increase.
- Favorable shelf locations or display space in stores will help. (Wineries and their distributors must use aggressive salespeople to get favorable positions.)

Know Thy Customer

The wise winery owner or brand manager will take some time to understand their target customer. Various New World countries have provided several ways to segment wine consumers, but one simple and useful method is that provided by The Wine Market Council (2000). They have researched the different types of wine consumers in the US and have come up with the following classification scheme of three categories:

- **Core wine consumers:** These core wine consumers account for approximately 86% of the table wine volume consumed in the US. Fifteen percent of the core wine consumers drink wine daily, 48% drink wine a few times a week, and 37% drink wine weekly. Sixty-three percent of these wine consumers are female.
- **Marginal wine consumers:** This group consumes the remaining 14% of the table wine volume sold in the US. Marginal wine consumers drink wine less often than weekly but at least as often as every 2–3 months. Forty-six percent of these consumers regard wine as a special occasion drink. However, when they do drink wine they drink about the same amount of wine as the core consumer, approximately 2.2 glasses per occasion. Sixty-four percent of these consumers are female.
- **Nonadopters of wine:** These consumers either do not drink wine at all or drink it less frequently than every 2–3 months.

The Wine Market Council (2000) found that an acceptable price range of wine for everyday use at home was US$6.50 to $19.00 and an acceptable price range in restaurants was US$12.00 to $29.50. There were no price sensitivities that differentiated the core wine consumer from the marginal consumer. For both types of consumers the most important factor when making a purchase choice was type or varietal of wine, followed by planned price range, brand, and country or place of origin.

Wine Brand Positioning

Positioning the wine brand is at the core of a successful marketing strategy. A good wine brand positioning helps to guide marketing strategy by clarifying what a brand is all about and how it is unique from other wine brands. The strongest brands deepen their points of difference from other brands by convincing the consumer that they can provide greater benefit or value on the attributes that matter to the customer. For example, Volvo and Michelin have positioned themselves as products that provide safety and peace of mind, Intel has positioned itself as performance and compatibility, Coke as Americana and refreshment, Disney as fun, magic, and family entertainment, and BMW as styling and driving performance.

Deciding on a positioning requires determining: 1) who the target customer is, 2) who the main competitors are, 3) how the brand is similar to these competitors, and 4) how the brand is different from these competitors. In the case of Volvo, their automobiles appeal to people who most value safety and reliability and are willing to pay a little more to ensure that they get it. Volvo owners are less concerned with styling and driving performance. An automobile cannot be all things to all people and neither can a wine. Wine coolers can be fruity, fun, and refreshing, but a customer who pays $200 for a bottle of wine is most likely looking for other product benefits, such as outstanding quality and the prestige associated with owning an expensive bottle of wine.

Brand positioning involves understanding long-term pricing strategy. Pricing strategy, whether it is US$3.99 per bottle or US$100.00 per bottle, requires that the winery understand the investment they have in the land, bricks and mortar, global competition, costs of goods sold, quality of the wine, style of the wine, quantity produced (limited supply?), etc. Wine over US$30.00 retail transcends just being an important wine. It is a luxury good and usually needs a powerful story with an emotional connection.

Once a brand has successfully positioned itself in the minds of the consumer, it is difficult to change consumer perceptions and that positioning. Therefore, the winery should carefully consider the positioning strategy. For example, there are several categories of wine: jug, popular premium, fighting varietals, classics, premium, ultra-premium, and luxury. Once a wine brand has been positioned as a jug wine, as in the case of Gallo, it takes years of good wine ratings and lots of advertising money to convince wine consumers that that winery can make an excellent premium wine, as in the case of Gallo of Sonoma.

The winery may not always have total control of the product's positioning in the minds of the consumers. Country of origin is an excellent example. Wine consumers may have the perception that all wines from Chile or Argentina are of inferior quality, when, of course, this is not the case. But convincing consumers to change their long-held beliefs is an uphill battle. The French still believe that wines from the "New World" are inferior to French wines.

Being Consistent With Brand Image

Once a winery decides on a positioning strategy, in other words how that wine is special and unique, then the winery must be consistent with promoting that image in everything it does. If the wine is going to be positioned as a luxury wine, then everything the winery does to market that wine must reinforce the perception of luxury. This starts with an expensive looking label and bottle, carries over into all of the promotion pieces, and is reinforced by the marketing staff with their distributors and in the tasting rooms. For example, luxury wine advertising should only be placed in magazines, restaurants, and events that are considered "upscale."

Building a brand image takes time. The winery must beware of too much emphasis on short-term sales growth and current promotions without regard to the overall brand strategy and the image it is trying to build. Everyone that works for the winery must be aware of the brand's distinctive attributes and be ready to always represent the brand to distributors and consumers with consistency. For example, if the winery's strategy is to promote an image of "family" that goes all the way to the Spanish Land Grants in Sonoma County, then every piece of literature must consistently convey that image.

During the process of building an image for the wine brand, the winery may decide it is prudent to give the brand a "personality." This can be a very effective method for helping consumers differentiate the brand from the thousands of others available to them. A wine brand, like a person, can be characterized as being modern, old-fashioned, fun, exotic, or irreverent. The tasting room staff and tasting room decor, labels, advertising, and special events should reinforce this personality as part of the image building campaign.

Characteristics of a Good Brand Name

A carefully selected brand name can reinforce the positioning strategy and also contribute to the brand's image. It can help tell something important about the winery or its products. Following are some characteristics of a good brand name (Perrault & McCarthy, 2002):

- short and simple,
- easy to spell and read,
- easy to recognize and remember,
- easy to pronounce,
- can be pronounced in only one way,
- can be pronounced in all languages (for international markets),
- suggestive of product benefits,
- adaptable to packaging/labeling needs,
- no undesirable imagery,
- always timely (does not go out of date),
- adaptable to any advertising medium,
- legally available for use (not in use by another firm).

Building Brand Loyalty

Every business tries to develop brand-loyal customers: customers who not only like their brand, but will repeatedly purchase it instead of another brand. Airlines try to build brand loyalty through their frequent flyer programs. American Express has its Membership Rewards program, which gives cardholders points based on the amount they charge. The points can be redeemed for a variety of items, such as airline tickets, jewelry, and electronics. Safeway has its Savings Club in which members receive discounts on certain marked items in stores. Wineries build loyalty through newsletters, clubs and member-only events, support of local schools and charities, protecting the environment, members-only websites, and quantity discounts.

Simply put, how likely is it that a customer will switch if the wine brand's price is changed, features are changed, or a competitor's products have perceived or actual superior features (their wine received a higher score than yours)? Strong brands have the highest level of brand loyalty.

In spite of easy switching costs, an onslaught of higher competitor ratings, new entrants into the market, and a vast array of lower price/value alternatives from New World countries such as Australia and Argentina, a winery tries to cultivate in its customers a nonspecific emotional attachment to the brand. Sometimes that emotional attachment comes from the special treatment the customers receive every time they stop by the winery or attend a special "members-only" preview of the new release. Other times, the loyalty comes from customer identification with the owners and the lifestyle they portray, such as Ravenswood consumers who identify with the "rebel" image of the winery and may actually tattoo themselves with the Ravenswood symbol. Another example is Bonnie Doon Winery, which cultivates an image of fun with irreverent labels and unique wine club member parties that appeal to a loyal group of consumers.

Following are some tips for building an effective loyalty program (Keller, 2003):

- **Know your customers:** Most loyalty programs involve the use of sophisticated databases and software to determine which customer segment to target with a given program.
- **Change is good:** Wineries must constantly update the program to attract new customers and prevent other wineries from developing "me-too" programs.
- **Listen to your best customers:** Suggestions and complaints from top customers must be carefully considered, because they can lead to improvements in the program.
- **Engage people:** It is important to make customers want to join the program. This includes making the program easy to use and offering immediate rewards when customers sign up.

Research has found that loyalty-building programs in themselves are not enough for the customer. Just as in the case of the airlines, in which the customer demands on-time service, well-maintained planes, and a fair price, the wine buyer demands consistent quality and a reasonable price. With over a thousand brands of wine in the

US alone, the customer has many options. Disappoint them once and they may never buy the wine brand again!

The Challenges of Taking a Brand International

Obviously, the challenges facing a company creating a national wine brand are considerable. In general, there is a lack of brand loyalty, and wine brands are usually fighting for shares of the market that would be unappealing to almost any other industry. At the international level, these challenges only become more difficult.

For most consumers, wine is an expression of personal taste and culture. In many markets, this means a primary interest in regional or local wines, with only rare explorations into the larger world of imported wines. In any market that produces wine, imported wines are going to have a smaller share of the market than local wines. And some markets, most notably those with slower economies and less expensive local products (Eastern Europe and Latin America), will always be a challenge.

The situation is exacerbated by the high cost of goods for most wine products, compared with the more traditional international branded products. There simply isn't the same kind of room in the budget for the traditional methods of international brand marketing, such as television advertising and major media promotions. Therefore, when attempting to establish an international brand, four major elements are critical:

- **Top quality:** The first is a top-quality product. This means a clear category leader that establishes the company as being in the top tier of international wines. This is the flagship behind which the rest of the portfolio will sail into each market. It must be among the greatest wines of its region, and compare on some level with the greatest wines in the world. This wine not only establishes credibility with the key influencers in the media and trade, but also creates the demand among consumers for rare and wonderful wines.
- **Brand story:** The second element is a strong story behind the brand: a way of capturing the imagination of the market and the attention of the media. This story must work in all of the target markets—and that alone may be a challenge. Because public relations campaigns offer more cost-effective ways to communicate to the various audiences than advertising, this story is critical. Personality is the key for long-term visibility and credibility.
- **International relationships:** The third element is relationship building. This means not only establishing relationships with key customers in each market, but also attempting to build long-term partnerships with critical distributors and retailers. The wine industry is a relationship-driven industry, and savvy players dedicate the time and people in each market to develop and maintain the relationships for the life of the brand.
- **Patience:** The final element is being realistic and patient. Building international wine brands can take years, even decades. A single wine brand will never be a dominant force in the market the way Coke and Pepsi are; but it is possible to build a brand that has real international cachet and uses that cachet to achieve goals in both profitability and volume. An example of a

very strong and old wine brand is Dom Perignon. The brand has been built over decades, but the owners have ensured that the quality, the special brand story (monk who discovered sparkling wine), and the relationships are in place to secure the brand's place as one of the most enduring in wine history.

A Tale of Two Brands

In 1996, *Chalk Hill* was a little known grocery store brand barely making enough revenues to keep the winery going. By 1998, they had repositioned themselves to be one of the top US Chardonnay producers, with a waitlist of customers wanting to buy their wine at over US$40 per bottle. How was this achieved? How was Chalk Hill Winery able to change the "brand image" of their wine in such a short time?

The answer lies in their decision to make the commitment and investment to realize a vision for a high-end Chardonnay. Working with a team of wine-marketing consultants, the owners and winemaker went through a process of identifying what was truly unique about their wine. What was the story behind the wine? How was it different from any other Chardonnay in the world. The answer came from the land—the special chalky soil in which their Chardonnay grapes grew was like no other soil in the world. It was a unique soil, from a very special appellation, Chalk Hill, in Sonoma County, California. Furthermore, the vineyards were situated in rolling hills, with 300 acres planted. The combination of all of these factors, plus a small production of cases, grew into the brand image of Chalk Hill.

Once this special, authentic image was realized, then the brand-building process began. A second label sold by the winery, which was eclipsing the Chalk Hill label, was pulled from the market. The Chalk Hill wine label was then updated to reflect the new brand position and story. Wine marketers and a public relations team then put together a communication strategy to describe the "story" to high-end distributors, retailers, and wine writers. The story of the special chalky soil and hillside vineyards was so appealing that high-end restaurants around the nation began to purchase the wine. Sommeliers and wine waiters told the story again and again to customers. Customers then repeated the story to friends, and soon Chalk Hill Chardonnay became a top-selling brand with a waitlist of customers trying to purchase it.

A second successful brand story is the one behind *Hanzell Vineyards*. Once a little know family winery in the foothills of the Mayacamas, today Hanzell is a prestigious, luxury wine that is sold only by allotment to high-end wine shops, fine wine restaurants, and an elite group of wine club members for US$65 per bottle and higher. Again, this was achieved by an in-depth focus and research into what made Hanzell Vineyards unique. What was the story that set them apart from all other vineyards and wineries in the world?

Similar to Chalk Hill, Hanzel made the investment into developing a world-class wine brand by hiring experts to help them "articulate their story." Fortunately, they didn't have to look far, because the quality of the wine was already there—and had been for more than 50 years. The issue, at the time, was that the winery was not that well known.

Hanzell's unique story is the "grand cru" farming standards that they use. Focusing only on the Burgundian varietals of Chardonnay and Pinot Noir, they use sustainable farming techniques, which are environmentally friendly to the special mountain vineyards of their Mayacamas, Sonoma Valley estate. With only 42 of their 200-acre estate planted, they use the same farming techniques as the top 2% of Grand Cru Burgundy. This includes stressed growing conditions and rigorous pruning to intensify the flavors of the wine, which results in very low yields—less than 3 tons per acre—and only 3000 cases produced per year. This creates a very rare, scarce, and exclusive wine that is sought after by wine connoisseurs around the world.

Wine marketing methods to support both brands include using only the finest materials for their embossed and engraved labels; expensive parchment letterhead and brochures; and bottles hand-polished and wrapped in tissue. Every detail of the grape-growing, winemaking, and wine-marketing process receives the utmost care and attention. Likewise, Hanzell Vineyards targets only the top 20% of wine writers, distributors, and retailers, who are invited to special educational events at the winery and other locations. During these meetings, the special story of Hanzell Vineyards is communicated in a relaxing and intimate environment to a very elite and influential group of buyers who will continue to "tell the story" to their customers. Thus, the brand grows successfully, with grace and exclusivity.

These two examples of wine brands illustrate the importance of understanding the uniqueness of the wine's story and then attempting to develop a complete brand strategy to communicate consistently the image and position of the wine. This takes much time, talent, dedication, and vision, but in the end it can pay off handsomely in customer loyalty and positive cash flow.

Summary

Creating a successful brand is a real challenge for wineries. Competition in the industry is intense. Before launching a brand wineries have to develop a long-term plan and be prepared to reinforce their brand image in everything they do. When consumers think of a wine brand they need to recall favorable images or mental associations about the brand. Creating strong, favorable, and unique associations takes time, money, and consistency. It requires that the winery understand its consumers. When consumers think of Coke they think "Americana and refreshment." Whey they think of Disney they think of "fun, magic, family entertainment." When they think of BMW they think of "styling and driving performance." When they think of a specific winery, what special image and perception comes to mind? That is the brand!

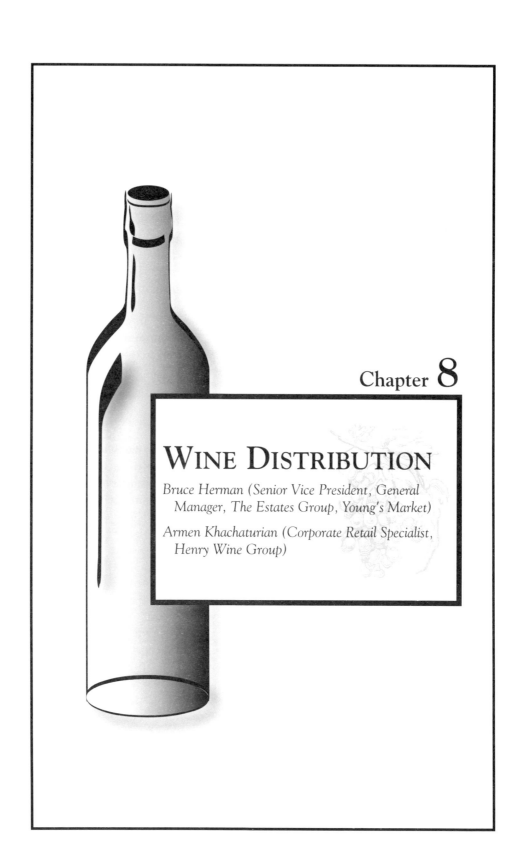

Chapter **8**

WINE DISTRIBUTION

*Bruce Herman (Senior Vice President, General
Manager, The Estates Group, Young's Market)*

*Armen Khachaturian (Corporate Retail Specialist,
Henry Wine Group)*

The distribution of wine from winery to customer has been occurring for centuries, with the earliest records describing the transport of wine in ancient Canaan via amphorae—large terra-cotta pots with a pointed base. Wine has also been transported via goatskin bags, in barrels on old British sailing ships, and today in large ocean freighters that haul it in large case shipments or bulk. Refrigerated trucks and train compartments also transport wine between countries, states, or territories all over the globe. The actual shipment of the wine is fairly easy. It is the complex regulatory requirements and identification of the proper distributor or broker that is more complex.

This chapter provides an overview of the process of wine distribution. It begins with a general description of the process for distributing wine on a global basis. Then it examines one of the most complex distribution systems in the world—that found in the US. Indeed, this system is so multifaceted that many in the wine industry say it is easier to ship wine from the US to England than it is to ship it between certain states. The historical premise for this system is described, as well as present-day distribution regulations and practices. This is followed by an explanation of the role of the wholesaler and broker, including information on how to identify one to sell your wine. Next is a list of tips on how to work successfully with wholesalers and brokers. The chapter ends with a description of "a day in a life" of a distributor sales representative.

Wine Distribution on a Global Basis

The basic requirement to begin distributing wine on a global basis is a *clear strategy* and *commitment* to global wine marketing (see Chapter 5 for more detailed information on this process). This means that the top management team of the company must have identified a reason to export and/or import wine from other countries and have committed the personnel and financial resources to do so. Without this preliminary foundation, attempting to distribute wine globally can be fraught with frustration and disappointing results.

However, once this basic requirement is established, the next step is to *identify a market* that matches the company's wine style, image, and price point. This will require market research on the part of the company, and can also be the first place of contact with potential distributors. According to Wine Vision (2003), some of the best ways to identify potential global distributors are to obtain recommendations from other producers who are already exporting, contact importers at trade shows and other wine events, and work with your local wine associations and agriculture trade offices. Embassies and consulates around the world also publish reports on various commodities, including wine and market share information.

In distributing wine globally, one has three *distribution choices*:

1. Identify an import *distributor* if one is interested in visiting the country to which you will export your wine and want to be involved in negotiation.
2. Use a *broker* if one does not have time to visit the country and prefers to have someone else represent the wines. This is the easiest method to start exporting.

3. *Sell* the wine directly by calling upon specific country distributors and retail establishments. This takes more time, but eliminates the margin made by the distributor or broker who is representing the brand.

The benefit of working with a global distributor or broker is their knowledge of the various markets. They will understand the legal structure of the distribution systems within the countries. In addition, they are knowledgeable about import tariffs, pricing, label requirements, and winemaking regulations. They also have established relationships with consumers, and know the specific cultural nuances of doing business in that country.

Another very important aspect of global distribution is *logistics*, or shipping wine safely so it is not spoiled by fluctuating temperatures. Most wine is shipped internationally by freight forwarders who use specially refrigerated trains, ship containers, and trucks. In addition, they take care that once the wine has arrived in the country that the proper shipping documents are handled and the wine is safely moved to a warehouse or other temperature-controlled environment. For this reason, having the appropriate insurance when shipping wine globally is very important.

A final consideration with global distribution is *payment*. Agreement on currency type, payment method (electronic, check, etc.), timing, etc., must all be negotiated and agreed to with distributors and brokers. Due do credit risks with certain customers, many experienced wine exporters will purchase insurance against nonpayment. Related to this is the issue of exchange rates. This can work for or against a winery. For example, several years ago when the US dollar was stronger than the Euro and Australian dollars, it was difficult for many US wineries to sell wine abroad because it was priced too high due to the exchange rate. At the same time, some European and Australian wine was being sold in the US at inexpensive prices, which cut into US wine sales. This situation has recently reversed, which allows some US wineries to sell their wine more cheaply abroad. However, chances are that the exchange rates will continue to fluctuate as they always do because of economic changes around the globe.

Wine Distribution Outside the United States

Distribution complexity and methodology vary across each market around the world, mostly due to local laws, regulations, and business practices. While this chapter cannot possibly cover every distribution system in even the most populous countries, it is meant to provide some basic knowledge of systems, practices, and challenges that cross many cultures. Some countries allow beverage alcohol, namely wine, to be distributed directly from the winery/supplier to the retailer or restaurateur. Some countries require going through a "middle" tier of some sort. Some countries, as in the US and Canada, have laws that vary among the states or provinces inside the country. Beyond the actual delivery of the products, methods of payment and collection vary as well. The most important understanding, wherever one is distributing around the world, is to recognize the local laws, nuances, and business practices that provide the means to deliver the wine from the supplier to the consumer in the most efficient and effective manner.

Wine Distribution in the United States

From Colonial times until the passage of the 18th Amendment in 1919, beverage alcohol was sold and distributed in a free-market system. There were few rules and regulations about who could own retail establishments and how business was to be conducted between the retailer and the supplier. It was common to have suppliers owning their own bars, saloons, and taverns or giving incentives to retailers to carry their brands exclusively. Incentives to the retail trade may have come in the form of interest-free business loans and mortgages; equipment such as refrigerators, dispensing systems, glassware, and other supplies; or direct rebates to the establishment when they sold the supplier's brands to the exclusion of the competition. Lawlessness, alcohol abuse, and corruption were commonplace when the suppliers were selling directly to the retailers, with a preponderance of saloons tied to the suppliers of beverage alcohol. This abuse of beverage alcohol, public drunkenness, and the control of retail outlets serving the public by the large distilleries and breweries led to the American Temperance Union and the Anti-Saloon League, which saw all beverage alcohol consumption, moderate or excessive, as evil.

The economic challenges suffered by the retailers, partly caused by the exclusionary practices of suppliers, along with the social issues of abstinence resulted in the passage of the 18th Amendment, commonly known as Prohibition. Prohibition did not end the consumption or sale of alcoholic beverages. It forced the practice "underground" and offshore, leading to a black market for beverage alcohol, which was dominated by organized crime. Bootlegging or smuggling of alcoholic beverages became a large and very profitable business. All levels of government lost the ability to control, regulate, and collect tax revenue from this now "illegal" activity. During the Depression, Congress focused its attention away from the moral and religious issues of abstinence and began to consider the potential revenue gains if wines, spirits, and beers once again became legal to sell and consume. Ending Prohibition, in the eyes of Congress and a majority of the American people, could add much-needed revenue to local, state, and the federal government as well as much-needed jobs for the American worker. The "Great Experiment" became a great failure, which both the public and Congress changed on December 5, 1933 when the 21st Amendment to the Constitution was ratified, ending Prohibition and giving the states the authority to regulate the production, importation, distribution, retail sale, and consumption of beverage alcohol inside their borders.

Shortly after the 21st Amendment was ratified, Congress passed the Federal Alcohol Administration (FAA) Act, which set broad limits on the rules states might establish to regulate the sales, promotion, and merchandising of beverage alcohol within their borders. Congress was also concerned with the historic abuses of pre-Prohibition when suppliers owned retail outlets through a tied-house relationship. To insulate the retail tier from the supplier, many states adopted the three-tier system of distribution by placing an independent licensed wholesaler in between the retailer and the supplier. These states are known as open states, of which there are 31. Other states chose to become the wholesaler and retailer (or a hybrid of this structure) and these states are commonly known within the industry as monopoly or control states, of which there are 19.

The control or monopoly states not only regulate beverage alcohol distribution within their borders, similar to open states, but they also sell alcohol beverages wholesale and in many cases act as the retailer selling direct to consumers through state-owned and -operated retail outlets. The control states are: Alabama, Idaho, Iowa, Maine, Montgomery County Maryland, Michigan, Mississippi, Montana, New Hampshire, North Carolina, Ohio, Oregon, Pennsylvania, Utah, Vermont, Virginia, Washington, West Virginia, Wyoming.

The goal of control states is to promote responsibility and moderation in the consumption of beverage alcohol. In the regulated environment present in the US, control states are an alternative to the open or licensed states. They have a controlled distribution system owned and run by state employees that, in essence, substitutes the state for private ownership. Figure 8.1 illustrates the differences between the open and control state process.

The Role of the Wholesaler

Simply put, wholesalers (tier 2) purchase wines and spirits from suppliers (tier 1) and sell, deliver, and service the retail customer (tier 3). Wholesalers also collect state excise taxes and provide gallonage and sales reports to verify usage, consumption, and tax collection. In most states, wholesalers are allowed by law to extend credit to licensed accounts, provide frequent deliveries, provide full case, split case,

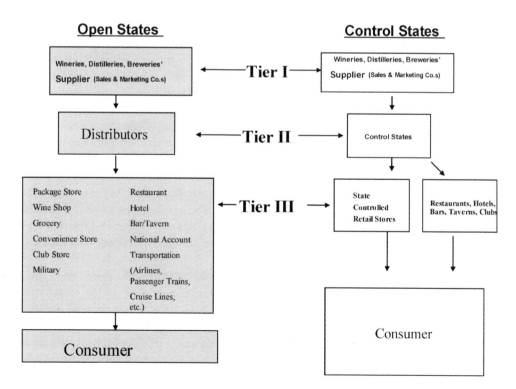

Figure 8.1. Distribution process in US open and control states.

or fill bottle requests to accommodate the needs of smaller retail customers and slower moving brands.

Wholesalers play an important role in the marketing and merchandising plans for the suppliers they represent. Wholesalers implement the suppliers' in-market point of sales programs by making product brochures, fact sheets, and posters available to the consumer through wine shops and package stores. They work with both suppliers and their retail customers to reset shelves, cold boxes, and place displays or wine racks in prime selling locations. Wholesalers train both on- and off-premise retail sales staffs on the use, taste, and food pairings of wines and spirits. They conduct sales seminars, tastings for wait staff, promote the latest cocktail recipes, print wine lists, table tents, and shelf talkers for both their retail customers and their suppliers.

Wholesalers also furnish the suppliers they represent with daily sales data, competitive market information, and category market expertise. Large wholesalers in major markets generally segment their sales force by trade channel (on-premise, off-premise, grocery, chain, club store, and national accounts); wholesalers in major metro-markets also provide specific ethnic market selling expertise about Hispanic, African-American, and Asian consumers. The information collected and given to suppliers, producers, and wineries by distributors, when pieced together throughout the country, gives them the ability to spot trends, target market their merchandising and selling activities, as well as anticipate problems, which gives these suppliers, producers, and wineries a competitive advantage for their wines and spirits.

The Role of the Broker

There are many different types of brokers who provide a service directly to wineries or wine suppliers. Brokers can act like wholesalers by providing the producer with a selling organization (sales people) that has a direct relationship with the retail tier. Brokers usually represent a number of different brands of wines and spirits, and focus their activities on selling their portfolio directly to restaurants, hotels, wine shops, package stores, or grocery chains in the marketplace. While the broker sells to the customer directly to the retail account, the producer usually bills the account directly instead of the broker.

Other brokerage organizations act more like sales and marketing companies, where they help to manage the relationship between the products they represent and the distributors chosen to sell these products within the open states. In this situation, the broker spends more time managing the distributor's sales force and trying to get as much selling time and attention focused on the broker's portfolio of wines and spirits.

Whether the broker sells direct to the retail trade or through a distributor, most brokers have one thing in common. Brokers do not take ownership of the wines they sell, but rather earn a commission from the producer once the wines are sold through to the distributor, the retail tier, or to the control state. This, you will note, is the fundamental difference between a broker who has a sale force that sells to the retail tier and a distributor. Distributors take ownership of the wines they represent by paying the producer or the sales and marketing company, usually within 30 days after an order has been processed by the producer. The distributor not only takes possession of the wine but also maintains the accounts receivables and assumes the risk of bad debts from the retail tier. Brokers, as stated earlier, generally do not take ownership of the wines they represent and do not take on the responsibility of the accounts receivables nor assume the risk of bad debts.

In large markets such as Metro New York and California, where there are many trade channels, ethnic markets, a large concentration of accounts, and a multitude of brands vying for distribution, brokers generally are present to fulfill a need not occupied by the traditional distributor. Brands on the periphery not represented by the first- or second-tier sales and marketing companies, as well as wineries representing their own brands, often utilize brokers to build their distribution and sales volume. Producers also utilize brokers because there is less competition within the broker's portfolio than within the distributor's selection of brands represented in the marketplace.

Generally, brokers do not represent major spirit suppliers or major wineries; therefore, smaller brands can gain a greater share of mind from the broker's selling organization than they can from a major market's distributor. In addition, some small restaurants and wine shops prefer to conduct business with brokers or small distributors because they believe that they are more important to the smaller broker or distributor and will therefore receive better service. Once brands grow in volume and begin to achieve momentum or greater critical mass in a market, brokers run the risk of losing brands as they move to a distributor. As brands grow, producers either decide to have them represented by their own sales force or represented by a larger sales and marketing company. In conclusion, brokers serve a need within the three-tier distribution system and generally represent smaller brands on their way up or more mature brands losing volume on the way down.

Finding a Distributor and Broker for Your Wine

First and foremost, it is important to have a vision for your brand or portfolio and understand who the target consumer is and what trade channels in each market you want to penetrate. Once you have a clear understanding and identity of who you are and where you want to go, it is much easier to choose a distributor or broker for your brand or portfolio of brands that align with your vision.

A good resource when starting out is to consult the Wine and Spirit Wholesalers Association (www.WSWA.org). They are a trade organization that represents most of the distributors throughout the country handling both wines and spirits. Another contact is the Wine Institute (www.wineinstitute.org), which is a trade organization that represents most of the wineries in the US. You will find a helpful resource section on their website and a link to other related organizations that may be used as a source for both distributor and broker leads.

The most effective, yet least efficient, way to identify potential distributors and brokers is to visit the marketplace and talk to both retail and restaurant customers whom you believe should be selling your bands. There is much information that can be gleaned from a market visit and talking to potential customers about who they like to buy wine from, who has the most knowledgeable selling organization, who services them the best, who has a compatible portfolio, and other key issues that would affect your decision-making process when deciding which distributor or broker you want to represent your brands.

Once you have identified a number of potential distributors or brokers, you will also need to have a clear vision of the competitive set and how you want the distributor or broker to approach the marketplace. Do you want them to be strong on-premise or off-premise? Is chain distribution a priority and do you need access to national accounts? Who in their current portfolio of brands may be your direct competitor and who may have the clout to demand more attention and therefore make the distributor or broker less effective on your wines? Remember that in today's consolidated marketplace competition cannot be eliminated, but how it is limited and managed could give you a greater chance for success. After you have sorted out these issues and interviewed as many distributors and brokers as possible, you will be in a good position to determine the best company to represent your brands.

Working Successfully With Distributors and Brokers

To work successfully with distributors and brokers, it is very important to *have a marketing and sales plan*. In addition, it is important to communicate with your distributor or broker early and often. Everyone is trying to get attention from their distributor or broker, and the sooner you can give them your plan, even if it isn't perfect, the better chance you will have of making certain that they don't forget about you and go on to selling someone else's wine. Your plan needs to include marketing as well as sales goals. For example, just telling the distributor your price and how many cases you want them to buy is not a plan—it's a sales allocation. Make certain that your distributor knows what your goals and objectives are for your brands not only for the current year, but also for the next 2 to 3 years.

Some questions to consider are:

- Do you want to be on wine lists, or poured by the glass?
- Does the distributor have copies of your latest and greatest wine reviews?
- Does the distributor know which items are highly allocated and which customers should be given the first shot at buying these sought-after wines?
- Have you effectively communicated which wines are going to be in short supply and which wines are going to be in long supply so that your distributor can manage them in a way that benefits your brands?

Review performance against the plan with your distributor or broker on a very regular basis. Nothing keeps your in-market agent's attention better than having brand review meetings every 60–90 days with management.

Stay focused not only on what your distributor or broker buys from you, but, more importantly, on what they sell to the trade. Although what you sell to the distributor or broker is what generates your revenue, what they sell through to the trade is the real indicator of how well your brand is doing in the marketplace. It is beneficial to not only know what they are depleting to the trade, but also to whom and at what price.

Distributors and brokers often spend too much time and money forcing out cases just to make a sales goal requested by the supplier. In the end, these efforts do not really help to build the brand for the future, but simply move inventory from one tier to the other.

You should have a *clear definition of your competitive set*; communicate it to your distributor and broker network so that they can use it to help guide selling and distribution activities. Also let your distributors and brokers know whether you want your wines to be sold in the chains or the club channel so that they can manage your distribution objectives efficiently and effectively.

Be consistent. Due to the size and complexity of the portfolios managed by distributors today, it is much more productive to present the goals and plans once and not change strategy in the near term. When directions or objectives change, the distributor can quickly lose focus or attention on the brand.

When dealing with the media, *don't limit your contact to just the wine press.* You should include lifestyle editors, and travel and leisure writers, as well as food and restaurant critics. Don't overlook the radio talk shows and cable food shows to promote your wines. We live in an information age and there are hundreds of stations looking for things to talk about to their audience. Once you get press be sure that you have a way to communicate this to your distributor and to your accounts, directly, if at all possible.

Stay in touch with the wine trade. Winemakers and winery principles should make regular visits to the marketplace to meet and greet the people who sell the wines. Much can be learned and accomplished by getting to know your customer face to face. You must always remember that the truth is on the street and not in the boardroom, so stay close to your customers and work the market with your distributor.

Develop a way to *communicate what's going on at your winery* during harvest and at other times of the year directly to your retail accounts and to the distributor's sales force. The wine business is a people business, and the more you can communicate with your customers and distributor directly, the greater the share of mind you will achieve for your brands.

Set up a "trade only" section on your website. This makes it easy for sales people to download winery events, wine reviews, shelf talkers, sell sheets, and the like. It also is less expensive for you because you don't have to print, mail, and/or ship these valuable selling tools to you distributors. They can get them off your website and customize them for their accounts and their market.

Encourage visits from the trade to your property. Don't limit VIP visits only to owners or to buyers, but encourage clerks and waiters to visit your properties as well. They are usually the ones who have direct contacts with the consumer and can suggest your wines for trial.

A Day in the Life of a Wine Distributor

Perhaps the heading is slightly misleading because there is no typical day for a wine sales representative. In fact, no two days will ever be the same due to the nature of the job. As a distributor sales representative, success comes from possessing skills such as time management, organization, follow through, interpersonal communication, and knowledge about your wine product book. It is important to realize that this job entails so much more than just selling wines. If you want to excel as a distributor sales representative you will need to establish good rapport with your buyers. The best way to achieve this is by building good relationships.

Building good relationships is probably the most challenging aspect of this job. You must first gain respect from your buyer. This can be achieved by demonstrating your aptitude for the products you represent, along with displaying a certain degree of professionalism. When you arrive for scheduled appointments, you should be punctual and be prepared to make good use of their time. Keep in mind that building strong relationships does not happen overnight, but with time and persistence this can be accomplished.

A "typical" day starts the night before. You will need plenty of time to plan your route. Your day's itinerary is not based on your own convenience, but rather on the schedule of your buyers. This is where good organization is crucial. Mastering this skill will enable you to perform the challenging task of meeting the time demands of each of your buyers. After deciding which accounts you will visit, you will need to prepare each account individually based on the goals for that store.

When you go to a retail account, such as a wine or grocery store, you will begin by conducting an inventory of your products on the shelves. While conducting the inventory, you might dust bottles, remove any damaged ones, and make sure that each wine label is visible for the consumer to see. Often the bottles will get shifted around, so it is your job to make sure that each product you represent is in its designated place.

After completing the assessment, you will give your buyer a suggestive order, including any new products that your company may have to offer and any special pricing. This is the time when you may have the opportunity to invite your buyer to taste some new wines or vintages, while providing technical and tasting notes. The purpose of giving buyers the opportunity to taste each wine is to allow them to determine if a particular wine can be integrated into their wine program. It also serves as a selling tool for the buyer or wine steward. They will have the information and knowledge to pass on to the consumer.

Once you have completed your assessment you should close the sale. It is at this time that you will telephone the order to the warehouse, where the order will be packaged and delivered to the account. It is always a good idea to follow up with either a phone call or a personal visit to make sure that the buyer is pleased with their purchase, and to answer any more questions they may have regarding the order. Many times, you may even deliver some of the cases of wine yourself, and help stock them on the shelves.

At the end of the day, you will have called on many accounts, but you may still be hosting a wine tasting dinner that evening. The hours can be very long during the peak seasons of summer and fall, but can be less during January and February. Most distributor sales reps are paid a base salary, plus commission, so the more wine that can be sold to an account, the more lucrative it can be. Sometimes the wineries will also provide incentives to distributors to sell more wine. Incentives can range from a bonus to a chance to participate in a raffle for a vacation to an exotic destination.

Due to the autonomous nature of the job, one of the ways for your employer to keep track of your performance is by requiring each sales representative to submit the proper paperwork each week. This report consists of your documentation of each account. This may include the date and time of each appointment, the name of the contact, and a brief summary describing the particular sales call.

In the big picture, the position of the distributor sales representative plays a major role in the wine industry. You bridge the gap between the supplier and the consumer and provide the education and accessibility that will enable the consumer to enjoy the lifestyle that wine has to offer.

Conclusion

In summary, establishing a successful process to distribute your wine is not necessarily easy, but with advance knowledge and perseverance, it will pay off. The wine industry is still basically a "relationship industry" all over the world. Therefore, it is necessary to build the relationships and learn the major regulations in each country, state, province, or territory to ensure your wine can be sold successfully. However, as this chapter states, there are associations that can help in this process, as well as brokers and consultants who can facilitate success.

Chapter 9

DIRECT WINE SALES

Janeen Olsen (*Professor of Wine Marketing, Sonoma State University*)

Curtis Eaton (*National Sales Manager, California Wine Co.*)

Don Getz (*Professor of Tourism and Hospitality Management, University of Calgary*)

Direct wine sales occur when wineries sell directly to the final consumer without the use of independent wholesalers and retailers. There are many methods by which wineries sell directly to consumers, including selling from a tasting room or cellar door, hosting special events and winemaker dinners, having a wine club, selling over the Internet, and/or using telephone and mailing lists. Many wineries also create newsletters and email promotions targeting potential customers. Related to direct sales, and supporting many direct sales programs at wineries, is the concept of wine tourism. Wine tourism is growing rapidly in importance around the world as a means to both educate tourists about wine and support revenue increase through direct wine sales.

With this in mind, this chapter describes the advantages and challenges of direct wine sales, reviews the various sales channels, outlines some of the regulations for direct selling, and provides an introduction to the concept of wine tourism.

Advantages and Challenges of Direct Wine Sales

There are many advantages as well as challenges in selling directly to consumers that must be weighed against each other. The primary advantage to selling direct is that the winery is able to capture the margin that otherwise would go to the distributor or retailer. This margin typically ranges from 25% to 50%. For this reason, many wineries find the profits per bottle of wine are much higher when sold direct. Another reason that wineries may sell direct to consumers and not use the services of distributors may be that the production volume is low and many distributors will not purchase small amounts. Smaller wineries often face this problem when trying to distribute wine and therefore are not able to sell to distributors. Some small wineries sell 75–100% of their wine solely through direct sales (Walker, 2002). V. Sattui Winery in the Napa Valley and Viansa Winery in Sonoma sell 100% of their wine production direct to consumers. Even larger wineries may have smaller amounts of unusual varieties or wine that was not used in their blends, and direct sales allows the wineries to find a market for smaller production lots. They may also produce these unusual varieties or small production wines just to add value for their wine club membership.

With increased competition it is becoming increasingly difficult for newer wineries to find room on retailers' shelves or restaurants' wine lists. It is also becoming more difficult to find major distributors who want to take on new wines. The additional problems within the distribution channel come from a lack of support on promoting products from the distributor's sales team who are overwhelmed with pressure to sell wines from the big producers. A new winery, whose marketing budget is relatively meager compared with the bigger existing wineries, is forced to rely on their direct to consumer sales strategy to overcome these challenges with distributors. These new ventures may find that initially the only method available to them to sell their wine is through direct sales. If they become extremely successful and their reputation grows, it may become possible for them to place their wine with distributors. Navarro initially was direct to consumer and only added distribution to ensure that their products were seen by gatekeepers in the A-tier restaurant and retail accounts.

Even though there are advantages in direct sales, these methods are not without their challenges. For example, even though the profits per bottle may be higher, there are still many additional costs associated with direct sales that must be covered. Money is required to build and operate a tasting room and to organize tours and special events. Internet and direct mail sales require the creation of promotional materials. Databases of potential customers must be created and constantly monitored. Packaging and shipping costs must be covered. Unless all of these activities are done well, direct sales may not turn out to be any more profitable than other methods of selling wine.

Channels for Direct Wine Sales

Direct selling includes a variety of methods available to a winery. It is not uncommon to find that wineries use several of these methods together. The following paragraphs describe the most common methods of selling directly to customers.

Tasting rooms, or cellar door operations as they are called in some regions, are a very popular method of selling direct. In California there are over 600 wineries that operate some form of tasting room. Some tasting rooms are operated at the same location as the winery, while others may be located away from the winery but in a popular tourist area. Both on-site and off-site tasting rooms allow the visitor to sample wines, learn about the viticulture and winemaking techniques, and purchase wine. Some tasting rooms that are located at the winery or near vineyards may operate tours for visitors as well. Many tasting rooms also offer other merchandise for sale besides wine. In some cases the merchandising efforts are minimal, perhaps focusing on wine openers, glasses, and other inexpensive wine-related gifts. In other cases, the merchandising effort may be substantial, selling products not related to wine, such as kitchenware, jewelry, art, and clothing. Many wineries report they earn a substantial portion of their revenues from nonwine sales. When winery merchandising is done well, products should be stocked and displayed in such a way as to support the overall brand image the winery is trying to achieve. Viansa and Beringer are two examples of winery tasting rooms that do an excellent job of merchandising to promote their variety of brands while bringing in substantial revenue.

Special events are another way that wineries can attract customers to the winery or build brand awareness and create customer relationships. Branding is most effective in the wine industry when a winery can sponsor an event that will resonate with that individual when they are making their wine-buying decisions. Special events most often take place at the winery; however, many wineries also participate in trade fairs, festivals, and other events located outside of the property as a way to promote their wines. Regulations often restrict the sale of wine from such off-site events; nevertheless, wineries can use such events to familiarize the participants with the wine, build brand image and awareness, and collect contact information for later direct sales attempts. The types of events that wineries stage are quite broad as event planners are continually coming up with creative themes and ideas to bring in new customers. Mardi Gras parties, Italian festivals, and cuisines of all types provide popular themes for special events. The concert series and Robert Mondavi Winery and Wente Vineyards are popular with visitors.

Wine clubs take on different forms, but typically a person agrees to buy a set amount of wine on a regular basis. The customer provides credit card and shipping information and the winery automatically ships the wine. Wine club sales can be a great asset to wineries because they are a predictable, ongoing source of revenue. Both budgeting and production levels can be improved when wineries know they can count on a certain level of club sales each month or quarter. Wine clubs also allow a winery to stay in touch with customers who live too far away to visit the tasting room on a regular basis. This is why many wineries consider wine clubs an excellent way to build brand loyalty. On of the biggest obstacles that wineries face is that, as of 2003, they are only allowed to ship to club members in 21 states. Yet 49% of all potential wine drinkers live in one of these states, creating a large market to serve (Ferguson, 2003).

Signing up members for wine clubs occurs in several ways. Often visitors to tasting rooms are asked if they would like to become a member. It is not uncommon for tasting room employees to receive a commission for each new member they sign up. Usually an employee receives $5 to $10 per sign up plus incentives tied into monthly competitions. Another way that wine club members are signed is through an Internet site. This allows people who have never visited the winery to receive wine shipments as well. Wine club members are also signed up at a consumer-based trade tasting where award-winning wines are poured and consumers can sign up to receive these wines as part of their membership. The San Francisco Wine Competition tasting provides wineries such as Stryker and Stonegate a place for sign-ups for wine club members.

As there are many wine clubs for consumers to choose from, not only those offered by wineries, but retail clubs as well, wine companies increasingly offer benefits to wine club members. Examples of benefits include additional discounts on wine purchases, waving tasting fees at the tasting room, invitations to winemaker dinners, and other special events and parties (Coppla, 2000).

Newsletters and direct mail campaigns can also be used to solicit wine sales. Wineries can keep customers informed of what is taking place at the winery, such as harvest and special events, and also let customers know when new wines are released. Newsletters often contain educational articles about winemaking and viticulture as well as recipes and human interest stories. The purpose of newsletters and direct mail campaigns in not only to sell wine, but many wineries find it an excellent way to develop brand loyalty among customers.

Telephone sales can be another means to reach customers. Although not as common, there are wineries that sell wine directly to customers over the phone. Many of these wineries have highly sought-after wines that are allocated, so the calls are primarily made to qualified customers so that they can place orders when the wine becomes available. Haffner is such an example of a winery in Sonoma Country that sells most of its wine through telephone marketing.

Internet sales can account for a small percentage of wineries' total revenues but still be an important means to create a strong brand image. Often the revenue is used to offset website expenses when a website's primary purpose is to support brand loyalty and build customer awareness. There are significant barriers to consumers making on-line wine purchases, such as: interstate shipping laws, lack of product knowledge, additional shipping and handling costs, the time delay in receiving the product, damaged wines shipped during unsafe weather conditions, and lack of on-line consultations at time of making the wine purchase. We must remember that wine is still a mysterious product to most consumers! On the other hand, Internet availability helps consumers who already possess product awareness to buy wines in areas where it is not readily available in retail outlets. Wines that have received good reviews or ratings are eagerly sought via the Internet. Small production or "cult" wines can sometimes be sought out using the Internet. The challenges in shipping wine still pose major challenges for consumer purchases via the Internet.

Regulation of Direct Wine Sales

Regulation of direct sales of wine to consumers is a very complex issue. There are currently 32 states that allow interstate shipping in one form or another. This is a very important means of reaching consumers as less than 17% of US wineries are represented in all states by distributors. Wineries often rely on consumer fulfillment companies, such as Consumer Direct Solutions (CDS), to manage their interstate ship-ment needs—storing inventories, managing the wineries' customer databases, and providing weather reports for shipping conditions. Some fulfillment companies are working within the three-tier system to provide shipping opportunities to more than the designated 32 states.

As shipping laws change, the wineries often are forced to wait for common couri-ers such as FedEx, UPS, and DHL to update their own shipping policies to reflect the current changes. This delay, sometimes months, can add to consumer aggravation within the states as eager customers try to get wine shipped to their state immedi-ately upon hearing of regulatory changes. Grass roots efforts such as Free the Grapes and high-profile attorney Kenneth Starr, working on behalf of the Wine Institute, are promoting the cause of overturning restrictions to interstate shipping in the remain-ing 18 states. The final decision as to whether to allow direct shipping will probably be determined by the Supreme Court if and when the case finally is heard. In the meantime, wineries must carefully monitor that they are in compliance with all di-rect shipping laws as the penalty for shipping illegally can be the loss of a winery's license to operate.

The Concept of Wine Tourism

Wine tourism is, simultaneously, a form of consumer behavior, a strategy by which destinations develop and market wine-related attractions and imagery, and a market-ing opportunity for wineries to educate visitors and sell their products directly to consumers (Getz, 2000). Wine tourism reinforces wine exports, as educated consum-ers who have visited a wine-producing region are more likely to become loyal cus-tomers and to spread a positive word about the wines (Chaney, 2002). Travel to wine regions is in part motivated by consumption of wines, leading to a desire to visit the producing areas (Sharples, 2002), and by the favorable image good wines create of the origin region.

Wineries are the core attraction in wine tourism. Even though many are not built or managed as attractions, there is increasing recognition that wine tourism works to the benefit of most wineries and they are adapting to this market. As noted by Dodd and Bigotte (1997), the majority of American wineries rely primarily on tourism for survival, reflecting both their inability to market widely and the fact that profit margins are highest at the source. More and more wineries are being built as architectural landmarks and tourist attractions, as hospitality and function centers, and even as self-contained vacation and conference estates.

In North America the most developed and popular wine regions are in California, especially Napa and Sonoma, but numerous other regions, from Finger Lakes in New York to Okanagan Valley in British Columbia, are aggressively marketing wine tourism, and the growth of visitor infrastructure and landmark wineries is truly impressive. Australia and New Zealand take food and wine tourism seriously, with regions like Marlborough and Barossa Valley becoming "must-visit" destinations for international wine tourists. The hands-down winners in Europe remain France and Italy, as they possess many wine regions known around the globe. Indeed, visits to Bordeaux and other famous wine appellations have taken on the dimensions of a pilgrimage.

Researchers have demonstrated that wine tourists are really cultural tourists searching for a "bundle of benefits" that include food and wine experiences, culture and recreational opportunities, all in attractive destinations (Charters & Ali-Knight, 2000; Williams & Kelly, 2001). Specific to wineries, research reported by Dodd and Bigotte (1997), using interviews with visitors to wineries in Texas, linked environmental and service perceptions as a factor influencing wine purchases, while M. O'Neill and Charters (2000) emphasized the importance of cellar door service quality. What else is needed for a successful tourist-oriented winery? The following elements will make for a complete wine tourist experience:

- access and visibility—signage and entry statement;
- parking and special access provisions, catering for the handicapped;
- design concept, views, the right ambiance;
- family orientation (play area, picnics);
- reception and direction;
- retailing;
- essential services for comfort and hygiene;
- tours (guided or self-directed) and an efficient internal visitor flow leading to sales areas;
- function areas (eating, tasting, meetings, events);
- departure management (provision for relationship building, mailing lists, sales).

Wineries have to work with destination marketing organizations and local communities to develop wine tourism. Formulating a sustainable wine tourism strategy, incorporating economic, environmental, and social goals, will be beneficial to all.

Conclusion

In summary, it is clear that as the wine industry has become more and more competitive, many wineries are looking for new methods of selling wine to consumers.

Selling direct to consumers has received more emphasis in marketing plans, and many wineries have made direct sales their primary method of distribution. The advantages of direct sales ensure the future growth of this marketing channel. But it won't be an easy road as regulations and costs structures make direct sales of wine a challenging venture.

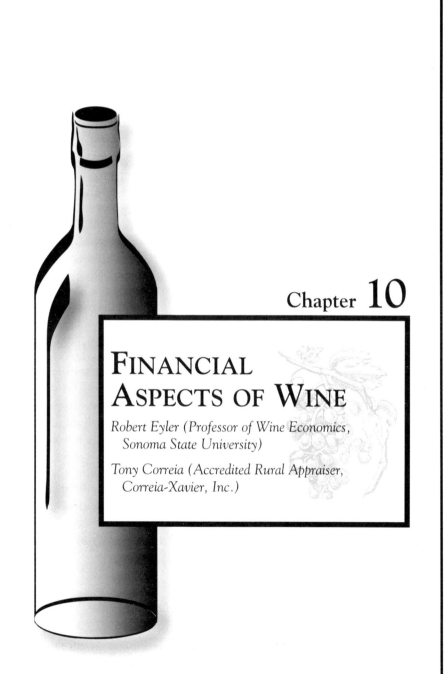

Chapter 10

FINANCIAL ASPECTS OF WINE

Robert Eyler (Professor of Wine Economics, Sonoma State University)

Tony Correia (Accredited Rural Appraiser, Correia-Xavier, Inc.)

Financing a winery, or projects like custom crush, vineyard purchase and development, or importation, all have one thing in common: the investor should only seek to engage in the project if expected to be profitable. Predicting the outcome of any project correctly uses a lot of diverse information.

This chapter looks at different aspects and models inside wineries and related projects, all with this constant theme. One important point to start: the wine business is not financially different than any other business. In a winery, there is a production facility, which chooses inputs and processes to optimize profit. Once the product is made, the wholesale price is determined somewhat by the market, somewhat by the firm; however, the bottle price dictates the winery budget. The models below show the interdependence of each stage of wine production and sale on the other, and how financial fundamentals act as our leitmotif. First, a brief refresher on finance basics provides a foundation for this chapter's ideas and conclusions. Then applications of these financial fundamentals show examples for different parts of a wine project. Finally, some ancillary topics on financing choice and other issues round out our look at finance in the wine industry. We use a winery project as an example throughout, with the idea that any other project is just a subset of a winery.

Financial Foundations in Theory

Finance is applied economics, related to making decisions concerning both real and financial assets. Real assets, such as grapes, machines, labor, etc., dominate production and day-to-day business at most wineries, while financial assets, such as trademarks, stocks, leverage, etc., dominate wine production administration and sales. For the most part, we focus on real assets here. In all cases, we are trying to maximize profit with respect to the constraints faced by the winery. In short, the decisions at each step of the winemaking process, from rootstock to the dining table, must be made with the same mentality. To analyze these choices, we use a net present value idea throughout this chapter.

Net present value (NPV) is a financial concept used generally for decisions concerning plant and equipment acquisition, or for gaining ownership in a firm through venture capital. The same rules apply in the case of financial assets, such as goodwill when buying a brand or label from another entity. The value today of future profits, less the initial cost to acquire the asset, is the NPV in terms (always) of cash flows. A simple formula for this is the following:

$$NPV = \frac{\sum_{i=1}^{n} ECF_i}{(1+R)^i} - I_0 \qquad \text{(Equation 1)}$$

where ECF is expected cash flows (cash profits), R is interest rate or rate of discount, I_0 is initial cash outlay for purchase of capital for time period $i = 1, \ldots n$, where period n is the last period of the asset's usable life or when the asset is fully depreciated.

This formula acts like a formula for profit. If the NPV > 0 (expected profits are greater than zero), the investment should be made; if the NPV < 0 (expected profits are negative), the investment should not be made; if the NPV = 0, flip a coin. For similar investment choices, the investment with the highest NPV is chosen. If no choices have an NPV > 0, a new array of choices should be sought, including additional search costs in the new figures, or the project should consider abandonment. Below, this idea is applied to different aspects of a winery's operation.

Vineyard Economics and Finance

Wine economics are little different than any other industry's economics. Wine is an agricultural by-product, an agricultural good, and must be treated as such fundamentally. However, it has large differences that separate it from most other agricultural products. The good's price on the open market for many firms is found by subjective judgments concerning wine quality rather than scientific means. There is a 3–5-year wait for the first crop after planting.[1] It is also an alcohol-based product, which subjects it to different, additional commerce laws than many other agricultural goods. From rootstock choice to trellising to trucking the harvest out of the vineyard, the choices made in all areas of the vineyard dictate how much the grapes are worth.[2]

Vineyard management choices must be assessed using the same methodology. Find out what the costs will be to maintain the vineyard and (if possible) get the companies to commit to a certain number per acre. There will be far fewer choices for vineyard management than any other choice in the vineyard. For your vineyard, you should assemble all the costs, all the potential revenues (starting in the year of first viable yield), and make a spreadsheet. The costs are by far the easiest of the cash flows to assemble and conceive in the initial stages. The revenue and the rate of interest to use in discounting future cash flows in the vineyard are more difficult. The next section begins with an overview of real estate cost issues regarding land, and then discusses issues of revenue and interest assessment in the context of vineyard investment decisions.

Real Estate Valuation Issues for Vineyards and Wineries

A major component of most winery investments is the underlying real estate: the land, buildings, and vineyards. Real estate has proven to be an attractive, stable, long-term investment, but it typically does not generate the rates of return sought for most winery operations. Also, the long period of time required for development of a winery and/or vineyard demands the devotion of the underlying land for many years with no return. Conversely, however, the real estate can typically be financed (or leveraged, or geared) at attractive long-term rates, amplifying the return to equity.

The question of whether a winery should actually own the production vineyards has long been debated, with many examples of successful wineries who own no, or few, vineyards, choosing to outsource their grape supplies. While vineyard land may be leased, or contracted, to allow the winemaker adequate control of the wine-growing process, many industry participants feel vineyards must be owned to allow for proper long-term decision making.

In the wine business, geographical indexes (GI) may be the most critical factor impacting real estate values. Location in a defined appellation—AOC in France or American Viticultural Area (AVA) in the US—may be an investor/winemaker's primary consideration in selecting a site or in considering the purchase of an existing winery or vineyard. The rights, or entitlement, to develop vineyards in such regions are tightly regulated. Hence, entitled land in the upper tiers of the recognized GIs will typically command high unit prices; however, such property will also tend to hold its value more consistently over the long term. Rates of return, then, tend to reflect the risk/reward factors of such investments.

External forces also play a key role in the value of most wine-related real estate, as land that is suitable for premium wine production is also likely to be attractive for other uses, most often residential estates. The value, or price, of land, then, is created by a complex matrix of location, climate, soil, water, and other legal and economic factors.

In terms of pure production potential, the usual agricultural factors come into play, with climate dominating the matrix in most cases. Vignerons will seek very specific climate characteristics to plant specific varieties. Once the proper climatic conditions are found, the next critical element is soil. Then the various physical characteristics of the land, slope, drainage, aspect, etc., are considered. Quality and quantity appear to be inversely related in grape production, with the highest quality grapes coming from areas of the lowest yields, and the highest yields commonly producing the lowest quality of grapes.

Water is perhaps the most interesting component of the equation, as vignerons seem always able to find water for sites meeting their climatic and soil criteria. Premium grapes are successfully grown without irrigation in many wine regions, albeit often at lower yields. Conversely, of course, in the commercial production regions, irrigation is a requisite component of the higher yields demanded.

Given all of the above, we see that real estate is a necessary component of the winery business, one that can be a significant increment of total investment, but also one that may be highly leveraged to reduce initial capital requirements. However, even when leveraged, returns on real estate prove to be lower than those desired of the total winery business.

Examples of Cost Issues With Vineyard Development and Grape Sourcing

Example #1: Vineyard Development

Anyone who has started a vineyard, or budded new rootstock onto old vines, knows the number of decisions in a vineyard project. Costs include stakes, trellising, irrigation, labor, equipment or equipment rentals, fencing, permits, etc. There is also an implicit cost of digging up a former apple orchard or land that was used for any other purpose. This *opportunity cost* is not a part of many expense tallies for vineyard development, but even if the land is not being used, it has an alternative use! Table 10.1 provides a list of cost categories in the vineyard segment. Once these costs are assembled, the owner can assess what is a realistic return on this

Table 10.1. Vineyard Cost Categories

Rootstock choice
Vineyard management fees
Budding
Frost protection
Trellis
Labor
Stakes
Harvesting
Irrigation
Trucking
Pest control
Permits
Weeding
Ancillary legal costs
Pruning
Vineyard acquisition costs
Fencing
Contingencies

investment by estimating revenue per ton, assuming a certain output per acre planted.

That price is the most volatile data in the project, as vineyard management techniques have advanced to determine a certain tonnage per acre very precisely. ECF represents the expected cash flows for each subsequent period (starting with the current period to its endpoint, whether that is a week, month, or year). It is prudent to run different scenarios under different prices, assuming you can identify most of your costs, and then run sensitivity analyses on a spreadsheet by changing the price per ton as revenue. This is easy to do on any spreadsheet package. Once you have this set up, the present value analysis described above is easily performed, allowing a decision between varietal, trellising, etc. The basic equation below summarizes the calculation of vineyard expected cash flows[3]:

$$\text{Vineyard revenue} - (\text{production costs} + \text{acquisition}) = \text{vineyard ECF} \quad \text{(Equation 2)}$$

The other choice if you want to produce and sell wine is to buy grapes or juice on the open market, but the financial assessment of that choice is basically the same.

Example #2: Grape Sourcing

If you find that vineyard development is not cost-effective, an alternative is to buy bulk juice or fruit and use it instead.[4] A contraction in grape prices has made the profitability of vineyard ventures initiated in the late 1990s questionable. However, the fundamental decision involved in making grape source decisions is similar to making vineyard development decisions financially. Most wineries know sources for bulk juice and grapes for specific varietals. Of course, there is a qualitative difference between buying bulk juice and contracting the grapes on the vine, but financially one must categorize costs and revenues specific to the grape purchase. The revenues from the grapes or bulk juice are not as manageable or as blatant. To a certain extent, your choice of bulk juice, grape, and vineyard dictates the price of your bottle. There is an interdependency that holds for most producers; it does not hold for all because of long-term contracts that change very little over time and also niche wines, whose price and market are somewhat stable.

The difference between these revenues and costs is, by definition, your expected cash flow. If you buy grapes before you see them (e.g., a winery contract with a new vineyard development where the first substantial crop is 3 years away), you are ostensibly engaging in a commodity futures contract and are betting on the contract price versus the spot price of grapes in 3 years. The point here is that no matter where you get your fruit, the model is the same. There are costs and revenues associated with all these choices and you must find the choice that maximizes your profit, given the cost and market constraints your firm faces. To summarize, a basic model is as follows:

$$\text{Grape or juice revenue} - (\text{production costs} + \text{acquisition}) = \text{grape ECF} \qquad \text{(Equation 3)}$$

Your pricing structure from winery to wholesale or sales force is normally FOB, or cost-plus pricing. This price is determined to deliver a certain retail price that lands you (hopefully at a profit) in your targeted price point. Financially, buying the lowest priced fruit may not necessarily provide the largest spread between revenue and cost, as the type of grapes you bottle affects the perceived quality of your wine. But you probably knew that. What you maybe did not know, because few people know this for sure, is the true mathematical connection between the grape price and the bottle price. Anecdotally, the basic linear relationship is that if you acquire grapes for $2000 per ton, the wine should be $20 per bottle retail. That relationship is ad hoc to point of fright. If it was that easy, I could buy futures in grapes and liquidate them at profit consistently. The grape cost is only a part of many input costs in the process that determines the price. The costs inside a winery are not a linear function of grape price, while the FOB price is a linear function of your production costs. This mathematical problem is addressed briefly below. The next three sections complete most of our needs by tying all the parts of a wine business together financially.

Once these expected cash flows are assembled, their present value can be assessed based on the timing of the revenue and costs. If you incur costs immediately, which is the most likely scenario in vineyard development, the costs are discounted differently than the revenues in that they begin in a different period. The message here is to set up your costs according to their timing. The viability of the present value calculation depends on how you set up these expected cash flows. Also, notice the use of the word "expected." You do not know the contingencies that are coming and both revenue and costs can easily change over time.

Vineyard Revenue and Interest Rates

While costs in vineyards and in most winery operations tend to be fairly standard, the revenues generated are difficult to initially assess. Two reasons exist for this uncertainty, especially if the vineyard is not established. First, until the yield is known, it is unlikely a wine producer will contract to purchase your grapes. Second, until you get your first crop, no one knows the grape's viability or how well your claims of quality will hold up. If you have planted Russian River Pinot Noir in Sonoma County, it is likely that wineries will want to get your grapes under contract due to the relative lack of supply compared with other varietals. If you plant Cabernet Sauvignon in Knight's Valley, you may have difficulty initially contracting the sale of your grapes for the same reasons.

The current market for grapes has a great deal of influence over the contract price of grapes into the future, with good reason. However, varietal choice, location, vineyard history, winemaker scrutiny, portfolio fit, and other details lead to changes in revenue. In 2000, it was easy to find Cabernet selling at $1500 per ton; in 2003, the norm was between $800 and $1100 per ton, with large variability. When thinking about the financial issues in the vineyard, one must consider the revenue derived from the grapes once they are salable. If an existing vineyard is purchased, uncertainty regarding yield and quality is not as large an issue.

New plantings can face timing problems. Unless contracted well in advance, the revenue to be derived from new plantings can be highly variable. It may depend on new market conditions, changes in local climate, changes in the consumer perceptions of the vineyard's varietal, etc. Because of the lengthy time between planting and viable crop, vineyard owners must take the present value of money into account, and also must remember that without a contract price, most revenue measurements are simply conjecture.

The interest rates used to discount future income into present value terms also may be problematic. Since the financial markets in the US lunged down after January 2002, the Federal Reserve has continuously cut interest rates in an attempt to revitalize the economy. As a result, many present value discount factors have shrunk to reflect the looser credit conditions. However, risks in planting new grapes or getting loans for vineyard/winery expansion have increased due to the economic downturn and changing market conditions. When looking at capital budgeting for winery projects, you have to choose some rate to represent, in the least, the opportunity costs of using any cash or of paying the interest on a loan. The mix of your loan rate, cost savings, and foregone interest income on cash used should lead to an interest rate that reflects reality. The importance of the interest rate, revenue forecasts, and very precise cost calculations cannot be overstated; they are the crux of finance. The prudent winery will not simply default to their loan rate or an average rate on its total leverage.

Winery Economics and Finance

Principles similar to those above apply whether you are a vineyard manager, cellarmaster, or the sole proprietor/winemaker/tractor driver/janitor for your own wine. Suppose you were going to buy new barrels to rid yourself of older barrels or to expand winery capacity. Would you not use the same principles as you use in calculating the viability of a winery project? Of course. The only thing that changes is the timing of revenue, as your hope should be that revenue and cost walk hand in hand inside the winery. The way we look at the winery, as different from the vineyard, is to think of the winery as small pieces amalgamated into one. This is known as segment analysis, and should be employed anytime you have joint processes taking place (which is classic in a winery), when projects have dual uses or feed into multiple products.

Segment Analysis

It is essential that the capital budgeting team for a winery subdivide the business into different parts and, if necessary, arbitrarily assign costs to different pieces of the business if not explicitly separated. There are two reasons why this should be done, under the auspices of generally accepted accounting principles (GAAP). First, it provides a more realistic view of your project's impact on the winery, its brands, and its functions. Overstating or understating the cost distribution means a potential mistake in the net present value calculation for the project. This is true even if the project affects the entire winery, like the construction and use of a tasting facility.[5] Most wineries have three major processes: *vineyard operations*, *winery operations*, and *marketing/public relations*, which includes the tasting facility, sales and distribution, and more. Any winery's capital budgets should begin with this trichotomy.

From this, each operation should be split into different parts, depending on the company's setup. The organizational chart should follow this three-way split, but if there are 10 vineyards, there should be 10 segments identified in vineyard operations. If there are two wineries, there are two winery segments. There will be multiple vineyards and brands involved in the least as a diversification strategy, especially if there are multiple varietals. However, it is likely all the grapes flow through the same winery, as a quality and cost control measure, if not for nostalgia and marketing reasons. There is likely only one tasting facility as well.

Next is the issue of pricing, both inside to the winery and outside to the consumer. While this is a marketing function, price determination does affect forecasting. Many wineries have a *transfer price*, or the price from winery to sales and marketing (including a tasting facility), which is bottle cost plus a markup. The FOB price is what the wine sells for at wholesale when administration and marketing markup are added to the transfer price. Many wineries price in their tasting room at FOB times 2. For a lot of wineries this makes limited sense, so long as the price is competitive in their price point, as it is easy and everyone understands the pricing.

However, is this retail price, FOB times 2, the optimal price? For most wineries it is not a price that maximizes profit. In fact, the analogy is like throwing darts. Making arbitrary price choices is like aiming for the bull's eye: you might hit it by chance, but there are techniques that hit the bull's eye more often than not. To hit the bull's eye of maximum profit with price is tricky and takes some analysis, but there are wineries that could do this analysis very easily by using historic revenue, cost, and quantity data for each brand or product that is priced separately. Statistically, the winery could get closer to economic optimization in price rather than just a guess, as $0.10 more or less on price could be the difference between no more profit and thousands of dollars of residual. This underscores the need to segment the firm and look at the winery or project as a series of smaller pieces.

The best way to split capital budgets at wineries is into brands and then varietals for these reasons. The cost of the winery and sales/tasting facility can then be easily assigned to each brand by percentage sales or grape cost, depending on any large differences between brands. Any project that the firm seeks can now have its revenues and costs easily allocated to the appropriate parts of the firm and its impact analyzed accordingly. Table 10.2 shows some of the basic costs in a winery, assuming that the capital exists initially and the winery is a going concern or project or is to be acquired. All other decisions are a subset of that larger acquisition.

For wineries, the issue is not budgeting as much as finding the source of funding. The next major section is on funding options and finance, and linking the ideas above with the financial markets themselves.

Equity Versus Debt Financing, Mergers and Acquisitions

One of the key aspects in finance over the last 50 years has been determining the optimal source and mix of funding for projects. Should a firm only use debt or loans, or should it go public, as just a few wineries and wine-related firms have done over the years? Should the firm use accumulated profits or retained earnings? Does it matter? We begin with this final question because it motivates the reason why taking bank loans has been the majority choice in this industry.

The hours brooding over the choice of financing a winery project may be a waste of time. There is a very famous theorem in finance called the Modigliani-Miller Theorem, which states the choice of financing mix is immaterial, if the cost of using each is the same. If the firm feels that the costs of each type of financing makes them truly indifferent between the choices, the theorem seems to be very easy to believe. How-

Table 10.2. Winery Cost Categories

Raw grape juice or fruit
Winemaker
Labor (other than Winemaker and Cellarmaster)
Cellarmaster
Maintenance
Waste disposal
Bottles
Breakage
Labels
Inventory costs
Corks
Sugar testing
Electricity, water, sewage, and other utilities
Transportation
Cooling systems
Oak chips (optional)
Barrels
Boxes

ever, it is unlikely that the choices will have the same exact cost, if certain financing choices are available at all. Debt financing seems to be constantly available to all firms, especially in the wine industry, where the market for ownership expansion or use of retained earnings is not as fruitful. However, we see later that a major concern of the industry may be finding enough financing through debt instruments to pay for large projects.

The ability to use equity is small in this industry. Firms such as Constellation have had great growth due their conglomerate strategy, but smaller wineries (Scheid and Williamette Valley) that are publicly traded have suffered greatly in the equity markets. A smaller winery, which is now a much larger producer, Ravenswood, was acquired by Constellation in 2001. We should see much more merger and acquisition activity, such as the Foster's Group acquisition of Beringer Winery in 2002, and Opus One between Mondavi and Rothschild. Mergers and acquisitions, as well as joint ventures, spread the cost of using equity among two or more firms, which makes the agreement beneficial to both firms. The only economic reason to engage in mergers and acquisition activity or agree to a joint venture is if both firms see a benefit.

While a lot is made of share prices, and what they really mean, the key is not the stock's price today, but if it is volatile upward. A flat-moving stock makes for little in capital gains and may, for this reason, bar the ability of the firm to finance future projects in the same way. The return on equity of wine firms is the key issue here.

Table 10.3 lists publicly traded companies and their ticker symbols, and Figure 10.1 shows the selected stock's price movements since July 20, 1998, which provides 5 years of data. In the figure, the Dow Jones index is represented by a solid line, the NASDAQ index by a dotted line, and the specific winery by the dashed line. For all three indices, they are based at 100, on July 20, 1998. Thus, in all the graphs, the lines start at the same place, which really provides a perspective on how volatile downward these stocks have been for the last 5 years, except for a couple of cases.

Table 10.3. Winery Stocks and Ticker Symbols

Company	Ticker
Chalone Wine Group	CHLN
Diageo	DEO
Williamette Valley Vineyards	WVVI
Brown-Forman	BFb
UST	UST
Louis Vuitton	LVMH
Mondavi	MOND
Constellation	STZ
Scheid	SVIN
Golden State Vintners	VINT
Geerlings and Wade	GEER
Todhunter	THT
Fortune Brands	FO
Allied Domecq	AED

Source: Yahoo Finance, Factiva Databases (2003).

Looking at the graphs should convince the reader, regardless of when you read this passage, that the growth rates of most wine stocks are low. Moreover, the faster growth rates come from companies that are conglomerates (Constellation).[6] Economically, funding projects through equity means the firm must convince a brokerage, who will underwrite the initial public offering (IPO), that the stock has a great deal of potential. The only way brokerages make money from underwriting new stock issues is if potential secondary investors see the stock's potential. Just because your winery is going through a label change or you have a passion for wine does not mean you will be able to raise funds through equity markets. Also, if you worked for a dot.com and saw riches made by the owners of these companies, those extremely high PE ratios and exponential growth rates do not exist in this industry en masse. Wine is an agricultural by-product and should be seen as such because that is how the equity markets see it. For that reason, only the largest and most diversified companies can truly have success in equity markets.

The cost of using retained earnings can also be very high. The key cost in using accumulated profits is what you could earn on the money versus the cost of debt financing. If you use retained earning that could have earned 7% in a mutual fund and debt costs 5%, why risk the earnings when the spread between these two numbers is positive. If debt costs more than low-risk investments, then the use of retained earnings is less at issue, unless there are forecasted cash needs that retained earnings historically fund at your firm. Generally speaking, the risk of losing your retained earnings, or losing the availability of those profits for cash use, makes retained earnings the last resort. That leaves us the least costly and most used option: debt.

Is Debt Financing Really That Bad?

Much has been made since the beginning of the recession in 2001 and the subsequent recoil of the stock market explosion that consumer, firm, and government debt was so high in the US that we are on the verge of another debt crisis that will rival the last major problem in the early 1980s. For those that remember 20% interest on home loans and sometimes higher on business loans, it took a long stagnation in the US, and really worldwide, to cause that problem. It was exacerbated by debt default of massive proportions in Mexico, Brazil, Argentina, and elsewhere in 1982. If rising debts act as a signal to financial markets to increase the cost of debt financing to businesses, and interest rates begin to rise again over this decade, one saving grace will be that many winery loans, except those to import and distribute, involve land.

The high land prices in Sonoma, Napa, and San Benito Counties are starting to affect (or infect depending on your perspective) all parts of California. While that increases the price of land, and thus the price of projects, it also gives a good picture to financiers that the project will appreciate in value over time, purely through supply and demand forces. Land has a finite supply, and vinable land even less, giving a high price. Demand in these counties, and in California, seems not to be waning, providing the other condition to sustained high prices. Most price bubbles, if you believe real estate is on that path, are burst by supply issues: equity market bubbles burst because stocks become available rapidly, based on uncertainty about stock prices in the future. How easy is land to sell? Not very, at least compared with stock, and a brand new region where wine projects are going to begin in earnest is difficult

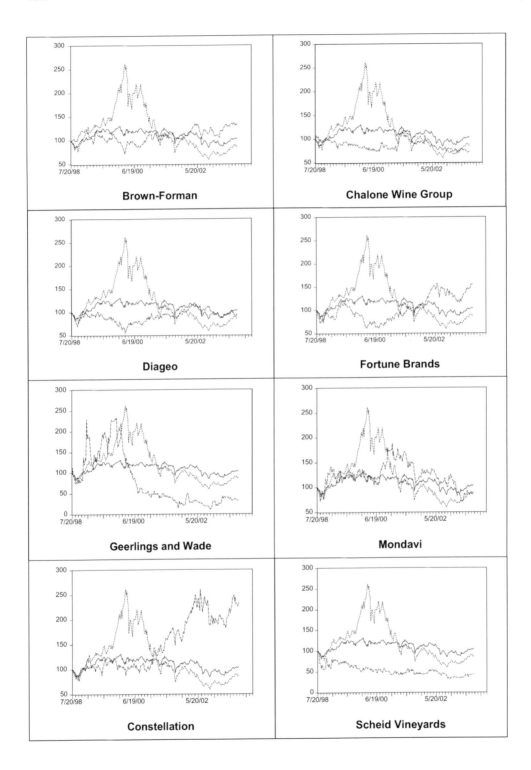

Figure 10.1. Stock price movements of public traded companies, US markets.

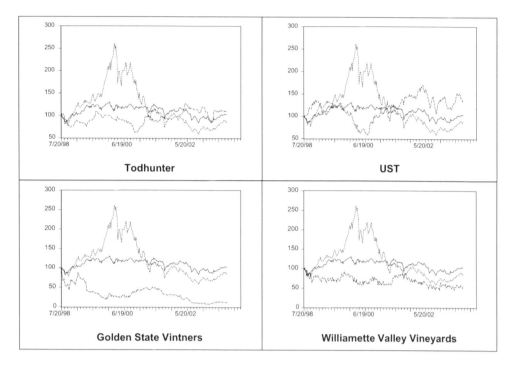

Figure 10.1 continued.

to imagine at this point. For these reasons, banks and financiers should feel confident in achieving a positive return on investment for a winery project based on land.

Three Big Issues in the Future of Financing Wine-Related Projects

Those in the trenches of making financial decisions or doing consulting have the best perspective on the future of capital budgeting and financing made in this industry. Regardless of your specific pursuit, from custom crush to bulk brokerage, there seem to be three big issues that permeate all these decisions. According to two industry experts in wine finance (author, personal interviews, summer 2003), there are three major issues in financing wine-related projects:

1. **Limited capital available to wine-related projects:** For larger projects, the risks versus the needs in dollars are starting to turn against winery projects. For this reason, the NPV calculation may be greater than zero for the bank to provide a loan, but at too small an amount. As the needs rise, banks are less willing to lend large dollar amounts.
2. **Low current return on investment:** The return on investments, because this is an agricultural product, is low, and banks see it as such. For certain wineries, this is less of a problem, but those same wineries are not seeking financing on a regular basis, or for cash flow needs.

3. **Lag time for revenue generation and to break-even point:** The issue of yield, especially for new plantings, is becoming more problematic, especially with forecasts of ongoing gluts in the US. If you intend to plant, and a glut is forecasted, the revenue stream may be smaller than what will make the vineyard economically viable. The more squeeze there is on grape prices due to oversupply, the more pressure there will be in projects getting to NPV > 0 in a timely way, if at all.

Conclusions

To summarize, wine finance is no different than other finance applications, except in two key ways. First, the nature of pricing in the industry, based somewhat on the subjective quality perception of the consumer, third-party experts, etc., forces the CFO of a winery to assume revenue streams in the future that can change quickly. Also, the lack of perfect overlap with cost and revenue, especially in a vineyard project, makes projections extremely problematic. Capital budgeting in this industry is very difficult, but it is generally like any other industry. Segmenting your project and identifying all costs is the key to a successful capital budget in the wine industry. In other industries, price forecasts are also imprecise, but the factors that go into pricing in this industry make budgeting a great challenge.

The type of financing available may be more a function of dollar need than project viability. It seems that banks are less likely to finance large vineyard projects due to shrinking margins, and because wine is an agricultural by-product national equity markets do not see much return to the projects. Unfortunately, historical data corroborate Wall Street's perception. However, merger and acquisition activity, as well as joint ventures, may be the best way for the industry to circumvent the whims of venture capitalists and keep financing within the industry. To a certain extent, that strengthens the equity and debt markets' perceptions of this industry's viability.

Notes

[1] Even though we know there is the "Australian Method," which promises a viable crop in 18 months, we will assume the standard 3–5-year window before significant revenue may be gained from the planting. Also, the prohibition hangover that many states remain paralyzed by dictates distribution.

[2] All agricultural crops have different "price points" based on perceived quality and average cost. The subtle difference here is that wine does not have different marketplaces for each price point, as $50/bottle wine may be sold next to $5/bottle wine. This variability is not intrinsic to any other food or beverage; the automobile industry is the best analogy.

[3] Including trucking, unloading, and any costs associated with the grapes per the contract. Bulk juice is available directly from large growers or through B-to-B websites such as www.WineryExchange.com, and the search cost should be included.

[4] Of course, if your winery has "estate-bottled" products, for example, one has to carefully consider the regulatory rules on changing the source of fruit and how it changes your products and prices. This shows the basic interdependency between

the marketing team and the vineyard manager.

[5]The example of a tasting facility shows all the different ways one project can affect many different aspects of the winery without disturbing vineyard operations and most likely having little effect on the cellar operations outside of inventory flows.

[6]We do not mention winemaking companies that trade on foreign markets, especially Australian and British companies.

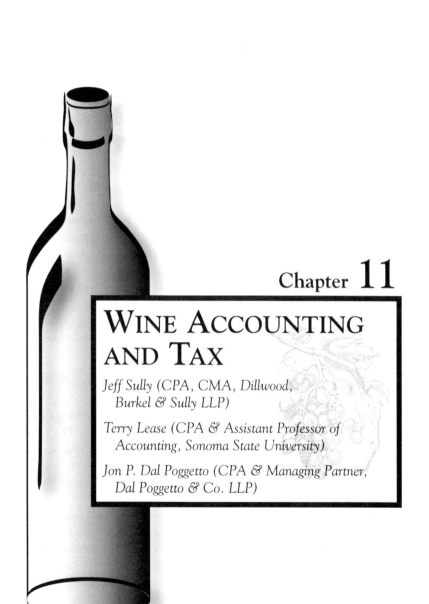

Chapter 11

WINE ACCOUNTING AND TAX

Jeff Sully (CPA, CMA, Dillwood, Burkel & Sully LLP)

Terry Lease (CPA & Assistant Professor of Accounting, Sonoma State University)

Jon P. Dal Poggetto (CPA & Managing Partner, Dal Poggetto & Co. LLP)

In a general sense, businesses in the wine industry use accounting information much like those in any other industry: 1) to issue financial statements to investors and banks or other creditors; 2) to file tax returns with federal, state, and local tax authorities; and 3) to assist management in planning and making decisions related to areas such as pricing and resource allocation. Rather than attempt to summarize basic accounting and tax principles in a few pages, this chapter focuses on issues that are unique or of particular importance in the wine industry. The purpose of this chapter is not to allow an owner or manager to do the winery's accounting; rather, it is to give the owner or manager an idea of how accounting information is developed and may be used. Its purpose is also to give the accountant a better idea of how to apply accounting principles and techniques to businesses in the wine industry. The point is not to turn winery owners or managers into accountants, but to help them communicate better with the competent accountants they engage or employ.

One of the most important but difficult issues a business in the wine industry faces is how to account for the costs of the various stages of wine production. Product costing affects the valuation of inventory and determination of cost of goods sold (thus, net operating income) on financial statements and tax returns, and influences any management decision that considers costs or profits. Accordingly, the chapter begins with that issue and devotes the majority of its space to it—providing a comprehensive costing example. It begins with an introduction to product costing, then describes the various cost centers for a wine business. From there it describes how to use cost centers, and then provides specific examples for farming and winery costs. The chapter concludes with an overview of the critical tax issues in the US wine industry.

Product Costing: Introduction

To understand inventory costing, the wine production process should be broken down into a series of steps within a continuous flow of processes. The winery crushes grapes at a desired degree of ripeness, ferments the juice or must, and clarifies the new wine. The wine ages until the flavors and balance achieve their greatest potential. Finally, the wine is bottled. At that point, the production process stops. The grapes arrive at the crusher and cases leave the loading dock.

Wine costing is the process of accumulating, allocating, and assigning both direct costs and overhead costs to wine inventory in a reasonable and consistent manner. Assigning a cost to this inventory, however, requires a slightly different view. The production process is consistent and definable. Within that process distinct stages of production activity can be defined. Each stage becomes a focal point for assigning costs.

For example, the *crush activity* has a collection of costs that are unique to crushing and fermenting grapes. *Bulk aging* is another area of unique costs, where labor activity may be minimal, yet utilization of building capacity may be significant. *Bottling* has costs associated with getting the finished wine into bottles. Finally, there are *overhead costs* that support all three areas. What makes each of these areas distinct from each other is that they have different activities from the same resource requirements.

During the harvest, there will be higher demands for cellar labor, utilities for tank refrigeration, specialized processing equipment such as crushers and presses, etc. The aging process requires barrels and space to store them, in addition to tank space for blending and chemistry adjustments. Labor will not be as high, although there will be a need for refrigeration during the warmer months. Bottling requires the use of equipment that has sat idle for 10 or 11 months out of the year. Now it will run 12 or 14 hours a day for a month or two, and during this time labor will be concentrated.

Each of the activities above deals with the same product. In some stages (such as crush), the product changes in substance; in other stages (such as bottling) its changes are more a matter of form. Yet each stage is a different activity and places different demands on the same resources, or *cost drivers* to support that activity. Stating it another way, even though an hour of labor is an hour of labor, the *cost objective* of that labor is different for crush, aging, and bottling. The cost objective is the accumulated measurement of cost drivers required to perform specific and related activities. Aging wines requires barrels; but once the wines are sent to the bottling tank, the barrels are empty. Identifying and separating the activities that occur in the production process is the first step in being able to segregate costs that are unique to that activity, which in turn allows for a more accurate determination of the costs that most directly relate to a specific wine.

Defining Cost Centers

Once the different activities have been identified and segregated, they become the basis for defining *cost centers*. A cost center is an accounting construct designed to accumulate the cost drivers during the time frame over which costs are collected for reporting. A given cost center should cover only one type of production activity. Cost centers are at the foundation of costing procedures.

"Thinking like a winemaker" will also help develop cost centers concepts. For example, farming costs are incurred to grow grapes. The costs associated with growing those grapes, plus harvest and transportation costs to the winery (along with costs for purchased grapes), become the initial costs for the resulting bulk wine. At harvest, the grapes come into the winery to be crushed, fermented, and made into wine. Crushing and fermenting add more costs to the new vintage, and cellar activities add further costs to the bulk wine in inventory. All of these costs become part of the bulk inventory, as measured by dollars per gallon. When these wines are bottled, the cost of bulk wine to be bottled comes out of bulk inventory and flows into bottled wine inventory, and bottling costs are added at this time.

Each of these stages represents four major cost centers: 1) farming cost center, 2) crush cost center, 3) production cost center, and 4) bottling cost center. Two more cost centers would be used for costs that support multiple stages of production: 5) facilities cost center and 6) payroll cost center. In addition, the business would have one or more cost centers for noninventory costs, that is: 7) for costs that are associated with selling the wine, or 8) with running the organization but are not associated with producing the wine.

In a well-structured chart of accounts, the accounts would be grouped and numbered by cost center to facilitate proper recording and efficient use of the cost information. Some costs, such as payroll costs and facilities-related costs (e.g., depreciation or rent, utilities, property taxes, insurance), would be recorded initially in the payroll or facilities cost center and then allocated to the cost centers for the different stages. This topic is covered in the next section.

Using Cost Centers

Each cost center contains the traditional grouping of cost classifications: *direct costs*, such as direct labor and materials, and *indirect costs*, such as supervisory labor and allocated overhead. The direct costs are those costs that are associated only with a specific wine. These costs include grapes, identifiable labor, and measured supplies.

Indirect costs are those costs that are associated with several different wines, because the same cost drivers may be shared by the different wines in the production process. The use of the resource by any specific wine is not measured directly, so the indirect costs must be allocated. The indirect costs may generate many different allocation methods. Some work fine, while others will generate inconsistent results. Different allocation methods are illustrated as part of the following examples of costing the different stages of production.

Costing in the Vineyard (Farming Costs)

This cost center accumulates data pertaining to the cost of growing grapes for the current year. There will be direct labor associated with traditional farming operations, such as disking, pruning, thinning, harvest, etc. There will be direct materials purchases, such as fertilizers and other chemicals. Finally, there will be indirect costs that need to be allocated, such as supervisory labor, property taxes, trellis repair, and insurance, to name a few. The question arises as to how to allocate these costs. Table 11.1 forms the basis for illustrating the most basic allocation method.

If all of the blocks are evenly spaced with 535 vines per acre, the cost of growing grapes could be viewed as being $4,365 per acre ($109,125/25). On the other hand, if each acre provides approximately the same yield, the cost could be viewed as being $1,180 per ton ($109,125/92.5) to grow grapes.

Table 11.1 takes the entire costs for this vineyard and divides it by the number of tons or acres to come up with a simple allocation rate. The allocation base is either tons or acres, but all grapes are treated equally. Changing the allocation base to vineyard blocks would refine this process because different varieties have different yields. Assume that each block represents a different variety, with the acres and yield (in tons) for each variety presented in Table 11.2.

Table 11.1. Example of Basic Cost Allocation Method

Total acres	25
Harvested tons	92.5
Total farming costs	$109,125

Table 11.2. Example of Cost Allocation by Block

Categories	Block CS	Block ZN	Totals
Acres	6.5	18.5	25
Block yield (tons)	26.65	65.85	92.5
Total farming costs			$109,125

It still costs $4,365 per acre to farm. The new information in Table 11.2, however, indicates that the Cabernet block CS cost $28,373 to farm ($4,365 × 6.5 acres), for a cost of $1,065 per ton ($28,373/6.5 tons). The Zinfandel block ZN cost the same $4,365 per acre to farm, but the total cost for Zinfandel block ZN is $80,752 ($4,365 × 18.5 acres). Having harvested 65.85 tons of Zinfandel, the cost per ton is $1,226 per ton ($80,752/18.5 tons) versus $1,065 for the Cabernet. The new allocation takes into account that different varieties will yield different tonnages. However, it still assumes that the varieties expend resources at the same rate for each block.

But what happens if the vineyard decides to replace the CS block of 535 vines per acre with 1,100 vines per acre using recently developed technology and techniques? Does continuing to allocate cost as before provide a reasonable result? The required amount of some resources will be significantly different for blocks that are radically different from each other, as indicated in Table 11.3.

The yields have gone up from the denser planting, but so have total costs. Using the allocation method in Example 2 above, it costs $4,662 per acre to farm, with $30,303 allocated to the Cabernet ($4,662 × 6.5 acres) for $814 per ton ($30,303/ 37.25 tons). The Zinfandel is allocated $86,247 of costs ($4,662 × 18.5 acres) for $1,310 per ton ($86,247/65.85 tons). Does it make sense that the cost of the Cabernet would have decreased by almost 25% while the cost of the Zinfandel has increased by over 6%? This allocation creates a very large discrepancy between the cost of Cabernet and the cost of Zinfandel. However, the Cabernet's increased vine densities should require more labor, more times through with the tractor, more spraying, etc., while nothing changed with respect to the Zinfandel. Also, a larger investment is required (with more depreciation) for the Cabernet.

Assume an examination of the various accounts reveals that there are variable costs associated with activities such as general labor, pruning, harvest, etc. Practical experience suggests that the newer planting methods require more labor simply because there are more vines to deal with. A simple way to measure the additional

Table 11.3. Example of Cost Allocation With Different Block Techniques

Categories	Block CS	Block ZN	Totals
Vines per acre	1,100	535	
Total acres	6.5	18.5	25
Block yield (tons)	37.25	65.85	103.1
Total farming costs			$116,550

resources required is to assume that the labor hours spent in an individual block is a measurement of all variable resources being applied to that block.

In addition to the costs described above, there are harvest costs that are more closely related to the tons of grapes harvested than to labor hours. Finally, there are fixed costs, such as property taxes and insurance, which do not relate to the vine spacing of the different blocks or the amount of grapes harvested. In order to arrive at an equitable allocation of the costs for this vineyard, as defined by the two blocks, three allocation bases are used to arrive at the allocation of costs, based on the information in Table 11.4.

The labor hours provides the basis for the allocation percentages for the variable costs in the vineyard. The Cabernet block uses 36.5% of labor hours (1,602/4,385) and is allocated that percentage of the labor-related costs. The remaining 63.5% will go to the Zinfandel block, even though the Zinfandel makes up 74% of the acreage. Consequently, the Cabernet would receive $21,081 ($57,757 × 36.5%), or $565.93 per ton. The Zinfandel would receive the remainder, $36,676, or $556.96 per ton.

The $23,611 of harvest costs is allocated based on tons. Using that basis, each ton harvested costs $229 ($23,611/103.1 tons). Finally, the $35,182 of other general overhead needs to be allocated. Because the general overhead applies to the entire vineyard in total, irrespective of the number of vines planted or grapes harvested, the remaining overhead is applied at the rate of $1,407 per acre, or $245.53 per ton for the Cabernet and $395.38 per ton for the Zinfandel. The final cost per ton calculation is listed in Table 11.5.

Different allocation methods or bases could be used, if management felt that a different approach would be more appropriate. The important thing to remember is that the allocation method must be understandable, cost-effective, and truly reflect the production in the field.

Figure 11.1 provides a big picture overview of a vineyard accounting worksheet. This is useful in understanding how all of the various components can be calculated.

Costing in the Winery

Overhead costs are those costs associated with keeping the winery operation viable. Overhead is the term for costs that are required to support production, yet are

Table 11.4. Example of Cost Allocation Based on Block Farming Costs

Categories	Block CS	Block ZN	Totals
Total acres	6.5	18.5	25
Vines per acre	1,100	535	
Yield (tons) per block	37.25	65.85	103.1
Labor hours per block	1,602	2,783	4,385
Total farming costs			$116,550
Labor-related costs			$57,757
Harvest costs			$23,611
General overhead			$35,182

Table 11.5. Example of Per Ton Calculation

	Cabernet Sauvignon	Zinfandel
Variable labor costs	$21,081	$36,676
Harvest costs	8,530	15,081
Fixed overhead costs	9,146	26,036
Total costs	38,757	77,793
Total tons	37.25	65.85
Cost per ton	1,040	1,181

not associated with a specific wine. These are costs that the winery will incur no matter how much wine is produced. For example, a winery may have a building that cost $2,000,000 to build and can store several thousand barrels. That building will cost approximately $50,000 per year in depreciation, regardless of the volume of inventory stored in it. In any given year, one third to one half of the barrel inventory

BlackAcre Vineyards
FARMING COST ANALYSIS

Variable farming costs			$	61,189
Harvest costs				23,611
Fixed farming costs				31,750
	Farming costs		$	116,550

Variable farming costs by variety

Labor hours, Cabernet	1,602	36.5%	$	22,355
Labor hours, Zinfandel	2,783	63.5%		38,834
	4,385	100.0%	$	61,189

Harvest costs by variety

Tons, Cabernet	37.25	36.1%	$	8,531
Tons, Zinfandel	65.85	63.9%		15,080
	103.10	100.0%	$	23,611

Fixed farming costs by variety

Total acres, Cabernet	6.5	26.0%	$	8,255
Total acres, Zinfandel	18.5	74.0%		23,495
	25.0	100.0%	$	31,750

Per variety analysis

	Cabernet	Zinfandel	Total
Variable costs	$ 22,355	$ 38,834	$ 61,189
Harvest costs	8,531	15,080	23,611
Fixed costs	8,255	23,495	31,750
Total	$ 39,140	$ 77,410	$ 116,550

Common size analysis (per ton)

	Cabernet	Zinfandel	Average
Variable costs	$ 600	$ 590	$ 593
Harvest costs	229	229	229
Fixed costs	222	357	308
Total	$ 1,051	$ 1,176	$ 1,130

Fact pattern 4

Figure 11.1. Vineyard accounting worksheet.

may be empty for several months during the year. Those barrels could have over $100,000 to $500,000 in depreciation costs each year.

A winery may have varying levels of activity, yet they still relate to the same basic cost objectives. While the assets (building and barrels) have varying utilization rates during the year (e.g., number of months the barrels are full this year compared with last year), accountants usually make an assumption that will simplify costing, so as to avoid getting bogged down in the process while providing reliable and meaningful information. One of the simplifying conventions that accountants adopt is to use the longest period of time to report costs that provides the desired level of information. The selected time frame is then used for all cost allocations. For the examples that follow, this chapter assumes a 1-year time frame.

Note that utilizing a yearly time frame "averages out" the nonspecific production cost differences that show up from month to month. Costing on a monthly basis would result in swings in per gallon costs from vintage to vintage, depending on differences in the cost objective for each bulk wine in the cellar. While perhaps technically accurate, the information presented may not be very meaningful. Because the production cycle is generally seen in terms of years, the costs per unit should reflect that same time frame. To summarize, the time frame chosen should be one that provides the needed level of detail without becoming overly burdensome.

One of the important types of overhead costs is the category of *facilities costs*. Facilities costs are those costs incurred to keep the building open, without producing a single drop of wine, such as utilities, insurance, property taxes, depreciation, and security. These costs are recorded in a facilities cost center.

These costs need to be allocated to the various activities within the business. Determining an allocation method begins with delineating the use of the facilities in terms of cost objectives. For example, assume that an entire winery is located in one building. Further assume that 55% of the floor space covers production prior to barrel storage. This will include the crush deck, the fermentation tanks, the lab, dry goods storage, etc. Another 25% of the winery building is devoted to barrel storage, and 5% to bottling. This will not include cased goods storage. Remember, the production process (and cost accumulation) stops when the wine is bottled. Nonproduction activities, such as case storage, tasting room, sales, and administrative offices, make up the remainder of the floor space.

In other words, in this example, 85% of the building supports production activities. Of all costs associated with keeping the building open and in good operating condition, 85% of those costs relate to production. Thus, using floor space as an allocation basis, 85% of all of the facilities costs are allocated among the various bulk wines in inventory, as well as wines bottled this year. The other 15% of the costs would be expensed as a period expense (Figure 11.2)

These percentages, once established, will not change unless the production flow is rearranged or the building is expanded. The percentages shown above contain some generalizations, but the purpose of the allocation process is to generate reasonably accurate but cost-efficient estimates of the costs of production. It begins with the assumption that 85% of the facilities costs go into production and that 15% are expensed as period costs (e.g., with 10% for retail activities and 5% for administrative activities). Assuming that facilities costs total $87,980, production would be

	Sq. Ft. %		Sq. Ft. %
Production costs		**Period costs**	
Crush	10%	Tasting room	10%
Cellar	45%	Offices	5%
Barrel storage	25%		
Bottling	5%		
	85%		15%

Figure 11.2. Facilities allocation summary.

allocated $74,783, retail activities would be allocated $8,798, and administrative activities would be allocated $4,399, as shown here in Figure 11.3.

The $74,783 applied to bulk wines is the estimated amount of facilities costs that the winery incurred over the course of the year to support crush, production, and bottling.

Payroll Costs

Before the example moves into the cellar, the payroll cost center deserves a brief mention. It is very common to have payroll entered directly into the respective payroll accounts residing in cellar, crush, marketing, etc. While there is nothing wrong with this method, it results in the loss of an important management tool. Winery owners are shocked to see what their total payroll costs are when presented as a whole. It's easy to miss when seeing payroll only in parts. The payroll cost center collects all direct payroll costs from the various activities, *plus* the payroll overhead accounts, such as taxes, health benefits, workers' compensation, and then allocates those costs to the other cost centers. A typical allocation basis would be a percentage based on direct labor costs.

Crush Costs

Many wineries fail to use a crush cost center and include the cost of crush activity with cellar costs. As a result, white wines tend to be undercosted, while red wines will be overcosted. The reason is that a wine that remains in the cellar for more than

Total facilities costs		$	87,980
Less: period costs			(13,197)
Allocated to production		$	74,783
Allocated to production (sq. ft.)			
Crush	10%	$	8,798
Cellar	45%		39,591
Barrel Storage	25%		21,995
Bottling	5%		4,399
	85%	$	74,783

Figure 11.3. Facilities allocation.

1 year (such as a red wine) will have cellar costs allocated twice. If the cellar costs include the crush costs, the wine will receive an allocation of the crush costs in the second year even though it did not benefit from those crush activities.

The problem is compounded because wines that remain in the cellar less than 1 year will receive less than a full allocation of crush costs, as some of the crush costs went to wines that have already been in the cellar for a year. The way to solve this problem is to have a crush cost center.

For purposes of the ongoing example, assume that crush costs total $66,655. (Remember that the crush costs would include an allocation of the facilities costs.) A simple way to allocate the crush costs would be on a per-gallon basis. For example, if Cabernet made up 25% of the new wine by volume (gallons), then it would receive $16,664 of crush costs. (For the sake of conserving space, the example will now track the costs allocated only to Cabernet Sauvignon.)

A variation on this allocation method could be used if the wines used labor disproportionately to their volume. In the variation, labor costs would be separated from other crush costs and allocated based on the labor hours employed for each type of wine. The remaining costs would still be allocated based on the total number of gallons. The important thing is to try to make the allocation assumptions accurately reflect what is going on in the production process while keeping the allocation process relatively simple to administer and understand.

Production Costs

This cost center covers the production process once the wines have been declared off fermentation. It involves cold stabilization, fining, filtering, barrel aging, blending—everything up until bottling. These costs apply to all wines in inventory, and in principle the allocation is straightforward, based on gallons in inventory. Simply take each wine's number of gallons and divided by total gallons to come up with an allocation percentage. A complicating factor in practice, however, is the time frame covered. Different wines will come off fermentation and into the production cost center and then out of the production cost center and into bottling at different times.

The allocation of production costs to inventory should take into account the amount of time a given lot spends in the cellar. For example, 5,000 gallons held 6 months will require fewer resources and, therefore, should absorb less cost in total than 4,200 gallons held a full year. To accurately allocate cellar costs, a weighted average system is needed. The allocation calculation also needs to consider that, by the end of the year, some wines may have been bottled and not appear in inventory at all! Table 11.6 shows a weighted average calculation and resulting allocation of production costs. Note that wines from the 2000 vintage that spent less than 12 months in the cellar were bottled and would not show up in the bulk wine inventory at the end of the year. The actual year-end gallons in inventory are 44,742, comprising all 2002 wines and those 2001 wines that were in the cellar for 12 months.

Administrative Costs

In some cases, where indirect costs have not already been accounted for in the production departments, it may be necessary to allocate a portion of the costs re-

Table 11.6. Bulk Wine Cost Summary (December 31, 2002)

Variety	Year	Gallons	Months in Cellar	Extended	Wtd. Avg. (%)	Yearly Cellar Costs
Cabernet Sauvignon	02	6,146	2	12,292	3.2%	4,649
Cabernet Sauvignon	01	5,701	12	68,412	17.7%	25,877
Cabernet Sauvignon	00	5,845	6	35,070	9.1%	13,265
Zinfandel	02	11,326	2	22,652	5.9%	8,568
Zinfandel	01	9,455	12	113,460	29.4%	42,916
Zinfandel	00	10,560	4	42,240	10.9%	15,977
Chardonnay	02	4,365	2	8,730	2.3%	3,302
Chardonnay	01	4,999	12	59,988	15.5%	22,691
Chardonnay	00	4,502	1	4,502	1.2%	1,l703
Sauvignon Blanc	02	2,750	2	5,500	1.4%	2,080
Sauvignon Blanc	01	3,289	4	13,156	3.4%	4,976
Total		68,938		386,002	100.0%	146,006

ported as administrative costs. For example, materials need to be ordered, compliance reports need to be filed, and repairs and maintenance need to be scheduled. To the extent these costs are included in administrative costs, part of the administrative costs should be allocated to inventory through the production cost centers. This could be a percentage of total actual administrative costs, or the sum of separately identified accounts within the administration cost center.

As a general rule, wineries try to mimic the amount of administrative resources devoted to production management, expressed as a percentage allocation. The part of the administrative costs allocated to inventory would, naturally, reduce the administrative expenses recognized on the income statement. The part of the administrative costs allocated to inventory should be further allocated to the different production cost centers (vineyard, crush, production, bottling) based on management's estimate of how much time they spend on each area.

Bottling Costs

Bottling marks the end of the production process. At this point, all of the production costs accumulated so far in the bulk wine inventory for the wine to be bottled are transferred to bottled wine. This cost center would contain account balances that tend to follow bottling activity. In other words, one would not expect to see a lot of accounting activity until the actual bottling, save for some depreciation and overhead allocations.

One of the bottling cost center accounts would be for bottling materials. All bottling materials would be added to this account and spread among all of the wines bottled. For example, if Bottling Materials has an account balance of $137,001 and 6,387 cases are bottled for the year, the cost per case would be $21.45. That method works and is fairly common.

A more accurate method, however, would reflect differentiated packaging costs for special or more expensive wines requiring a more "luxurious" package. In the Prepaids section of the balance sheet, there would be separate accounts for glass, corks, labels, etc. The recorded cost per unit for each item ($0.42 for corks, $7.05 for glass, etc.) would be used to transfer costs from prepaid bottling supplies to the bottling cost center for the materials used in the bottling run. Differentiating packaging materials in this way allows those costs to be analyzed in a meaningful way (e.g., compared to budgeted costs).

This is a good place to discuss an idea that applies in all areas, but probably has the biggest impact in bottling: *overhead should be allocated to the production cost centers based on budgeted costs and in such a way that equal activity bears equal costs*. Otherwise, the allocation of costs could be badly disproportionate to the use of resources.

Bottling, for example, generally occurs a few times a year, and the heaviest bottling may be early in the year, with a smaller run just before harvest. If overhead costs were allocated on a monthly basis as the costs are incurred, the first bottling run would be light on overhead, and the later one would be excessively burdened with overhead costs.

From an annual bottling budget, the overhead costs may be used to develop a set of standard costs that would be applied to each bottling run on a per case basis. Any difference between the overhead applied based on the budget-derived standards and the actual overhead allocated to the bottling cost center should be minor and would show up as a variance in cost of goods sold.

The next step is to bring in the costs from the bulk wine inventory and add them to the packaging costs. During the course of bottling, some wine will be lost from what was last recorded as the gallons in inventory. Keep in mind that the costs accumulated to date will become part of the final bottle cost. There is no need to expense spillage or filtration losses as they will be absorbed by the bottled wine as part of the final cost. The following example looks at the bottling of the 2001 Cabernet Sauvignon. Assume an estimated 5,701 gallons, with $121,477 of costs accumulated from other cost centers, will be bottled. The bottling report shown in Figure 11.4 below brings forward all costs from previous activities and adds the final costs from this last stage of production.

In the worksheet in Figure 11.4, a percentage of the costs of bulk wine is designated as fixed costs, based on a previous study of cellar costs, but the percentages may vary from winery to winery. Breaking costs into fixed and variable components allows for contribution margin analysis and variable budgeting. Also note that cased goods storage is not included in these calculations. Cased goods storage is a period cost, and should be expensed as a distribution or marketing cost. It is important to remember that once the wine is bottled, all production costs stop. In the example worksheet, the product cost is $73.71. That is the cost that should be used to reduce inventory and charge cost of goods sold for each case of the 2001 Cabernet Sauvignon sold.

Tax Issues in the US Wine Industry

Book to tax differences in the wine industry are focused around several critical areas. Generally, uniform capitalization rules (Unicap) apply under IRC §263A, whereby all farming and production costs, as well as interest and storage costs,

Example 5
BOTTLING INFORMATION

							Cost Analysis	
Date Bottled		January 15 - 16, 2003						
Product Bottled:		2001 Cabernet		Code	CS750-01			
Cases Bottled			2,343	*2.3775 =		5,570		
							Fixed	Variable
Gallons removed from bulk			5,701					
Estimated Losses			(131)					
Cost of Gallons removed from bulk					Cost	121,477.00	66,812.35	54,664.65
Glass (cases)	2,348	Unit Cost	$7.350		Cost	17,257.80		17,257.80
Packaging		Unit Cost			Cost	-		-
Corks	28,500	Unit Cost	$0.420		Cost	11,970.00		11,970.00
Capsules	28,500	Unit Cost	$0.260		Cost	7,410.00		7,410.00
Front label	30,500	Unit Cost	$0.180		Cost	5,490.00		5,490.00
Back label	28,250	Unit Cost	$0.080		Cost	2,260.00		2,260.00
				Direct Materials		44,387.80		
Other								
	Direct Labor				Cost $	4,428.27		4,428.27
	Supervisorial				Cost		-	
	Facilities Allocation				Cost $	2,399.23	1,758.64	640.59
	Other bottling overhead				Cost $	2,066.53		2,066.53

Total Bottling Costs		$	51,215.30	68,570.99	106,187.84
Total Costs		$	172,692.30	
Total Cases Bottled			2,343	
Materials		$	18.94	FOB	186.00
Labor			1.89	
Overhead			1.02	Cont Margin	140.68
Bottling Cost per case			21.86	Cont Margin %	75.6%
Total Bulk Wine Cost per Case			51.85	Gross Margin	112.29
				Gross Profit %	60.4%
Total Cost per Case		$	73.71	

Figure 11.4 Example of bottling information worksheet.

must be capitalized. However, there are some exceptions that allow wineries and growers to use the cash method to expense certain costs in the current year, as opposed to the accrual method where costs will not be recognized until the wine is actually sold.

One unique tax advantage of farm accounting is the ability to deduct certain soil and water conservation expenses for vineyard development [IRC §175(a)]. Under the code, costs incurred for leveling, conditioning, grading, terracing, contouring, and soil conditioning need not be capitalized. Additionally, the construction of diversion channels, irrigation ditches, and earthen dams may also be expensed. Finally, the eradication of brush and planting of windbreaks also fall under this section.

In order to qualify, the conservation methods used must be consistent with a plan approved by the Natural Resources Conservation Services (NRCS) of the Department of Agriculture (2003). There is a limitation on the amount of deduction that may be taken in any one year. The deduction is limited to 25% of gross income from all farming operations, with a carryover of any unused deductions. It is also important to note that the election must be made in the first year the soil and water conservation expenses are incurred, otherwise the deduction is lost.

Generally, Unicap applies to farmers with respect to establishing a vineyard, in that the preproductive period is more than 2 years [IRC §263A(d)(1)(A)(ii)]. If farmers are not required to use the accrual method of accounting, they may have the option to expense or capitalize certain preproductive expenses (including interest cost) when establishing a new vineyard [Reg. §1.162-12(a)]. Capital expenditures cannot be deducted. However, if the election is made to expense (which must be done in the first year) all depreciation must follow the alternative (straight-line) depreciation methods of IRC §168(g)(2).

Up until recently, wineries had to be on the accrual basis for accounting for tax purposes. A majority of wineries also grow some grapes. Any farming costs incurred would become part of inventory and not recognized until the wine was sold. This could be as long as 4 years later, depending on the wine. Individuals, or certain small businesses, may use the cash method for farm accounting. Reg. §1.263A-4(a)(4)(ii)(B) provides that the farming of a commodity up to the time of processing qualifies for cash basis, even if the entity is a winery using accrual accounting. Thus, a winery may expense farming costs. The result is that the tax-based inventory would be at a lower basis than the GAAP-based inventory. The expenses would be recognized up to 2 years earlier. The down side is that the tax-based gross profit margin would be higher when the low-basis wines are sold.

A recent exception to Unicap was Revenue Procedure 2000-22. It was available to taxpayers whose average annual gross receipts from all sources during the last 3 years was less than $1,000,000. This revenue procedure allowed wineries to use the cash method and not account for inventories. However, there was also a conformity requirement, in that the financial books had to be reported on the same basis. The banking industry cried "foul" immediately. Because of the flaws in 2000-22, the IRS issued Revenue Procedure 2001-10; 2001-10 removed the conformity requirement and refined the inventory accounting issues in that only *purchased* raw materials and supplies should be capitalized.

There is also a simplified production method available whereby the additional §263A costs divided by the traditional §471 costs times the ending §471 inventory costs equal the amount of §263A costs to add to ending inventory. For example, if §263A costs were $150,000, §471 costs were $500,000, and §471 ending inventory costs were $450,000, the amount of §263A costs to add to inventory would be ($150,000/$500,000) times $450,000 equals $135,000. There is also a de minimus rule. If total indirect overhead costs are less than $200,000 for the year, then only direct materials and labor need by capitalized. Everything else would be expensed.

Tax inventories must apply interest capitalization under the avoided cost rules if 1) the production period is greater than 2 years, (2) the production period is greater than 1 year and the cost is more than $1,000,000. The production period is measured

Table 11.7. Comparative Depreciable Lives

Asset	GAAP Years	MACRS GDS Years	MACRS ADS Years
Vines	20	10	20
Trellis & irrigation	10	7	10
Tractor	10	7	10
Building	40	39	40
Crusher	10	7	10
Barrels	5	3	4
Refrigeration	10	7	10
Bottling line	10	7	10

from the time the grapes are crushed until the wines are made available for sale. The avoided cost rules assume that interest expense from any borrowings must be applied to inventory first. For example, if inventory requiring more than 2 years' production were $1,500,000, and the net book value of equipment used to produce those wines were $2,800,000, and your average borrowing rate was 6.2%, the amount of interest to capitalize would be $266,600 (6.2% of $4,300,000).

As a final step, the capitalized interest calculation cannot exceed the interest actually paid. The calculation above takes into account debt required for production assets. The interest rate is a weighted average borrowing rate for all debt.

In addition to book-tax inventory differences, where capitalized production costs and costs of goods sold are generally higher, there are significant differences in depreciation. While GAAP uses straight-line and is preferred (although MACRS is acceptable), tax depreciation follows the Modified Accelerated Cost Recovery System (MACRS). Tables for MACRS depreciable lives can be found in Revenue Procedure 87-56. Table 11.7 illustrates some comparative depreciable lives.

Table 11.8. LIFO Calculation Example

Inventory	Quantity	Base Year Cost	Extended at Base Year Cost	Current Cost Index
Bulk	50,000	$10	$500,000	$600,000
Cased	15,000	$45	$675,000	$750,000
Total			$1,175,000	$1,350,000

1.15 Beginning inventory at base year cost	$1,075,000
Increase at base	$100,000
Index for increment	1.15
LIFO value of pool addition	$115,000
Beginning LIFO value	$1,075,000
Ending LIFO value	$1,190,000
Ending FIFO value	$1,350,000
LIFO reserve	$160,000

Many wineries use the *last-in, first-out (LIFO)* method of inventory accounting to reduce their current taxable income. The LIFO method charges operations with current production costs. In periods of increasing costs, inventories are stated at prior, lower costs and cost of sales includes higher costs.

The most common LIFO method used is the double extension method, in which inventories are extended at base year costs (the costs of cased goods and bulk wine at the point in time LIFO was first adopted) and the resulting base year cost of the current inventory is compared to the current FIFO cost to compute an index for the current year LIFO pool. An example for a LIFO calculation is illustrated in Table 11.8, assuming LIFO was elected the previous year. (In the example, LIFO has resulted in a cumulative reduction of taxable income of $160,000.)

Taxpayers using LIFO for tax purposes must also use it for financial reporting purposes; however, supplemental FIFO information can be provided to users of the financial statements. Not all inventory items need be under LIFO. If a winery was producing its own wines, as well as importing bulk wine subject to foreign currency translation adjustments, it might choose to value only the domestic wines under LIFO.

Chapter 12

WINE SUPPLY
CHAIN MANAGEMENT

*Tom Atkin (Assistant Professor of Operations
Management, Sonoma State University)*

*Jon Affonso (Assistant Winemaker,
Dry Creek Vineyards)*

The wine business has experienced huge changes over the last two decades in terms of advances in technology, globalization of markets, and stabilization of political economies. As nationwide manufacturing capabilities improved in the 1990s, managers realized that material and service inputs from suppliers had a major impact on their organization's ability to meet customer needs. Firms such as IBM and Chrysler now purchase over 70% of their cost of goods sold from outside suppliers. This has led to an increased focus on the supply base and the organization's sourcing strategy.

As a result of these changes, companies now find that it is no longer enough to manage only their own organization. They must also be involved in the management of the network of all upstream firms that provide inputs (directly or indirectly) for the organization. They must also be involved with the network of downstream firms responsible for delivery and after-market service of the product to the end customer as well. From this realization emerged the concept of the "supply chain." The wine industry has followed suit in this need to focus on managing its supply chain to reduce costs, improve quality, and meet customer needs.

This chapter provides an overview of how the wine industry interacts with its supply chain. It begins with a definition of supply chain and its management function. It then describes the process of determining your core competencies to determine which aspects of your business process to outsource to suppliers, and then reviews a commodity strategy to assist in doing this. Next the chapter reviews the major supplies for the wine industry, and the decision points used to determine which supply strategy to use. Finally, the chapter concludes with a review of supply chain management issues and trends for the future.

What Is a Supply Chain?

The *supply chain* encompasses all activities associated with the flow and transformation of goods from the raw materials stage (extraction), through to the end user, as well as the associated information flows. Material and information flow both up and down the supply chain (Handfield & Nichols, 1999). Supply chains are essentially a series of linked suppliers and customers that handle the product until it reaches the consumer and beyond, if recycling or disposal is involved.

Supply chain management is the integration of these activities through improved supply chain relationships to achieve a sustainable competitive advantage. The path to sustained growth involves managing costs across these multiple enterprises. Figure 12.1 illustrates a supply chain, with the "plan" portion depicting the "management" aspects.

Each organization has to define its own position in the supply chain. The wine industry exhibits a wide variety of supply chain designs, from the complete control demonstrated by the vertically integrated supply chain of larger wineries (i.e., E.&J. Gallo), to the fragmented marketplace of the smaller wineries. Several issues make the wine supply chain distinctive. First, the production of wine is very fragmented, with a large number of small wineries operating very independently. For example, there are currently over 1,000 wineries operating in Sonoma and Napa counties alone. This has resulted in a lack of coordination between producers and suppliers.

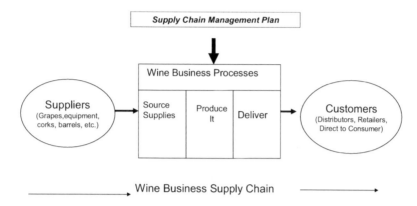

Figure 12.1. Supply chain management.

Second, the distribution system is unique due to the laws controlling the sales of wine in each state. This body of law requires a three-tier system that demands that wineries sell only through approved distributors in each state and limits sales direct to customers. This has led to a situation where a large number of wineries are competing for the attention of a handful of distributors who have become very powerful. These two factors, combined with the vagaries of an agricultural product, make the wine supply chain different from all others.

Determining Your Core Competencies

The development of a supply chain is essentially a series of make versus buy decisions. Any and all aspects of wine business activity can potentially be outsourced. The grapes can be grown on the private estate of the winery or they can be obtained from a grower's vineyard. The bottling of the wine can be handled in-house or performed by a mobile bottling operation. Custom crush facilities can perform any and all winemaking operations from crushing the fruit to fermenting, ageing, bottling, and even marketing the final wine. Firms will develop different supply chain strategies depending on their corporate mission and competitive advantages.

First, each organization has to decide whether to provide the product or service in-house or to outsource it. In order to decide, a firm must determine their core competencies. What is it that they do better than their competition? In addition, what materials give the firm a strategic advantage over their competitors? These two factors constitute strengths within the company and are activities that should remain inside the company. The current thinking is that the firm should concentrate on developing or enhancing these strengths. These are the things that are critical to the end product and that the firm has a distinct advantage in providing. These advantages may be due to economies of scale, higher quality, or a favorable cost structure.

Similarly, the firm should also look for weaknesses in areas where they do not produce an item as effectively or efficiently as their suppliers or competitors. In this situation, a company can develop the item into a core competency by bringing in skilled experts and investing in equipment to produce the item in-house. This is often expensive and time consuming. As long as the material is not a core competency, direct quality control is not a serious issue, and if it is less expensive to buy it than make it, then outsourcing is the preferred solution. Many firms have recognized that anything that is not part of a firm's core competence is a candidate for outsourcing. If a supplier can do a better job on a product or service, then it makes sense to buy from the supplier rather than make it in-house.

Commodity Strategy

A commodity strategy is the next step in deciding how to deal with all of the inputs that are required to provide a bottle of wine to a consumer. Inputs can generally be classified across two dimensions: the profit contribution of the input and the supply risk (Monczka, Trent, & Handfield, 2002). These two dimensions combine to form a 2 × 2 matrix, as shown in Figure 12.2.

Using this matrix as a guideline, we can see how best to manage all of the required inputs. Each cell of the matrix calls for a different set of techniques for obtaining it. For instance, the most valuable input for a winery to obtain is the grapes. This would fall into the strategic category so the winery would communicate extensively with those suppliers and continuously review performance. Some of the techniques that can be utilized for each category are listed below and an analysis of the key inputs for wineries appears in the following sections.

Major Supplies in the Wine Industry

The following sections describe the five major supply components for a winery. These are: 1) wine/grape source; 2) winemaking equipment—both fixed and variable costs; 3) storage; 4) distribution; and 5) inventory control management. A dis-

HIGH Profit Contribution	**STRATEGIC** – High supply risk and high profit contribution • Limit suppliers • Develop partnerships • Involve suppliers early • Closely manage price/cost • Continuously review performance	**LEVERAGE** – Low supply risk and high profit contribution • Multiple sources • Maintain competitive pressure • Seek waste elimination • Monitor performance
LOW Profit Contribution	**ACQUISITION** – High supply risk and low profit contribution • Ensure supply • Focus on service • Frequently review • Minimize acquisition cost	**MULTIPLE SOURCES** - Low supply risk and low profit contribution • Use multiple sources • Procurement cards • Automate • Give minimal attention
	HIGH – Supply Risk	**LOW – Supply Risk**

Figure 12.2. Supply chain decision matrix.

cussion of the many subcomponents of each category and its decision points is included.

Wine/Grape Source

Buying Bulk Wine

The first make versus buy decision in the development of a winery's supply chain is to determine if they are going to produce the wine or buy it on the bulk market. I would suspect that most wineries categorize the production of their style of wine as a core competency. I say most but not all. Some companies have vast distribution channels. Others specialize in unique packaging or are able to react quickly to changes in consumer preferences. Any of these core competencies creates a situation where it might be better to buy some or most of their wine in bulk, from another producer. The main factor in buying bulk wine is the availability of the wine. How specific of a wine style and type is the company looking for? Is the company simply looking for red or white table wine or are they looking for a 2001 Old Vine Zinfandel from bench land areas of Dry Creek Valley in Sonoma County? The specificity of the wine relates directly to the availability, which is the dominating factor in the market value of that wine.

Price is not determined by how much it costs to produce the wine. Price is really only an expression of what the market will bear. This of course creates a certain amount of volatility in the market, causing the supply to become an ocean of inexpensive good-quality wine or a desert of poor wine. The wine industry has formed wine brokerage companies that specialize in the buying and selling of bulk wines. They are excellent sources of information as to what the market has available as well as forecasting what will be available. They help in reducing the level of price volatility; however, it is still a free market system.

Producing Wine

As I stated, I suspect most wineries consider wine production in their style to be a core competency. Therefore, I suggest that most wineries should produce most if not the vast majority of their wine. This allows the production to remain in-house where the company can retain constant control over the quality of the product.

In an ideal world, the entrepreneur would have enough money to build the perfect little jewel of a winery to accommodate exactly what the winemaker had in mind. That million-dollar investment to start up a winery is out of reach for most of us. There are a couple of ways of avoiding that investment, however.

One of the evolutionary changes that occurred in the wine industry over the past 20 years is the business relationship called "custom crush." It is the leasing or renting of excess space in a winery facility to individuals who want to make their own wine without having to make the financial investment needed for a winery. This gives smaller wineries the capacity to grow and allows them access to state-of-the-art equipment. These facilities offer a wide range of services, including:

- crushing and fermenting,
- winemaking and tank storage,
- barrel storage,
- analysis,

- filling and packaging,
- regulatory compliance,
- business services.

"Shared premise" is a similar arrangement in which an established winery shares the use of its facilities with other winemakers. By alternating the use of winery space and equipment with an established producer, a grape grower or brand builder can become a vintner without the major investment. This arrangement offers more stability in winemaking style and more control over costs and pricing than custom crush.

The capital expenditure for building a winery is significant, and it is often difficult to produce wine without some financial backing. In order to obtain backing, you may have to show that your product is viable in the marketplace. Custom crushing facilities make it possible to offer a wine in the market before the winery is built. By outsourcing the production of your wine, you can avoid or at least postpone the enormous capital cost of your own facility and the equipment needed to crush, ferment, press, age, and bottle your wine. This allows the winery to produce a product, earn some revenue, and prove to the bank that its product is worthy of financial support.

With financial backing, a production facility can now be built. To develop a new winery, at minimum a facility, pressing equipment, food grade tank storage, and climate control systems and hoses are required. More often than not, grape crushing/destemming equipment, filtration equipment, pumps, as well as barrels, are additional items, all of which are fixed costs used to produce wine.

Buying Grapes From a Grower

Now it is somewhat obvious to suggest that producing wine should be a winery's core competency. Is the same true of the suggestion that a winery should produce its own grapes? This is not as clear. There are several reasons why outsourcing would be a good, if not a preferred, option for obtaining this strategic resource.

Many private growers produce high-quality grapes and sell them to wineries. The vast majority of wineries in the US purchase some grapes from private growers because the growers have a unique expertise and a close understanding of the grape vines on their property. They often have more experience and their close proximity to the vines makes them better equipped to respond to infection or infestation. In many cases, the growers are more focused and better suited to produce quality fruit than the wineries.

Due to the temperate climate in most winemaking regions of the world, vineyard land is in high demand. This increases the average price per acre to enormously expensive amounts. In addition to this, the winery must consider the large capital cost of the farming equipment, the trellis system, the irrigation system, labor, and the vines themselves.

The down side to purchasing fruit is that there is an inherent adversarial relationship between growers and wineries. Growers want more money per ton and higher yield. Wineries want less money per ton and lower yield for quality. Due to the importance of the commodity, a close strategic relationship is required. Constant negotiations are extremely important between growers and wineries to ensure a mutually beneficial relationship. If the relationship is close and mutually beneficial, there are few problems. However, if communication breaks down or the specifications are not clearly stated, there is a possibility of producing grapes that do not meet the requirements of the winery. This lack of communication often results in wineries that are forced to purchase inferior grapes or growers losing an entire year's income. It is for this reason that the winery should be in constant contact with the grower throughout the growing season as well as after harvest to discuss the quality of the fruit. This not only increases the likelihood that the fruit is maintained correctly during the current growing season, but it allows for improvement by both parties for the future.

Growing Grapes From Estate Vineyards

While the initial capital expenditure of planting a vineyard is high, in the long run it is often more cost-effective to plant your own vineyards. It is important not to grow too quickly so that the company is able to absorb the debt and still remain healthy. Unless someone began as a grower before they started their winery, many wineries do not initially own their own vineyards. In time, wineries gradually begin to purchase land and plant their own vineyards. Wineries often initially outsource the labor and expertise by hiring a vineyard management company instead of purchasing their own equipment and employing the labor. As the winery continues to plant more and more vineyards, it will be more cost-effective for the winery to purchase its own equipment and hire a vineyard manager and labor to maintain them. While in the long run it is more cost-effective to grow grapes, the main advantage is that it eliminates the adversarial relationship between the grower and the winery. This allows the winery to have absolute control over how the fruit is grown, which further helps to achieve the fruit specification and quality the winery is looking for.

Winemaking Equipment: Fixed Costs

There is a large amount of equipment to purchase if the winery has decided to produce the wine in-house. First, a building will be needed somewhat close to the grapes so the grapes won't suffer damage in transit due to temperature. The following items will be needed to outfit that building to produce wine.

Tanks

Tanks are necessary for fermentation and storage of wine. Although most are constructed of food-grade stainless steel, some wineries still use cement or wood tanks. Newer technologies are developing food-grade plastic tanks. Stainless steel has become the worldwide standard because of its strength, long life, and the ability of its surface to be easily sanitized. The cost of tanks can vary depending on whether they are fitted with a jacket (to control temperatures) or other specific features that have been added (such as cleanout doors). Jacketed tanks are double walled to allow a hot or cold liquid to pass around the tank without being in contact with the wine. The liquids are able to reduce or increase the temperature quickly to stabilize the wine. Currently, a good rule of thumb is that tanks will cost about US$2.00 per gallon. Therefore, a 6,000-gallon tank represents an investment of about US$12,000.

Newer tank technology is helping to improve the quality of the wine and speed up the fermentation process. The most recent designs serve to reduce fermentation time by one half through modern methods of pumping over and breaking the cap. Tank designs such as Selector System allow cap wetting in which the cap is steeped, remixed, and disintegrated. This improves the extraction capacity of color, bouquet, and taste and avoids the formation of solids. It also means less time spent in the tank so the tanks can be used more efficiently. Additional features allow the tank to empty completely so laborers don't have to crawl inside to perform dangerous cleanups.

Barrels

Barrels differ from tanks in that they are not only a storage vessel but they are an aging tool that dramatically affects the flavors, tactile impressions, and the aromas of the wine. Barrels are described by the origin of the wood used (i.e., French, American, Eastern European), the grain size of the wood, the volume it stores, and the amount of toast (how long the inside of the barrel is exposed to fire). The grain size also dictates the amount of oxygen that passes through wood into the wine, which dictates how fast a wine will age. All of these factors directly influence the amount and type of oak extraction that influences the wine. Every cooper is different and each barrel type imparts different characteristics. These factors will have a large influence on the style of wine and the winery should take care to purchase the correct barrels and a diversity of barrels to create the style they want to achieve.

Like everything else, barrels are very expensive. The type of oak and the expertise in building it are the two main factors that determine the cost. Barrels are still largely assembled and toasted by hand, which makes them labor intensive. Most barrels are either French or American oak, but many cooperages are sourcing some of their wood from Eastern Europe and even China. While French oak is generally twice as expensive as American oak, French oak may or may not be the type of oak that fits your style. On the other hand, while cost is a factor, the style of the wine should be the dominating factor in deciding which barrels to purchase rather than simply buying the least expensive barrel.

Another difference between barrels and tanks is that barrels have a much shorter life span. On average a barrel will last 3 to 7 years depending upon the winery's style. This means that new barrels must be constantly cycled into the program as older barrels are culled out. This creates a more complex management dynamic that must be monitored. The shorter the life span of the barrel, the larger the influx of new barrels and the higher the expense. This shorter life span makes the item almost a variable cost, but because the item is used for several different wines and different vintages it is often considered a fixed cost.

Of course, like most commodities, there are some price breaks for larger volumes. However, because most wineries purchase barrels from several different coopers, their volume of barrels is not as large as if they bought all of their barrels from one cooper. Therefore, there is less advantage for the supplier to provide significant price breaks and thus the savings are not very significant.

Oak additives (i.e., chips, beans, or dust) have been developed as substitutes for barrels. They come in French or American varieties and at any desired toasting level and grain size. These additives can be added directly to the wine or come in muslin sacks that act as tea bags to infuse the oak into the wine. Also, barrel innerstaves can be placed inside older barrels to increase their life span. This allows the use of older barrels while imparting compounds from the new oak. In addition, tank innerstaves can be used in the same fashion to impart oak character in stainless steel vessels rather than barrels. All of these alternatives can have a substantial cost savings.

Presses

Technology has taken hold in the process of pressing the grapes. The hydraulic vertical basket press and the horizontal bladder press are by far the two most common types of presses. The hydraulic vertical basket press operates by placing the grape skins into a slotted cylinder with a hydraulic lid that presses down from above. The wine is then allowed to flow between the slots and is collected in a pan at the base. The horizontal bladder press is the more modern version and it exerts the pressure by inflating a bladder mounted to the inside of the cylinder. Wine is then allowed to flow from slots in the cylinder on the opposite side. Because of the relatively low pressure exerted on the pomace and gentle mechanical treatment of the skins, the solid content in the juice is low. Automated control systems on both models drive the process to allow maximum yield and decreased stress on the juice.

Another type of press, the continuous press, is essentially a screw auger that presses the pomace toward a small outlet. This is efficient because it saves loading and unloading of the container, but a big disadvantage is that it causes tearing and breaking of the skin's tissue.

Cellar Equipment

There are several pieces of equipment that are used to varying capacities and they vary drastically depending upon the wine's style and price point. Items like crushing/destemming machines, filtration devices, pumps, hoses, and fittings are all commonly used in wineries. However, how and if they are used is more a discussion of winemaking than supply chain management. Suffice it to say that they are all expensive fixed costs with relatively long life spans. These pieces of equipment must first be decided upon based on wine quality and then their cost can be factored into the development of the facility.

Bottling Line

Setting up a bottling line is expensive but there are choices available. The bottling activities only take place part of the time so many smaller wineries use custom crush facilities to bottle their wine. A very creative solution is the mobile bottling line, which is essentially a trailer that can be moved from winery to winery for short filling runs. These facilities can also be used if the winery has exceeded its in-house bottling capacity.

Winemaking Equipment: Variable Costs

Winemaking Supplies

There are hundreds of different products that contribute to the production of thousands of different wines. It is beyond the scope of this chapter to discuss all of the different products and how they are used, but some of the more common supplies are listed in Table 12.1.

Many of these products have several different substitutes and can be purchased from a few or even one supplier. This consolidation gives the winery a little more leverage when it comes to pricing. There is a significant advantage for a supplier to

Table 12.1. Common Winemaking Supplies

Yeast
Yeast nutrient
Diammonium phosphate
Potassium metabisulfate
Tartaric acid
Fining agents
Settling enzymes
Caustic cleaning agents
Citric acid
Lactic acid bacteria
LAB nutrients
Lab analysis
Diatomaceous earth
Filters

sell a single winery a large volume of materials, which translates into the ability to offer significant price breaks. The better a winery is at reducing the number of suppliers providing items, the more efficient their supply chain will be, the better customer service they will receive, and the lower the price per unit will become.

Bottles and Alternative Containers

Tradition from Western Europe has dictated the form of most wine bottles. The three most common shapes are: the Bordeaux shape (long cylinder with a short shouldered neck), the Burgundy shape (shorter cylinder with a long unsholdered neck), and the Alsace shape (longer and narrower cylinder with a long unsholdered neck). Traditionally, certain wines are used in certain bottles. Therefore, the actual shape of the bottle helps described the wine it contains. Red wines typically are packaged in a dark green or dark brown glass to protect the wine from the damaging effects of light. The vast majority of bottles have a volume of 750 milliliters. However, smaller 375-milliliter and larger 1.5-, 3-, and 6-liter bottles are common and other sizes do exist. The neck opening design of most bottle types has standard dimensions to fit the standard cork size.

Glass bottles are by far the norm but substitutes are available. Glass is susceptible to breakage and the quality of the wine deteriorates if not consumed fairly quickly. The bag-in-box container has a cubicle shape that is economical to ship, maximizes shipping space, and can survive a fair degree of rough handling. The box contains a vacuum-sealed bag that prevents oxidation so it can keep the wine fresh for up to 4 weeks after opening.

Another option that is in experimentation is to store the wine in easy-to-open cans. Similar to beer and soft drinks, this container might make the product more accessible but will drastically affect the perception of quality of the product. Another issue is the infusion of aluminum flavor into the wine. The cans would have to be Teflon coated to prevent the product from being in contact with the metal. However, this may be especially useful on airplanes and in the catering industry.

Whichever container is used, the winery will be purchasing a very large quantity and will have some leverage with the manufacturer. While leverage can be used, I would not recommend going too far as it might begin to affect customer service. Many glass companies work with cardboard suppliers and they will package the bottles into the winery's finished boxes as part of their service before they arrive at the winery. This greatly increases efficiency of the bottling line as the cases are emptied and then refilled with the box they arrived in. It also eliminates the use of unnecessary packaging material. The glass company might also work closely with the winery to improve efficiency of materials by operating on a JIT basis. This assists in cash flow by not tying up money in inventoried supplies. Because bottles can be produced in large amounts fairly quickly and the material is easily recyclable, most glass suppliers have to keep very strict quality control programs to stay competitive and this is another key element to good customer service.

Labels and Foils

Labels and foils are devices that can really make a wine stand out on the shelf. They are a key component of the marketing effort for any winery. Foils are simple tin capsules that cover the top of the bottle. They provide little practical function but drastically improve the appearance of the product. Labels inform the consumer as to the content of the bottle. Some wording on the label is required by federal regulation and needs to be scrutinized to ensure that all information is in compliance. However, there is still plenty of space for brand identification and graphics. Close communication with the printer is needed during the design phase to achieve the desired presentation. Glue labels and pressure-sensitive labels are the most commonly used. The equipment and expertise needed to produce high-quality image is well beyond the core competency of the winery. It is not a loss of strategic advantage to outsource and it is still easy to maintain control of the design of the labels. It is important to choose a printer that will provide the range of materials and the assurance that the label will, in fact, work in conjunction with the labeling machine and the container utilized.

There are several manufacturers that provide these services but often the companies that offer the most service tend to be the most expensive. Therefore, the winery should determine how much service they are willing to pay for. A winery does purchase a significant amount of labels and can use them as promotional materials as well. If you can limit the number of suppliers, this again will allow the winery to maximize the amount of leverage it can have without affecting the customer service.

Corks

For centuries cork was the absolute closure of choice for wine. It seals the bottle as the liquid forces the cork to expand and some believe cork also allows small amounts of oxygen to enter the wine to assist in aging. In the 1980s the incidence of cork taint began to increase in a certain percentage of bottled wines. It was a taint that could, depending upon its intensity, cause a reduction in fruit character of the wine or even cause an outright moldy smell similar to wet cardboard.

Beginning in the 1990s several companies began to manufacture and sell synthetic corks that mimicked a cork as far as the ability to seal a bottle of wine. Questions have arisen concerning their ease of opening and the ability to maintain a tight seal

over several years' time. But, once thoroughly tested and evaluated, a number of wineries deemed synthetic corks quite acceptable replacements for true bark cork and
they are now widely used. Other wineries have opted to remain with the traditional
natural cork closure due to tradition and consumer perception.

By the beginning of the 21st century another closure method was being considered by some wineries. The long-skirt Stelvin screw top has been used in Australia for
a number of years, but only recently in the US for a premium wine. Technological
advances have enabled screw tops to perform well in preserving the freshness of the
bottled wine and it is much more convenient for the consumer. A recent entrant in
the closure arena is the MetaCork, a twist-to-uncork wine opener. It is hoped that
this type of closure will improve the consumer's overall wine experience by reducing the hassle of opening the bottle. It consists of a twist-capsule that is anchored to
a cork for easy removal.

In most cases, the decisive factor in a decision on closures revolves around consumer acceptance. Will the consumer react negatively to the use of an alternative
closure? How important is the issue of cork taint to consumers?

Suppliers in the cork industry have made strong efforts to increase the quality of
their products. They have begun to vertically integrate the supply chain so that more
control of the harvesting and production of the corks can be achieved. Batches can
now be tracked from the forest to the warehouse. More sanitary processing methods
and facilities have been established. Peroxide is now used instead of bleach and the
bark is stored on concrete rather than dirt during curing. All of these services are
controls to look for and should be demanded as a criterion of purchase. Again, many
suppliers provide these services and it allows the winery some leverage. However,
cork is not a quickly renewable resource and it is being depleted. Over time, the
price of cork will increase as the source of raw material decreases.

Storage

Bottle Aging

Even though the majority of wine purchased in the US is consumed within 48
hours after purchase, wineries must still be concerned about bottle aging. Bottle
aging is any chemical reaction that goes in the wine while it is in the bottle. Wine is
often filtered at the time of bottling to inhibit the wine from spoiling. As a result, the
wine is "shocked," which suppresses wine's flavors and aromas for a month or two.
Once the wine recovers it begins to express the characters of the fruit and what the
winemaker crafted into it as well. In time the wine will continue to age as the tannin
ages and the fruit characteristics will become more prevalent. The wine will ultimately become more complex and interesting to the senses.

Environmental Conditions

With the amount of evolution the wine undergoes in the bottle, a winery must be
concerned with the bottle environment from the time it is bottled to the time when
it is consumed. Extreme heat, extreme cold, light, and humidity are all important
factors to control in wine storage. Temperatures around 90°F and light can rapidly
accelerate the aging process. Heat will dry out the closure and allow the wine to
leak, oxidize the wine, or cause the wine to cloud. Extreme cold at around 30°F can

slow down the aging process or cause the wine to precipitate crystals. It is important that wine storage be between 50°F and 70°F with an elevated level of humidity
to prevent the cork from drying. It is for these reasons that trucking, retailers, and
consumers often go to lengths to maintain this environment.

These conditions should be maintained from case storage to consumer. This means
the winery should ensure the case goods storage for the winery, the transportation
of the wine to the distributor, the case good storage at the distributor, the transportation from the distributor to the retailer, and the retailer case storage are all climate
controlled. It is a tremendous amount of refrigeration.

Distribution

Three-Tier System

The three-tier system is a by-product of prohibition that forces all alcohol sales to
travel from a producer, through a distributor, and on to a retailer before it can be sold
to the consumer. Distributors are organizations that either act as a broker or take
possession of the product and act as an agent of the winery. As an agent they are
supposed to actively promote and sell the wine. However, as time has passed, most
of the distributors have consolidated, leaving only a handful, and they often have to
sell hundreds of brands. It is difficult to ensure the kind of customer service that is
commonly provided with other service providers when dealing with so many brands.
In the end many distributors are not able to actively promote every brand so the
winery is forced find other ways to gain attention.

Options in this area are quite limited due to the three-tier system imposed by
government regulation. But even within this system there are opportunities to promote the wine. These include winemaker dinners, tasting rooms, active public relations, wine clubs, private tours and/or parties at the winery, and special auction lots.
These activities will help to create a bond with the distributor, the retailer, and even
the consumer, all of which makes it easier to move the wine through the system.
These should be core competencies within the winery. There are services that will
allow you to outsource these promotional aspects. However, the whole purpose is to
build a direct relationship with the distributor, retailer, and consumer. By outsourcing
this service, it places an intermediate between them and decreases the level of close-
ness. It is far more effective to service these entities directly and personally. Even
with the benefit aside, the cost is not expensive and the result is very profitable.

Internet

The Internet provides an additional channel for reaching consumers. Direct communication with the end user is established and the wine is delivered to their doorstep. This allows the winery to develop a long-term relationship with its customers
and keep them informed about new vintages. Small package carriers typically take
care of the delivery, making it very convenient for the customer. Direct delivery from
California is now legal in 32 states and wineries are lobbying hard to make this channel available in more states. If the wine is purchased in the tasting room at the winery, tourists can now ship wine to the residence anywhere in the US. The wine club
management can also be outsourced, but the purpose is to have a direct relationship
and an outsourced service will be an additional layer.

Tasting Rooms

Direct access to customers is also provided by wine tasting rooms. Customers can sample the wine before purchasing it. This can often be the beginning of a longer relationship that can be enhanced by wine club membership and Internet promotions.

Wine Shipping

One function that can be outsourced is the warehousing and shipping of the wine. Many wineries use specialized public warehouses and co-ops to store their product and prepare it for shipment. These suppliers have also developed expertise in handling the paperwork and government reporting requirements that accompany the shipping process. They also provide the proper environmental conditions for transporting and ensuring wine quality is maintained. Using refrigerated trailers, heaters, and insulated quilts can provide temperature control during transportation.

Inventory Control Management

Monitoring the inventory of case goods allows for visibility of the entire stock of product that is ready to be sold. This ensures that the little or no product is lost or stolen. This is a service that a storage warehouse will provide, but the level of accuracy is often not as good as if the winery does it. This is another area that should be a core competency of the winery. There is software available that makes this much easier, but a specialist is preferred to ensure efficiency and accuracy.

A specialist will monitor rates of depletion in all markets where the wine is sold. This information can be passed on to marketing and even the production department to act as a type of feedback loop. If sales are up or down in specified markets, it might allow marketing to reallocate their promotion to areas where sales are down from areas where sales are high. It might also indicate to production which wines are preferred and what production levels they should predict for the next season. Again, this is all proprietary information that is essential to the winery's strategy, which further underlines why this service should be one of the winery's core competencies.

Supplier Quality Management Issues

Cost of Quality

Given that a large portion of the action takes place outside the winery, it is important to be able to manage activities taking place at the supplier. A good example is the supply chain for corks. For years wineries just accepted the fact a certain percentage of wine would suffer from cork taint. Wineries would try to identify tainted lots of cork and reject them, but little effort was made to force suppliers to change their handling methods and reduce the level of taint. Cork producers have recently reacted to the problem by instituting new methods of sorting and cleaning the cork. Producers are now making it right the first time rather than letting poor-quality product make its way to the customer.

Many of these issues are tied to corporate goals in achieving high quality. Dr. Joseph Juran developed the concept of cost of quality. He was able to show managers that poor quality was actually more expensive than making things right the first time. Products made with high defect levels are costly to the company in terms of product that has to be thrown out, loss of future sales, shipping goods back, inspection of incoming goods, and materials consumed in destructive testing.

Organizations have found that, in order to achieve better quality, they have to take an active role in the measurement and management of activities at the supplier. The first requirement is to clearly communicate the expectations and specifications for the item. In addition, many firms are reducing the size of their supply base to facilitate closer relationships.

Supplier Certification: ISO 9000

It is critical that a winery selects and maintains only those suppliers capable of providing the highest quality products. Certification is a process in which suppliers' manufacturing and quality processes are thoroughly evaluated to make sure they are in "control." Certification is implemented in stages beginning with supplier-provided information. A team will then visit the supplier to assess their management capability, cost structure, information systems, and total quality management philosophy. A cross-functional team usually performs this audit. A positive outcome means that the supplier is able to do more business with the customer. After a period of time, incoming inspection of the supplier's goods may no longer be necessary because systems at the supplier are well developed. The primary purpose is to work only with suppliers capable of continuous quality improvement.

This is a huge effort, however. In the absence of the resources to perform such an audit, a smaller winery may want to rely on an audit framework like ISO 9000. This is an international set of standards that tests the qualifications of the applicant to ensure conformance quality. Many purchasing managers recognize ISO 9000 standards as a necessary foundation for the implementation of total quality management.

Trends in Supply Chain Management

Total Quality Management

One of the keys to achieving customer satisfaction through total quality management is an emphasis on monitoring quality at the source. This means that wineries will have to develop systems for measuring supplier performance. These systems can be used to help make supplier selection decisions and determine where to commit supplier development resources. For instance, software has been developed that allows the winery to track activities at their grower's vineyards.

Information Sharing

Information is the lifeblood of any supply chain. A free flow of information is necessary to minimize inventories and maximize customer satisfaction. An example is the sharing of information between wineries and distributors. As we saw earlier, wineries can help to manage inventories by tracking depletion rates while distributors can help wineries by providing consumer profiles and analysis of sales information. Systems such as electronic data interchange (EDI) and vendor managed inventory (VMI) will help to accomplish this.

More Outsourcing

Firms will continue to outsource activities that are not part of their core competency. In the extreme, this could even result in the virtual winery, a winery that utilizes suppliers for everything. One local winery sells private label wine to a large retailer. The juice is imported from Chile, fermented and bottled at a custom crush facility, and shipped directly to the distributor. No bricks and mortar.

Longer Term Contracts

Nationwide, the percentage of long-term contracts continues to increase. Firms often combine supply base reduction efforts with the use of longer term agreements to reduce transaction costs and gain the benefits of closer relationships, such as improved quality and design assistance. Reference contracts between wineries and grape growers are typically multiyear contracts that stipulate certain activities to assure quality and consistency. Price changes can be tied to the county crush report. An evergreen contract renews itself automatically unless one of the parties cancels or renegotiates it. Per-acre contracts give the winery a large amount of control over vineyard farming decisions (Gallagher, 2003).

Conclusion

This chapter presents supply chain management in the wine industry as a dynamic endeavor. Firms in the wine business have many options available to them in designing a supply chain that will give them a competitive advantage. It takes constant monitoring and communication to keep the supply chain running as effectively as possible.

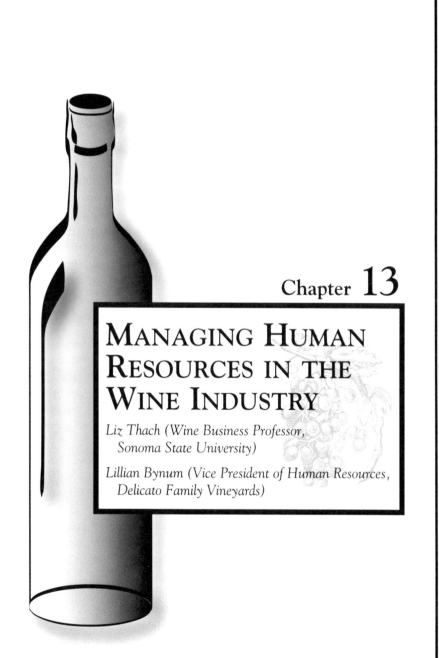

Chapter 13

MANAGING HUMAN RESOURCES IN THE WINE INDUSTRY

Liz Thach (Wine Business Professor, Sonoma State University)

Lillian Bynum (Vice President of Human Resources, Delicato Family Vineyards)

Thousands of people are employed in the wine industry in the New World. Many are attracted to it because of a love for wine and all its beneficial properties, such as being a unique product of nature, art, and science; enhancing food and health; and inspiring collaboration and friendship. However, working in the wine industry is not always filled with romance. It is still a global business, like many other businesses, and, as such, is bound to management policies that are linked to legal and regulatory control. In many cases, these policies protect the welfare of workers and the environment, but in the successful companies, they are also part of the very culture and are based on the premise that satisfied employees not only are more productive, but produce a higher quality product for the consumer.

With this in mind, this chapter focuses on how to manage human resources within the wine industry. It begins with a historical perspective on wine industry labor and then moves forward in time to modern-day practices. Specifically, it 1) provides an overview of the common employee positions within a vineyard and winery, as a business grows in size and production; 2) defines human resource management (HRM) in the wine industry; 3) describes the five major categories of HR (staffing and recruiting; training and development; employee relations, compensation and benefits; and record keeping and legal issues) as well as the special issues regarding these HR categories in the wine industry; and 4) highlights future HRM issues in New World countries.

Wine Labor Issues Through the Centuries

It is theorized that wine was discovered by accident sometime around 6000 BC. Supposedly someone picked some wild grapes, put them in a large clay pot to be consumed later, and then forgot about them for a while. Subsequently, when someone looked into the clay pot, he/she discovered the grapes had naturally fermented and turned into a unique liquid that tasted lovely and provided a rather euphoric effect.

Books on the history of wine all agree that this event took place somewhere near Mesopotamia, though authors argue about the exact location, with different authors suggesting modern-day Turkey, Iraq, and even Georgia as the actual birthplace of wine (Grist, 2003). Regardless of the location, once wine was discovered, people began to cultivate it, and immediately the issue of labor in making wine arose.

This issue was not easy to resolve, as tending the vineyards, bringing in the harvest, and overseeing fermentation and storage of the wine took an incredible amount of people and work. However, eventually a solution was found, and that was the use of *slaves* in making wine. Indeed, in ancient Egypt, where we find the earliest "wine labels" dating from 3200 BC, there are also many drawings of slaves working in the vineyards and bringing in the harvest. Interestingly, these drawings also depict the winemakers to be *priests* or someone of high knowledge and nobility (Grist, 2003).

The use of slaves to make wine on a large scale continued throughout much of early history and can be found in the records of early Syria, Canaan, Greece, and the Roman Empire. Indeed, as the Romans expanded into Gaul—modern-day France—in the early first century AD, in many cases they used slaves to plant the first of some of the famous old vineyards.

As wine made its way to the New World, the practice of using slaves to tend the vineyard continued in almost every country. In South Africa, offspring of the local tribes and European settlers were obligated to work the vines of the old vineyards. In Argentina, Chile, and California, the native Indians were required to work the vineyards, which were established around the old Spanish missions. Ironically, here again, the priest served in the role of winemaker and overseer of the production process.

A notable exception was Australia, where they never succeeded in convincing the native Aborigine tribes to work in vineyards. During some of the early years in Australia, they did employ the use of convict labor in the vineyards. Indeed, convicts originally planted the famous Dalwood vineyards along the Hunter River outside of Syndey in the late 1820s (Simon, 1967).

Historical Impact on Wine Labor Issues Today

The history of the labor situation is still felt in New World wine operations today. For example, because Australians could not rely on a cheap local labor source, they became very innovative in developing mechanized methods to harvest their vineyards. Today, they are one of the world's premier wine-producing countries, using more than 90% mechanization. This practice lowers labor costs, so the production cost of the wine is less.

In Chile, Argentina, and South Africa, much hand-harvesting is still done in the fields, but the labor costs are lower than those found in Canada and the US. Because of this, their final wine production cost is also lower. The US and Canada rely primarily on migrant labor forces from Mexico, who work in the vineyards for part of the year and then return to their homeland. Strict regulations on pay keep labor costs higher in the US and Canada and, therefore, the total production cost of the wine is higher in these countries.

The trend in many New World countries to use mechanized harvesting is not feasible in all vineyard locations. Steep hillside vineyards, or those in very prestigious appellations, still use hand labor, either because harvesting machines don't work on steep hills or because of the cachet of "hand-harvested" grapes. Many top winemakers in Europe and the US still insist on hand-harvested grapes for their wines, because of the perception that it results in higher quality fruit—even though many studies have proven that quality results are generally equal between mechanized and hand-harvested wines.

These same practices are reflected in Old World countries as well, such as France and Italy, where growers use mechanized harvesting for lower and medium-priced wines, but the high-end wine producers still use hand labor. A trend that is different in the Old World, however, is that they often hire "wine students" to work harvest and/or rely on "ecotourism participants." In both cases, they capitalize on people who are drawn to the romance of wine to provide inexpensive labor in return for being allowed to experience harvest in a famous wine region.

Common Employee Positions in the Wine Industry

Like many other industries, the number of employees in a wine business depends on the size of production in the venture. Although several large wine companies have operations in many countries around the world, such as Constellation, LVMH, Gallo, Allied Domecq, Beringer Blass, SouthCorp, Mondavi, and others, most wine businesses, at one point in time, began as a small family business. Indeed, in looking at wine countries around the world, many small and medium-sized family wine businesses still thrive. Though they may not have the global distribution might of the large companies, many do well serving a small niche within a state, region, or country. They may specialize in a certain grape varietal or style. Some may refer to themselves as a "boutique" winery and only sell direct to customers who visit their private tasting rooms or to local restaurants. Regardless of their size, certain work functions must be performed, and these dictate the number and skill level of employees needed.

Table 13.1 provides an overview of the four major job categories within an integrated wine business. These are vineyard, wine production, marketing/sales, and management/administrative. Within each category, various job titles and positions are listed. The existence of the position depends on the size of the business. In some cases, one person may perform the function of several positions. In other businesses, the position may be outsourced to a labor contracting or consulting firm. As a company grows in size and complexity, it usually adds more positions to handle the increased production and regulatory requirements. For example, in a recent Western Management Salary Survey for the US wine industry, they list more than 200 independent job titles. However, most of those titles are subsets of the four categories described in Table 13.1. The following paragraphs highlight some of the key positions within a wine business.

Employee Functions in the Vineyard

A common phrase in the wine industry is that "the best wine is made in the vineyard." Indeed, an old joke claims that the best winemakers "will set up a tent and camp in the vineyard," because the quality of the grape is the most important component of a fine wine. Obviously, the making and blending of wine requires much skill, but the health and operation of the vineyard is critical. Thus, the job of the *vineyard manager* (and *supervisors*) is one of the most important. This individual oversees

Table 13.1. High-Level Job Categories in the Wine Industry

Vineyard	Wine Production	Marketing/ Sales	Management & Administration
•VP of Vineyard Operations	•Winemaker	•VP of Marketing & Sales	•General manager/ CEO
•Client Relations	•Asst. Winemaker	•Marketing & Sales Management & Supervisors	•CFP/Controller
•Vineyard Managers & Supervisors	•Laboratory Technicians	•Sales Reps	•Accounting
•Vineyard Workers	•Enologists	•Public Relations	•Human Resources
	•Cellar Masters & Supervisors	•Hospitality Staff (Tasting Room or Cellar Door)	•IT
	•Cellar Workers	•Direct Sales	•Administrative Staff

the annual cycle of the vine and the performance of the *vineyard workers* who prune in the winter, sucker in the spring, thin in the summer, and harvest during the fall. During harvest, vineyards usually hire additional part-time vineyard workers to help bring in the grapes.

Throughout the year, additional work includes potential applications of fertilizer, pesticides, and water—depending on the country and legal issues regarding viticultural practices. For example, in some vineyards in South America, flood irrigation is still practiced, whereas in the US, drip irrigation is prevalent. Furthermore, some vineyards utilize organic or biodynamic farming methods, which don't allow for the use of most pesticides. Finally, a new trend is the installation of scientific equipment and monitors in the vineyard, such as weather-monitoring stations, neutron probes, and GPS systems. This technique causes the work of the vineyard managers, supervisors, and workers to become more highly skilled in computer applications and data analysis. However, the traditional vineyard skills remain very important. These include not only the physical ability to complete the required work, but knowledge of viticulture, grape diseases, and other environmental conditions. A worker with good knowledge of the vine, who has a long history in a particular vineyard, can be a very important asset to a wine business.

Other roles in vineyard operations may include *client relations*. If a vineyard is privately owned and not part of a winery, the vineyard owner needs to sell grapes to a winery. This task calls for skills in sales and relationship management with winemakers and winery owners. In many cases vineyard owners establish long-term contracts with wineries, which require the vineyard to be farmed in a way that meets the winery's criteria. For example, the winery may expect a certain tonnage of grapes from the vineyard, which could cause the vineyard owner/manager to thin the crop more strictly than he/she would on their own. This requirement may demand additional work in the vineyard, and therefore increases labor costs. Customer relations, sales, negotiations, and contract management skills are required for this function.

If the winery owns their own vineyard, the vineyard manager will farm the vineyard according to the needs and specifications of the winery. In a large corporation, this function is usually assumed by the *VP of Vineyard Operations*, who oversees many vineyards, each with their own vineyard manager and crew. They may manage the vineyards in such a way that specific grapes are designated for specific wineries, as is often the case in large global companies.

In many cases, a winery will manage their own vineyards and also buy grapes from independent producers. This arrangement calls for a *manager or VP of Vineyard Relations* who negotiates long- and short-term grape contracts with a portfolio of independent grape growers. Finally, some wineries choose to outsource the complete vineyard operations side of the business to a vineyard contractor, who supplies all the labor and equipment, and oversees the complete vineyard farming process.

Employee Functions in Wine Production

Perhaps one of the most crucial positions for any winery-based business is the *winemaker*, who is often compared to a star player or quarterback. Indeed, the names of top winemakers are referred to in reverent terms and are considered celebrities in their own right. In a small family-run wine business, the owner is often the winemaker, general manager, and vineyard manager combined into one—with perhaps a son, daughter, or spouse helping with some of the other administrative and sales roles. Another option in a small family-run business is to hire a consulting winemaker of top billing to assist in making the wines. This practice occurs commonly in newly established wineries, in which the owner has sufficient funding to pay the high salaries demanded by the top winemakers.

Larger wineries usually have a head winemaker, as well as several *assistant winemakers*. The global wine corporations may have a different winemaker for each winery in their portfolio, or have a cadre of winemakers who work across facilities, specializing in certain price points or varietals.

Winemakers possess a very specific skill set. Generally, they must have graduated with a bachelor's or master's degree from a top winemaking university, or have worked years as an assistant winemaker, learning the craft from an expert. Their background usually includes chemistry, math, and viticulture, plus practice in the art of blending. Some describe winemaking as an art; others as a science; some as a little of both. Regardless of the definition, the skills of a winemaker and quality of the grapes are both very important to the excellence of the final product.

Other important wine production functions include the *enologist*. This is someone who runs the various lab tests on the wine to test for quality, consistency, and specific components. In smaller wineries, the winemaker may also fulfill this function or it may be outsourced. Larger corporations may have whole staffs of enologists and *lab assistants*.

Finally, the cellar crew in a winery is very critical. Again, depending on the size of the operation, there could be a *VP of Operations, Cellar Masters* (managers), *supervisors*, and a large crew of *cellar workers*. The work involves a variety of processes, ranging from handling the crush during harvest season to cleaning barrels and tanks, racking the wine, testing, topping, blending, fining, and eventually bottling. Other functions may include inventory control, warehousing, and shipping logistics. Again, in a small family-run winery, these functions might be completed by the winemaker and family/friends. Other companies choose to outsource such work to a custom crush operation. It is a labor-intensive operation, requiring physical strength and flexibility, as well as good math and logic skills. Managerial and supervisory roles require leadership and organization skills, plus being willing to pitch in and help do the work when needed. During crush, when the grapes are being processed after harvest, the size of a cellar crew swells with part-time workers to handle the additional work.

Employee Functions in Marketing and Sales

Marketing and selling wine is a very complex process, and is an issue that many New World wineries grapple with on a daily basis. Most New World countries, with the exception of the US, produce more wine than their population can consume. Therefore, exporting wine to other countries is necessary for survival. Fortunately, in most of these countries, the governments provide assistance by establishing policies which assist in exporting. Because of the importance of marketing and sales, every winery has someone who performs the function of *VP of Marketing/Sales*. In a small family-run winery, the owner may perform this function and also serve as winemaker and general manager. In larger wineries, it will be a full-time job, and in global corporations it may be broken into two separate positions, and include a large staff of marketing and/or sales *managers, supervisors*, and *representatives*. Some wineries may also choose to outsource some or all of this work to a marketing/sales consulting agency.

Sales and marketing skills in the wine business require more than traditional sales and marketing knowledge. Professionals also must have a good knowledge of wine, know the competition, but even more important, be well schooled in the legal regulations of shipping and sales in certain regions, states, and countries. This knowledge includes not only special label requirements, but also the distributor network through which wine is sold in different countries. For example, in the US where wine is still sold through the three-tier system in many states, the winery *sales professional* (Rep) must use relationship skills with distributors to get their wine placed in prominent retail locations. This is because the winery cannot be directly involved with sales to the customer in certain states. Many wineries hire a cadre of sales reps to work certain states and develop relationships with the distributors and retailers who serve those areas. This is also similar with international sales, in which a sales rep who speaks the language of the country and understands its culture is located in-country to promote positive relationships.

Traditional wine marketing activities, which include market research, brand development, pricing, and advertising, are usually performed by a different group of employees located within the winery headquarters. Finally, another area of marketing and sales for many New World wineries is direct sales to consumers. This is often performed through the use of a tasting room or cellar door sales, and requires employees who are skilled in wine hospitality and sales. A *Tasting Room or Hospitality Manager* is usually hired to oversee the operations of the tasting room. *Tasting room employees* are trained in how to let customers taste wine and encourage them to purchase both wine and wine-related merchandise, if available in the tasting room. This requires direct sales and customer service skills. In the past, these positions were viewed primarily as public relations positions, but in more recent years wineries have begun to see the benefits of training these employees in sales skills to improve revenues. For small wineries, this is often a primary method of wine sales.

Finally, other marketing and sales jobs within the wine industry, which are newer in practice, may include *wine club manager, Internet sales manager, public relations manager*, and *special events coordinator*. Again, these functions can all be performed by the same person in a small winery or be separate positions with direct reports in a larger operations. Finally, these can also be outsourced to an external consulting firm or agency.

Employee Functions in Wine Management and Administration

Oversight of a winery calls for the position of a *general manager or CEO*. This position requires traditional leadership skills, as well as good operations management, strategic thinking, marketing, and financial skills. The general manager oversees the smooth functioning of all the operations within a wine business, including collaboration and coordination between vineyard, wine operations, marketing, sales, and other administrative functions. In a small winery, the owner may assume this role. In larger companies, there may be a general manager for each winery in the portfolio, as well as a CEO for the whole company. In addition, many wine businesses have a *Board of Directors* to which the general manager and other executives report. The Board of Directors is often comprised of investors and/or shareholders in publicly held companies.

Reporting into the general manager or CEO is usually someone from the other three categories described in the previous paragraph, as well as three other important areas. The first is the *CFO* and/or *controller* function, which is responsible for finance and accounting. In larger companies, there will be a department of accountants responsible for tracking finances, paying invoices, and balancing the books. In smaller operations, this role may be handled by the spouse and a hired CPA.

The *human resources manager* is another function reporting to the general manager. This role includes overseeing the hiring, training, salary/benefits administration, employee relations, and legal record-keeping process for all employees. In small companies, it is often performed by the general managers and other supervisors, and/or may be outsourced. In larger corporations, there is usually a VP of HR, as well as directors, managers, supervisors, HR reps, and HR assistants. Also, there is often a *legal representative* on staff or a retained service agreement with a law firm to support the HR function regarding labor laws.

Another important administrative function is *IT (information technology) professional.* The role of this function is to oversee the effective operation of the company's computer and software infrastructure. As wine companies grow, it is becoming increasing critical to be networked globally to suppliers, distributors, and customers. The role of the IT function is gaining increasing importance, and in larger wine businesses this is reflected in new titles of CIO (chief information officer), as well as full-time directors, managers, supervisors, and reps to support the function. In small companies, this role is often outsourced.

Finally, every well-performing wine business has a cadre of *administrative support staff* who support all of the various functions mentioned above. They can be compared to the glue that holds everything together by effectively handling office communications, paperwork, computer input, and a variety of customer service functions.

Defining Human Resource Management in the Wine Industry

Human resource management (HRM) can be defined as *the management policies and practices in the wine industry that impact employee satisfaction and performance.* Specifically, this covers the five categories of: 1) staffing and recruiting; 2) training and development: 3) employee relations; 4) compensation and benefits; and 5) record-keeping and legal issues.

Like other industries, the function of human resources in the wine industry is one that has only achieved prominence in the last several decades. Because so many wine businesses begin as family businesses, they often treat employee as "extended family." Indeed, when interviewed, one of the major reasons employees enjoy working at small and medium-sized wineries is because of the "family-like culture" (Thach,

2002). Because of this, most of the HR functions have traditionally been handled by the owner, or general manager. *Good HR practices are actually good management practices.* Companies that treat their employees with respect and dignity are naturally engaged in world-class HR practices.

However, once a wine company has at least 100 employees on the payroll, it is highly recommended that a full-time human resource professional be hired to oversee the function (Davison, 2003). This is because increased size brings increased complexity regarding legal issues and performance management, but more importantly because there is a need for more intense focus on the strategic issues of human resource management. The costs of labor are high, and the impact of satisfied and productive employees on customer service and revenues has been proven time and again. Therefore, savvy wine businesses realize they need to professionalize by hiring people with HR knowledge and experience. Indeed, many of the large global wineries have recruited HR professionals from other industries to help them remain competitive in the following five major HR categories.

Staffing and Recruiting

Strategic staffing involves analyzing the strategy of the company and forecasting the type of skills and number of employees that will be needed currently and in the future to keep the company operating productively. For example, if a winery plans to double case production within 5 years, they will also need to determine how to handle the corresponding labor needs. Some of the questions they need to answer are: What types of skills will they need to accomplish this? How many people do they need to hire? Can they retrain and/or promote? Will it be more cost-effective to outsource? Or a more relevant question in today's consolidation mode is: Can I acquire another winery and use the skill set of the employees already working there? A reverse side to this issue is the potential need to downsize a company, and develop a plan to assist impacted employees in finding new jobs.

Once a strategic staffing plan has been put in place (and is updated on an annual basis), a wine business needs to focus on the day-to-day recruiting needs. This involves developing a strategy and procedure around how they will replace employees who may leave, as well as hiring for new positions. In the New World wine industry the most common recruiting method is *networking*, or word of mouth. Often by just getting the word out internally among a workforce, or via the supplier and distributor network, a wine business can solicit many resumes.

However, in cases where a specific skill set or years of experience are needed, the following types of recruiting methods are most commonly used: *advertising* in wine-related journals and newspapers; advertising via the *Internet*; and/or use of *search firms*. This is almost always the case with higher level management and executive positions.

Once a good selection of resumes has been received, the HR staff will evaluate them against the job requirements. In most cases, prior wine experience is a plus. Candidates will then be invited to interview with HR staff and the hiring manager(s). Next, testing and reference checking may occur, as well as analysis regarding any legal hiring requirements and "culture fit." More sophisticated companies use a standardized set of interview questions to evaluate a candidate on specific competencies, which may result in a numerical score. Once the candidate successfully passes the above processes, they are welcomed to the company through a series of orientation programs that may include training, tours of the facility, and matching with a mentor or buddy. In small companies, this is often an informal introduction to other employees and perhaps a welcome lunch.

Unique Wine Industry Issue

A major staffing and recruiting issue unique to the wine industry is the need to hire a large number of contingent workers during harvest and crush. This is the case in almost every New World wine country. Even those who primarily use machines to harvest still need to hire some part-time workers to assist in the cellar with crush. Much time and effort goes into hiring employees to do this work each year. In some countries, wineries have established special housing to house the contingent workers; in others they hire buses to pick up workers at their homes in near-by towns and then return them at the end of the work day. Another practice is to hold a Harvest Job Recruiting Fair, as well as to recruit at local universities for "part-time harvest interns."

Training and Development

Training and developing employees in the wine industry is very important to worker satisfaction and productivity. The most common type of training is *technical or job related*. Examples include vineyard maintenance, cellar operations, wine knowledge, computer software training, as well as a variety of training on different job procedures. This type of training is offered either in a classroom format or one-on-one with a supervisor or peer demonstrating the proper technique.

One of the most important types of training in the wine industry is *safety training*. Winery workers are exposed to a variety of workplace hazards and must know programs like respiratory protection, confined space, hazard communication, and lock-out/block-out that are designed to keep them safe. Past practices, which assumed that all workers have sufficient common sense and will endure a significant level of pain and suffering just to be in the work force, have dramatically changed. Today, winery and vineyard employees need to be taught and learn the correct common sense ways to work safely.

In addition, in most New World countries, employers also have the ethical and legal responsibilities to ensure the correct job safety information is provided to every worker. For example, in California, safety training "tailgate sessions" often occur once a week. These involve the vineyard manager or supervisor teaching vineyard workers a "safety tip" for the week. In many cases the training is conducted in both Spanish and English, as many of the workers speak only Spanish.

Teaching safety to employees can be a big financial investment for wine businesses, but it provides a tremendous positive return. When employees work safely and without injuries, then they are happier, healthier, and more productive; medical and workers' compensation insurance costs are reduced; and employee replacement costs are reduced. By keeping everyone working safely, the efficiency of the company increases and profits can be made, which creates a win–win experience for both employees and owners.

Other types of wine business training include *customer service* and *sales, supervisory and management skills*, and updates on *industry and regulatory issues. Language* training is also important in some New World countries. For example, in both North and South America, winery employees are sometimes offered training in either English or Spanish language skills, so they may be come bilingual.

Wine Industry Training Issues

There are several training and development issues in the wine industry. One of these is *career development* and *succession planning*. Because there are so many small, family-owned businesses, employees who are not related to the family sometimes complain that there are no upward career opportunities for them. Therefore, some employees will transfer to another winery in order to advance. Related to this is the issue of succession planning, because family members do not always want to take over a wine business. Therefore, determining who will succeed as head of a wine business is a common issue.

Another issue is the need for *advanced skill levels.* As the industry becomes more global and complex, additional skills are needed, such as computer knowledge, data analysis, global sales and marketing skills, and even basic literacy skills such as reading and writing for some field workers. Because of this, in some areas of the industry there are talent shortage issues. For example, in many wineries a cellar worker is an entry-level labor position. Applicants for such positions often lack the ability to advance to higher skill levels without a structured, well-designed training program.

Leadership and management skills are also an issue in this culturally diverse, ever-changing, competitive industry. Highly sought-after technical skills can be offset by a lack of leadership and management skills, which can put a company in a compromising position. Therefore, wine businesses continue to seek and develop employees who have both the technical and leadership skills to move their businesses forward in the global market (Thach & Shepard, 2001).

Employee Relations

Employee relations includes providing clear goals, feedback on performance, and two-way communication. Ideally, this is a joint partnership between line managers and HR staff. Clarity on goals is provided via employee meetings and other communication tools, such as an employee handbook and notices. Feedback on performance is provided via informal discussion, performance appraisals meetings, discipline conversations, and recognition and rewards for a job well done. Two-way communication is encouraged as part of the culture, and may be formalized in "open door" policies, grievance processes, and/or standard meetings between employee(s) and manager. Wine businesses that implement these processes well and treat employees with respect and dignity find that employees are more satisfied, productive, and contribute innovative ideas to help the business succeed.

For example, in some wine businesses, practices have been established to encourage employees to continually look for ways to streamline processes and improve quality. They do this out of a sense of ownership and pride, because of the open culture and communication in the company. They will go above and beyond to ensure success, and truly are a company's competitive advantage.

Employee Relations Issues

One issue in this area, which is not unique to the wine industry, is *union activity*. Though some New World wine countries are required to use union employees, others are not, and prefer to keep owner management control of employee policies. The best way to do this is to treat employees better than union-required practices. Another issue is increased *turnover* in the wine industry, especially among certain jobs, such as tasting room employees, assistant winemakers, and some field worker positions. The cost of turnover, in terms of recruiting and retraining workers, can take a toll on company profits. Turnover is also a morale issue that can lead to decreased productivity and increased production costs also affecting a company's bottom line.

Compensation and Benefits

Designing fair and competitive compensation and benefits systems is another major function of HR professionals. This often begins with a compensation and benefits strategy, ideally developed jointly by line management and HR. The strategy describes how the wine business will position itself in comparison with the competition. For example, a strategy may state, "we will pay 5% over market average." To establish a strategy, most wine businesses will participate in *salary surveys* to establish ranges for key job positions. In addition, HR staff will monitor any advertised salaries and benefits for both domestic and international job listings posted by their competitors.

Salary generally includes base salary, and any bonuses, overtime, stock options, savings plans, commissions, and other perks, such as company car, loans, and memberships, which impact salary. Benefits may include health, dental, vision, life, and disability insurance, as well as vacation, sick time, holiday pay, child care support, flextime, counseling support (EAP), gym, meals, employee discounts, and other options.

Designing a compensation and benefits system requires much effort, and is often regulated by law in different New World countries. For example, Australia, New Zealand, and Canada have socialized medicine, so benefit plans look much different there than in the US. Also, currency, exchange rates, minimum pay, overtime, and cost of living differences between countries impact system design. All of these salary and benefit issues impact both employee satisfaction and the overall production costs.

Unique Salary and Benefits Practices in Wine Industry

One practice that is unique to the wine industry in this area is the use of creative perks and bonuses. For example, many wineries in New World countries give employees free or discounted wine, and often schedule celebrations and parties with wine and food around the cycles of the vine, such as pruning parties, budbreak, harvest, barrel tasting, and release parties. Related to this are special bonuses for working through harvest, returning early for pruning season, or selling a targeted amount of wine in a tasting room (Thach, 2002).

Record-Keeping and Legal Issues

Governments in the New World wine countries have different policies on how employee records are to be filed and maintained, as well as laws regarding employee relations. Many agree that the strictest legal policies are in the US, where auditors can review employee records at any time and verify that proper permits and identification are on file for each employee (e.g., social security card, I-9 permit, etc.). If errors are found, employees can be dismissed and the business fined.

There are also laws about discrimination and worker treatment that vary by country. One interesting example is in South Africa, where workers have lived for years in winery-provided housing on the vineyard property. Recently the South African government introduced a new policy that required property owners to give the house and the land on which it resides to the workers—if they had lived there for a certain number of years. This prompted many South African winery and vineyard owners to buy houses for workers in a nearby town, so they could retain ownership of their vineyard property (personal interview by L. Thach with Dr. Phillip Freese, vineyard owner in South Africa, Fall 2002; Voss, 2000).

This is different from practices in the US, where housing for migrant workers from Mexico is a growing social issue. Because many of the workers migrate to the US during harvest and pruning season and then return to Mexico, they do not have permanent housing. To save money, some will rent a small apartment or hotel room and then crowd 10 or more other workers in to sleep on the floor. Others may sleep in cars, under bridges, and in barns. Community concern over this has lead some groups, such as the Napa Vintners Association, to build migrant worker housing so they workers have clean, warm, and safe quarters in which to stay.

In Chile, the worker treatment situation is a bit different. For years, workers lived on the large "hacienda style" grounds of the winery and vineyards. Often they were paid in wine as well as currency. However, after a social movement within the country to limit alcohol consumption, many workers left the vineyards to move to the cities and acquire different jobs. This caused winery owners to hire buses to go to the local cities and towns to pick up workers and transport them to and from the vineyards to their home each day.

Worker treatment and discrimination issues continue to be a subject of debate in many New World countries, and are one of the human resource issues to which special attention should be paid. Positive efforts are under way in many wine-producing countries, but a consistent focus on these issues should be emphasized. In the long run, this will benefit wine businesses by not only providing more positive public relations press, but also in improved worker satisfaction and morale, which can lead to increased productivity and company profitability (Davison, 2003; Ulirch, 1997; Yeung & Berman, 1997).

Future HRM Issues

As the wine industry becomes more globally competitive, additional human resource issues will become more visible, in addition to those listed above. Following is a short list of some of these potential future HRM issues.

- **Increasing Use of Mechanization and Impact on Workforce:** The rise of technology in the vineyard and the use of mechanization is expected to grow in the future. This is similar to other industries, which have replaced workers with technology. The impact is a forced "reskilling" of the labor pool in these industries. Though there will always be some wineries doing hand-harvesting and pruning of vineyards, the rising labor costs coupled with the increased quality of mechanized methods are forcing this issue in many New World countries.

- **Rising Costs of Worker Benefits:** Related to the above issue is the rising cost of workers benefits—many of them government mandated. The main issue is around health care costs. Even wine businesses in countries with socialized healthcare systems often find they still have to purchase private healthcare as a benefit for some employees, especially those in the professional ranks. In California, new legislation is being pushed to force all employers with 50 or more employees to buy health care for each employee, even though this is not legally required now. The burden of this cost may force many small businesses to go under.

- **The Impact of Vineyards in Asia:** Currently both China and India are planting hundreds of acres of vineyards, and are using inexpensive labor to do so (Gastin, in press). Though many argue that these Asian countries currently do not have the climate and appellation to produce world-class wines, each year the quality improves. In addition, wine consumption rates are rising in this part of the world, whereas they are declining in many other parts. China has an excellent past record of being able to produce other agricultural crops of good quality at much lower costs because of its inexpensive labor force. A good example of this is the apple crop, which China now produces more efficiently than any other country in the world. This has had a very negative impact on the apple industry in the US and other countries. It is possible that China and India could do the same with the wine grape industry.

- **Merger and Acquisition Activity:** A final issue impacting HR in the wine industry is that of increasing merger and acquisition (M&A) activity all along the wine business chain (Gilinsky, McCline, & Eyler, 2000). Large wine corporations continue to purchase and add other wineries to their portfolio. In addition, vineyard management firms, distributors, and wine retailers are also consolidating through mergers and acquisitions. Each time this occurs, there is an impact on the human resource function, as some employees become redundant in their roles and must be let go or retrained to assume other needed positions. In addition, current HR systems, such as record keeping, pay structures, and benefits, often must be consolidated into one system—just other financial and business systems in the companies must be merged. Many experts predict that M&A activity will continue in the wine industry for many years to come. Therefore, this will have an ongoing impact on human resource management.

Chapter **14**

THE LEGALITIES
OF WINE

Cyril Penn (Editor, Wine Business Monthly)

Wendell Lee (Attorney, Wine Institute)

Due in part to their popularity and to their inherent intoxicating properties, alcoholic beverages are often regulated and taxed more heavily than other products in many countries around the world. Because of this, interesting legal production, distribution, and sales systems have been developed to control and monitor not only the sale of high alcoholic beverages such as gin, whiskey, and vodka, but also wine. These regulations identify provisions for many aspects of wine, including labeling regulations, level of alcohol, trade restrictions, winemaking practices, documentation, currency conversions, and many other legal issues that must be considered in the marketing, sales, and distribution of wine in a global environment.

With this in mind, this chapter provides an overview of some of the major issues regarding the legalities of wine. It begins with an historical look at US wine laws, and then moves forward in time to describe taxes and compliance issues, trademark and label matters, and farming and land use. The chapter then expands to a global view of some of the specific legal issues impacting New World countries. It concludes with useful information on trade and international shipping issues

The Historical Context of US Wine Legalities

There is a saying in the wine industry that it is often easier to ship wine between two different countries than it is to ship wine between two different states in the US. This is because, in the US, alcoholic beverages are regulated and taxed more heavily than other products. Until recently, wine, beer, and spirits were regulated, for example, by the same federal agency responsible for regulating firearms. The legalities of wine in America start with Prohibition and the eventual Repeal of Prohibition embodied in the 21st Amendment to the US Constitution. In the US, the 21st Amendment is the mother lode of all US state and federal regulations and laws. All roads come from it, and all roads lead to it.

The temperance movement in the US started in the 19th century as various states passed laws restricting alcohol. By the time the 18th Amendment to the US Constitution was passed in 1919, a majority of 33 states already had laws on the books prohibiting the sale of alcohol within their borders. Repeal came with the 21st Amendment in 1933. By then, Prohibition had devastated the US wine industry.

Had the 21st Amendment simply ended Prohibition, much of today's wine regulations would not exist. While Section 1 of the 21st Amendment effectively repealed Prohibition, Section 2 of the 21st Amendment gave plenary power to individual states to determine the manner of alcoholic beverage production and distribution within their own boundaries. Over the years, Section 2 of the 21st Amendment has been interpreted to mean individual states have absolute power to regulate and control alcoholic beverages in their boundaries and that the federal government must take a "hands off" approach. That assumption is why the regulation of wine, beer, and spirits is so disparate among various states. It is why Pennsylvania and Utah exert such control that they act as exclusive importers, wholesalers, and retailers of alcoholic beverages; why other states have created elaborate licensing and tax systems for alcoholic beverages; why statutes require alcoholic beverages to go through wholesalers; why elaborate "Tied House" restrictions separate producers from wholesalers and retailers; why some laws prevent wineries from choosing what distributor they work with; why Texas has "wet" and "dry" areas scattered across the state; why grocery stores sell wine in some states but not others; and on and on.

Alcoholic beverage regulation may have started out with the noble purpose of addressing temperance issues in the individual states, but these interests are fueled largely by politics; regulation has evolved into a form of political manipulation, if you will, of the *assumption*. State statutes are justified, at times, in terms of public safety but are also too often also motivated by profit.

In the topsy-turvy world of US alcoholic beverage law, the Supremacy Clause, which holds that federal law reigns supreme over state statutes that may conflict, at times appears to be standing on its head. While some of these state alcoholic beverage regulations would be seen as violating antitrust laws in any other industry, these laws exist today due in large part to the 21st Amendment. Franchise security laws, unique to the alcoholic beverage industry, provide statutory protections to wholesalers of alcoholic beverages and places suppliers at a contractual disadvantage. These laws perpetuate a three-tier distribution system that strongly protects the wholesale tier, maintaining a wholesaler's economic interests as a matter of law by making it difficult for a supplier to terminate its relationship. Indeed, if one found a way to effectively and profitably eliminate the middle distribution level in another business it would be considered a stroke of genius: in the wine sector it would be considered criminal.

Wineries need distribution and distributors. The three-tier system looks to be here to stay but the wholesale tier has seen rapid consolidation. There were 100 wineries shortly after Prohibition and more than 50 distributors, for example, in California. The top 10 wineries make about 90% of the wine, yet there are nearly 1,000 wineries just in California and two large distributors account for most of the business. Nationally, the 10 largest distributors account for about 90% of all wine sold. Wineries must compete for distributors to help them gain exposure and increase sales. The largest wineries have an advantage here. Smaller wineries can have trouble hooking up with distributors and are often forgotten in large distributor portfolios. Sometimes a distributor must decide what winery's numbers they're going to make and who's going to grow and who isn't. Wineries can depend on their distributors to take orders but not to sell the wine. They must do the selling themselves. At the same time, consumer demand for hard-to-find wines and the higher margins they provide make direct-to-consumer shipping increasingly attractive to the wineries.

The *assumption* has led to a mish-mash situation where about half of the states now allow people to order wine and have it shipped to their doors but the rest of the states do not. In some states, shipping directly to a consumer remains a felony. Wineries have been making some progress in the legislative arena as well as in the courts. There is an expectation that the issue could reach the US Supreme Court. The 6th Circuit Court of Appeals has ruled that Michigan's ban on direct-to-consumer shipments from out-of-state wineries is unconstitutional, overturning a lower court ruling, and a similar ruling overturned Texas's ban on direct shipping. There are also active lawsuits in Florida, New Jersey, and New York.

Taxes and Compliance

Alcoholic beverage "licensees" must be sensitive to federal and state regulations. Failure to comply with the Federal Bureau of Tax and Trade (previously the Federal Bureau of Alcohol, Tobacco and Firearms) and their respective state alcoholic beverage control agencies could lead, among other things, to the revocation of the required alcoholic beverage license. Also, the corporate, limited liability company and partnership companies some other industries use to achieve tax, liability protection, and other goals can also be problematic in the wine business, because these structures can violate state and federal alcoholic beverage regulations.

Some wineries hire outside consultants to assist with regulatory and compliance issues while some of the largest wineries have entire departments dedicated to this area. One such consultant has assembled the following list of agencies that a person establishing a new winery can expect to deal with. It is by no means exhaustive:

- Each state has a state control authority similar to the California Department of Alcoholic Beverage Control. A directory of these control authorities is maintained by the Federal Tax and Trade Bureau and can be found online at http://www.ttb.gov/alcohol/info/faq/subpages/lcb.htm.
- The US Tax and Trade Bureau (TTB, previously the Bureau of Alcohol, Tobacco and Firearms) issues federal alcoholic beverage basic permits for the production and wholesaling of alcoholic beverages, including permits for alternating proprietors. The Bureau grants label approval, regulates production and trade practices, and collects excise taxes from producer and wholesaler permittees.
- The IRS assigns federal employer identification numbers.
- The county clerk registers fictitious business names for wineries using alternate brand names or for brand names specified by negociants.
- The U.S. Patent and Trademark Office registers trademarks.
- State taxing agency collects employer, income, and excise tax accounts.
- County or city planning departments provide information on zoning and use permits.
- Building departments issue building permits.
- State or county transportation authorities, depending on whether access is from state or county roads, administer parking and access requirements; may require possible improvements or encroachment permits.
- Forestry and Fire Services Department regulates fire protection requirements and hazardous materials use.
- State, county, or city water agencies regulate stream setbacks, underground tanks, wastewater monitoring, and issues required permits.
- Public/environmental health department regulates waste water disposal and issues a variety of permits relating to health concerns.
- Federal, state, and county agricultural agencies issue weighmaster licenses and grape purchase licenses, and oversee pesticide use.
- City business license tax office, if site is in city limits, issues business license.

Whether you hold a Tax and Trade Bureau-issued Bonded Winery basic permit or store wine in a licensed Bonded Wine Cellar (BWC), there are different Tax and Trade Bureau requirements governing the movements of wine in bond, tax paid removals, and wines shipped for export. When it comes to paying taxes, accurate record keeping is essential. Documentation and transfer records need to be held on site for 3 years or more and can be randomly chosen for review if a facility is selected for a random TTB audit. It is a challenge training staff on the changing compliance regulations, record keeping, and tax reporting requirements. TTB has a helpful Internet site and holds educational seminars that cover requirements for record keeping, reporting, and export documentation. If one's export documentation is inadequate, one may be held liable for the taxes and interest. Fraudulent reporting is subject to criminal penalties.

Many wineries hold their wine in storage after bottling in the bonded area of their winery or bonded wine cellar, and do not pay the required excise taxes until the wine actually is shipped. This helps to preserve cash flow, helps control inventories, and can prevent accidental mistakes. However, it is not unusual for wineries to pull bonded or unreleased wines for quality control checks, samples, or prerelease shipments. When this occurs, the wines must be transferred from in bond to tax paid status, and it is important for a winery to understand how to do this.

Trademark and Label Issues

One legal area any prospective wine industry professional will want to know about is trademark law. It is amazing how many trademark infringement suits wineries have been involved in. Infringement lawsuits arise when the use of a trademark, usually a wine brand name, conflicts with an already existing brand name. These situations can often be avoided with a trademark search conducted by a professional search firm or attorney. Searches can be extremely intensive and should be left to professionals, but there is a lot that can be learned about a potential trademark by searching three freely available online databases. While a search of these databases will not conclusively resolve whether a name is available, these searches can tell you a lot about whether a brand name is *un*available.

First, the US Patent and Trademark Office maintains an online database of all trademarks that have been registered or are pending registration. When searching this database, it is important to keep in mind first that the test for trademark infringement is whether its use would result in the likelihood of consumer confusion. Similar names in different product categories may not cause consumer confusion (e.g., Plymouth Arrow and Arrow shirts). The USPTO trademark database can be found at http://tess2.uspto.gov/bin/gate.exe?f=tess&state=3k91j9.1.1 and the general home page is at http://www.uspto.gov. Secondly, it is important to remember that registration of a trademark is not mandatory. There are countless trademarks that are currently in use as winery brand names that are not registered as trademark—a search of the USPTO web site alone will tell you only if a trademark is registered or attempting registration.

It is also important to remember that geographic names are generally considered generic and not capable of being a registered trademark. However, one can search the Tax and Trade Bureau's Public COLA (Certificate of Label Approval) database to determine whether a geographic brand name is currently in use. The Public COLA database actually contains data for all label approvals from 1990 to the present and can be found at https://www.colasonline.gov/colasonline/publicSearchColasBasic.do. Unlike trademark registration, which is not mandatory, label registration is required. Still, there are limitations with a search of the TTB COLA registry because of its incompleteness and because there are many labels that are approved but yet never used in the marketplace. The fact that a brand name may be on a COLA may not necessarily preclude use.

Finally, a search of general online databases such as Google or Lycos may be able to uncover some potential conflicts with existing trademarks. Advanced search techniques on these databases can reveal information useful for a determination of whether a trademark is available for use.

In recent years we have seen many trademark lawsuits. The most well-publicized case involved Kendall-Jackson, who sued E.&J. Gallo claiming Gallo's Turning Leaf brand appeared too similar to its label (Gallo prevailed). There was Galleron vs. Galleron-Lane, Thunderbird (E&J Gallo) vs. Thunder Mountain Winery. In Michigan, Leelanau Wine Cellars sued the parent company of Chateau de Leelanau. Leelanau is the name of a sparsely populated county, a township within that county, a peninsula and a lake, all of which are just northwest of Traverse City in Michigan's northern Lower Peninsula.

The industry is place oriented and the debate over geographic brand names could fill its own chapter and even its own book. Conflicts arise partly because lawyers measure the legal strength of a mark by how readily it can be protected from knockoffs and near-miss imitators, and defended against charges of infringement or deceptiveness. Marketers, on the other hand, measure strength by the extent to which a mark enhances sales volume and margins—a goal that tempts many to seek a boost by making a prestigious geographic origin part of the brand name. There is sometimes some uncertainty about where the legal line lies.

The primary brand name on a wine label is a trademark. Slogans and package graphics are also trademarks, subject to the same legal criteria. Trademarks that say nothing about the nature of the product are strongest in the legal sense. To marketing and sales management, however, the ideal mark gives consumers additional information—typically, something about the product's characteristics or imagery.

Farming and Land Use Issues in the US

Water and air quality laws and land use regulations represent an entirely different set of legal issues for wineries. Winemaking is a manufacturing and packaged goods enterprise but is also an agricultural enterprise. Further, federal and state laws governing the daily operation of the wine industry often interrelate and overlap, making regulations hard to decipher.

There are laws relating to pesticide regulation, air pollution control, solid waste management and water quality, and noise control. In California, the EPA enforces compliance with California Air Pollution Control Laws, the California Clean Water Act, California Code of Regulations, and the Porter-Cologne Water Quality Control

Act embodied in the California Water Code—which empowers the State Water Resources Control Board. In California, there are nine regional water quality control boards under the umbrella of the State Water Resources Control Board. They may impose waste discharge and storm water discharge requirements, and regulations specific to land disposal of wastes, groundwater discharges, and non-point source pollution.

The National Endangered Species Act of 1973 can restricted land use on agricultural land, evidenced by the endangered status recently given to the California tiger salamander, an ongoing issue that has delayed some vineyard and winery projects. In addition, wineries that grow their own grapes will need to comply with laws concerning farm labor contractors. Vineyard management company operators may need to register as farm labor contractors or have current contracts reviewed for compliance with the state enforcement.

A Global View on Wine Legalities

The US has the most complex web of legal requirements to navigate. Canada runs a close second. As in the US, Canada's federal government handles health and legal issues while most Canadian provinces have their own liquor control board governing the movement of alcoholic beverages. These entities are similar to "control" states in the US. Even hotels and restaurants in Canada must purchase wine through these liquor control authorities. As with distributors in the US, small and medium-sized wineries often have difficultly getting any attention from the massive governmental entities.

New World countries such as Australia and New Zealand are less restrictive, though, like the US, they have labeling requirements that include such things as health warnings about sulfites. There are distribution issues too, as it can be difficult, for example, to obtain an import license in Australia. Chile and Argentina are less restrictive in terms of their regulatory requirements and though Chile has taxed imports disproportionately when compared with the US, this trade barrier is being eliminated. There are also issues with respect to South Africa, with restrictions on licensing and labeling as well as steep import tariffs.

US producers do not ship much wine to these other New World wine-producing countries. These producers make good wine themselves and are not considered large target markets. Though building a winery can involve legal and regulatory hurdles in many countries, most New World countries are considered relatively easy to invest in. The most challenging land use regulations are probably found in California, particularly within Napa County.

It is important to note that virtually all of the US wine companies that have looked to expand their production into other countries have done so by entering through joint ventures. Having a joint venture partner to deal with local legal and regulatory as well as cultural hurdles is highly effective. It works particularly well when there is a reciprocal relationship. If a joint venture partner is shipping wine into the US, for instance, the US winery is likely to handle distribution, licensing, and trademark issues for the partner. This approach has worked well for a number of wineries but the Robert Mondavi Corporation is probably the best example. Joint venture partners include

Opus One with the Baroness Philippine de Rothschild of Château Mouton Rothschild (France); Luce, Lucente and Danzante with Marchesi de' Frescobaldi (Italy); and Caliterra, Arboleda and Seña with the Eduardo Chadwick family of Viña Errázuriz (Chile).

Trade Issues

International trade issues, while they are slow to change, are very important to the wine industry, which continues to globalize. Some of the most restrictive trade barriers on wine have been imposed by the European Union. This is a concern to New World wine producers because the United Kingdom is the largest market for imported wine. The US is continually working on trying to get more harmonization on common issues, such as how wine should be labeled. There are numerous ongoing trade issues. One of the largest and most complex involves "geographic brand names." The Europeans have long complained that the US should disallow the use of geographic brand names such as Chablis, Champaign, and Port, terms that are used generically in the US but that have more specific meaning to European producers.

One of the most recent international trade issues the wine industry is dealing with is the US Bioterrorism Act and its related regulations. The Public Health Security and Bioterrorism Preparedness and Response Act of 2002 was passed in that year by Congress to track America's food supply both in terms of its domestic distribution and imports into the US. The objective of the Act is to improve the ability of the US government to prevent and respond to bioterrorism. It appoints the Food and Drug Administration as the lead agency for developing regulations that will carry out the provisions of the Act. There are three main requirements of the Act. The Act requires members of the food industry (wine and other alcoholic beverages are considered "food" under the Act) to:

- register with the FDA by December 12, 2003;
- submit prior notices of imports with the FDA effective December 12, 2003; and
- maintain and establish adequate records.

Final regulations for food facility registration and prior notice were issued in October of 2003. Final regulations for record keeping and administrative detention were due in March of 2004. The FDA expected about 400,000 US and foreign food facilities to have registered by December 12, 2003, and is on record as stating that the first 4 months after December 12 will be spent attempting to educate and assist companies in achieving compliance. After that grace period, the FDA may exercise its enforcement authorities in other ways. Violations of any provision of the Act can result in food imports (including wine) being held at the port of entry and can subject a company to both civil and criminal penalties. The Act also authorizes the FDA to administratively detain food that raises a threat of serious adverse health consequences or death.

Shipping Internationally

Wineries interested in conducting business internationally will need to be aware of international label requirements and will need to stay up to date on label changes and documentation for shipping internationally. They are going to need to pay excise taxes. Most countries impose excise taxes and this is typically based on alcohol content.

There are some good information sources available via the Internet and there are consultants who specialize in helping wineries with this. One source is www.winescience.com, which includes concise listings of regulatory and winemaking requirements for 25 countries. The US Department of Agriculture maintains a website which includes useful information about how to do business abroad. Many countries have resources that are available online, such as Australia's Wine and Brandy Corporation. Finally, WineVision has developed a very comprehensive website regarding how to export. It can be accessed at http://www.winevision.org/globalexporting/ or from their main portal, www.winevision.org.

Chapter **15**

ENVIRONMENTAL AND SOCIAL RESPONSIBILITY ISSUES

Jeff DeLott (Owner & President, SureHarvest)
Kari Birdseye (Vice President of Sustainability
  Programs, SureHarvest)
Karen Ross (President, California Association of
  Winegrape Growers)

Customers around the world are increasingly demanding products that are organic in nature and are produced in such a way that they are kind to the environment and people that help create them. Testaments to this growing need can be seen on food product labels that verify they are grown organically; shampoos and cosmetics that state the products were produced without harmful testing of animals; and boycotts of coffee, chocolate, and clothing companies that have been accused of less than desirable human resource practices. This trend is also impacting the global wine industry, and already there have been several successful programs implemented in various locations around the world to assist wineries and vineyards in moving forward to embrace environmental and social responsibility issues.

This chapter describes this fascinating trend and resulting practices by providing an overview of sustainable winegrowing efforts. It is organized into the following four sections: 1) definitions of sustainability; 2) a description of California's Code of Sustainable Winegrowing Practices; 3) an overview of international sustainable winegrowing efforts; and 4) a forecast for sustainable wine-growing practices in the next 5 years.

Defining Sustainability

Since the late 1980s there has been an exponential use of the terms "sustainability," "sustainable development," and "sustainable agriculture" in academia, government, nonprofits, and the private sector. Most definitions of sustainable development and sustainable agriculture hold three key principles in common, approaches that are environmentally sound, socially equitable and economically feasible. The combination of these three principles has become known as the three "Es" for *environment, equity*, and *economics*. Figure 15.1 illustrates this principle. As the overarching principle of sustainability has become more widely adopted in the private sector, the three "Ps" has emerged as an increasingly popular way to refer to sustainability: people, profit, and the planet.

Much of the historical roots to the current widespread use of sustainability definitions that include environmental, social, and economic components can be traced to the 1987 report *Our Common Future* from the World Commission on Environment and Development. This influential report presented the following definition: "Sustainable development is development that meets the needs of the present without compromising the ability of future generations to meet their own needs." This definition was a guiding force in the formulation and adoption of Agenda 21 during the United Nations (UN) Conference on Environment and Development held in Rio de Janerio, Brazil, 1992. As defined by the UN, "Agenda 21 is a comprehensive plan of action to be taken globally, nationally and locally by organizations of the United Nations System, Governments, and Major Groups in every area in which human impacts on the environment."

Agenda 21 specifically addresses social and economic issues related to the environment including poverty, human health, housing, and consumption patterns; conservation and management of resource issues including impacts on land, water, and air resources, agriculture, forestry, fisheries, transportation, material use and waste

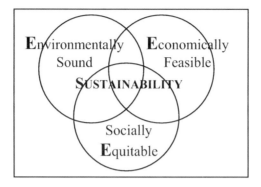

Figure 15.1. The three "Es" of sustainability.

disposal, etc.; the roles of the public, private, and nongovernmental sectors; and implementation issues including the roles of science, education, financial resources, decision-making, and legal systems. Ten years later at the UN World Summit on Sustainable Development held in Johannesburg, South Africa, in 2002, the commitment to fully implement Agenda 21 was reaffirmed.

Given the diversity of individuals, organizations, and sectors working on sustainability, no one definition has emerged to adequately address this diversity of interests. In fact, the number of sustainability definitions has grown steadily to the point where there are many online resources that provide multiple definitions of sustainable development (e.g., http://www.unescap.org/drpad/vc/orientation/awareness/sustainable_development/sd_definition.htm), sustainability (e.g., http://www.ecy.wa.gov/sustainability/more_defns.htm), and sustainable agriculture (e.g., http://www.nal.usda.gov/afsic/AFSIC_pubs/srb9902.htm). Regardless of the definition one chooses or creates, turning principles into practices is far more challenging that deciding upon the "right" words. An example of using an overall definition of sustainability and turning into practical action steps to implement is provided later in this chapter.

Wine-Growing Practices

One excellent example of how environmental and social responsibility practices are being implemented in the wine industry can be found in the California Code of Sustainable Winegrowing Practices. It began in the Fall of 2002, when the Wine Institute and the California Association of Winegrape Growers (CAWG) began holding workshops throughout California to introduce the California wine community to a code of best management practices through a 490-page workbook promoting social responsibility and environmental stewardship.

The "Code of Sustainable Winegrowing Practices" is a voluntary self-assessment tool for California's vintners and growers with information on how to conserve natural resources, protect the environment, and enhance relationships with employees, neighbors, and local communities.

John De Luca, the Executive Vice Chairman of the Wine Institute, a public policy advocacy group, representing more than 600 California wineries, describes the impact of the Code as follows:

> With California's population growing at half a million people annually, we are taking steps to assure that California winegrowers will have viable and outstanding land for growing winegrapes and producing world-class wines. In an increasingly competitive global marketplace, with growing consumer environmental awareness, it is in our interest to farm responsibly with the best science available.

The California Department of Food and Agriculture has recognized the importance of this project by recently awarding a $280,000 grant for widespread implementation of the Code's sustainable practices. Wine Institute and CAWG work closely with regional groups throughout the state to hold educational workshops to help the industry adopt the Code.

The California Environmental Protection Agency announced a partnership with Wine Institute and CAWG, called Performance for Sustainability (PFS). This partnership includes representatives from the Department of Pesticide Regulation, the California Integrated Waste Management Board, the Air Resources Board, and the Regional Water Quality Control Boards, among others.

The workbook includes 13 chapters of practical guidelines, with a self-assessment tool for users to evaluate their current implementation of practices and receive a final score. From there, they identify development areas on which to focus for improvement. Table 15.1 shows a list of the 13 chapters included in the Code.

Stephen Schafer, of Schafer Ranch and CAWG chairman, explains the vineyard owner's perspective of the Code: "This project is important to my family. If we are going to maintain a winegrape growing operation, we have to be able to sell and compete against foreign competition. This is the 'leg up' that will help our operation as well as improve winegrape quality."

Table 15.1. The Chapter Topics in the Code of Sustainability

Viticulture
Wine quality
Soil management
Material handling
Vineyard water management
Solid waste reduction management
Pest management
Purchasing
Ecosystems management
Human resources
Energy efficiency
Neighbors and community
Winery water conservation

More than 50 members of the Wine Institute and the CAWG worked on the document for 2 years. Environmentalists, regulators, university educators, and social equity groups provided expertise to the project as well. The workbook will be updated periodically to reflect current industry advancements.

"This industry driven project recommends best practices that have been pioneered by many California vintners and growers. We believe the wine community will embrace the Code because it is the right thing to do and improves wine quality at the same time," said Michael Honig, chairman of the committee that developed the workbook and general manager of Honig Vineyard and Winery.

Within the first year of implementation, more than 65 informational workshops were held throughout the wine-growing regions in California. Vintners and growers met together to review the workbook and use the self-assessment criteria to evaluate their vineyard and winery operations. More than 500 growers and 50 winery operations participated in the workshops and more than half submitted their evaluation forms to the project.

The primary audience for this workbook is California winegrowers and vintners. The workbook content is also useful to a wider audience including employees, suppliers, wine grape and wine buyers, neighbors and local community members, members of the environmental and social equity communities, policy makers, regulators, and the media.

A key desired outcome for the SWP project is the widespread development and execution of sustainability strategies in the California wine-growing community. Business strategy is often defined in terms of an operation's mission (the business purpose and fundamental reason for existence), vision (future desire, long-term goals), and values (core ideals, beliefs, and actions). It is important for all businesses committed to corporate social responsibility, from the small family-operated vineyard and winery to the multinational corporation, to clearly define and implement a sustainability strategy.

The Sustainability Mission

The mission for the development and implementation of the workbook is to provide winegrowers and vintners with a tool to voluntarily:

- assess the sustainability of current practices;
- identify areas of excellence and areas where improvements can be made; and
- develop action plans to increase an operation's sustainability.

The overall, long-term mission for the Code of SWP project includes:

- Establishing voluntary high standards of sustainable practices to be followed and maintained by the entire wine community.
- Enhancing winegrower-to-winegrower and vintner-to-vintner education on the importance of sustainable practices and how self-governing will enhance the economic viability and future of the wine community.
- Demonstrating how working closely with neighbors, communities, and other stakeholders to maintain an open dialogue can address concerns, enhance mutual respect, and accelerate results.

Sustainability Vision

The vision of the SWP project is long-term sustainability of the California wine community. To place the concept of sustainability into the context of winegrowing, the project defines sustainable wine growing as growing and winemaking practices that are sensitive to the environment (environmentally sound), responsive to the needs and interests of society at large (socially equitable), and are economically feasible to implement and maintain (economically feasible). The combination of these three principles is often referred to as the three "Es" of sustainability (see Figure 15.1).

These three overarching principles provide a general direction to pursue sustainability. However, these important principles are not easily translated into the everyday operations of wine growing and winemaking. To bridge this gap between general principles and daily decision making, the workbook's 13 self-assessment chapters translate the sustainability principles into specific wine-growing and winemaking practices.

Sustainability Values

This project is guided by the following set of sustainability values:

- Produce the best quality wine and/or grapes possible.
- Provide leadership in protecting the environment and conserving natural resources.
- Maintain the long-term viability of agricultural lands.
- Support the economic and social well-being of farm and winery employees.
- Respect and communicate with neighbors and community members; respond to their concerns in a considerate manner.
- Enhance local communities through job creation, supporting local business and actively working on important community issues.
- Honor the California wine community's entrepreneurial spirit.
- Support research and education as well as monitor and evaluate existing practices to expedite continual improvements.

To date, the Code of Sustainable Winegrowing Practices has been very well accepted in California by wine businesses, environmental groups, and consumers. The California wine industry has recognized the need to adopt progressive environmental and social responsibility practices to remain competitive in a global environment. Since its introduction, many other businesses, from both within and outside the wine industry, have requested copies of the Code as a model for the implementation of their own sustainability programs.

Overview of International Sustainable Wine-Growing Efforts

The US is not the only country to embrace sustainable wine-growing practices. Indeed, there have been several other commendable efforts in both the New and Old

World. Following are descriptions of programs in New Zealand, South Africa, Australia, and parts of Europe.

New Zealand Wine-Growing Program (SWNZ)

After conducting a review of international sustainable viticulture schemes, the New Zealand industry developed a program using the Wadenswill (Swiss) scheme as a model. A working group of growers and industry representatives developed a pilot Integrated Winegrowing Program scheme first implemented in 1995–96 on a trial basis in five vineyards. With a Sustainable Management Fund grant of $150,000 and additional support from Winegrowers of New Zealand, membership in the program grew to 120 vineyards in 1997–98. In the 2001–2002 growing season, there were 260 members in the program representing approximately 60% of the vineyard acreage.

The positive points self-audit scorecard has 77 questions covering practices associated with all of the major production issues. A ranking on each practice evaluates whether it has negative impacts (either unsustainable or –10 points); is sustainable (ranked at 0 points); or is an area for desired improvement over the current practice (ranked +10 or +20 points). Scorecards are collected from all members at the end of each season and an analysis of the regional trends in vineyard management practices is reported back at regional member meetings (Manktelow, Renton, & Gurnsey, 2002).

The SWNZ program now has a national coordinator and is guided by a steering committee whose goal is to see the program adopted as a minimum production standard across the whole New Zealand wine industry. Plans are to integrate both vineyard and winery sustainable production practices and to develop new recording and analysis tools. Additional information on this program can be obtained from the SWNZ national coordinator at tessa@winz.org.nz.

South Africa's Integrated Production of Wine (IPW) System

At the start of the 2001–2002 harvesting season, all but one of the 69 cooperative cellars, 90 out of 95 estates, 177 out of 186 private cellars, and all seven producing wholesalers and all four bottlers had signed up for the IPW. This makes up almost 96% of all cellars and represents more than 99% of all wine grape production (Tromp, 2003).

South Africa's IPW program for grapes includes: IPW training; Farm and vineyard management; Soil and terrain; Cultivars' rootstocks; Vineyard layout; Cultivation practices; Nutrition; Irrigation; Pruning and trellising; Crop and canopy management; Growth regulators; Integrated Pest Management; Handling of chemicals; and Record keeping.

Practices are rated as either good (5 points), average (2–3 points), or poor (0 points). To qualify as IPW grapes, the grower must achieve 75 points out of a possible 150 (or 50%). Only registered chemicals may be used within the specified safety periods. Residue analysis must show no prohibited substances. At least one representative of the operation must attend an IPW course.

South Africa's IPW program for wine includes: IPW training; Grape quality; Harvesting and transportation; Equipment; SO_2 levels; Substances added to wine; Fermentation; Cooling; Waste water management; Disinfectants and cleaning agents; Management of solid waste; Noise and air pollution; and Packaging materials.

To qualify as an IPW wine, the grapes must be IPW produced; total points must be above 50% for the wine guidelines; no prohibited residues should be found upon analysis; and cellar records must be maintained (Broome, 2003). Information about South Africa's IPW program is available at: www.ipw.co.za.

Australia's "Sustaining Success" Strategy

The Cooperative Research Centre for Viticulture (CRCV) is Australia's viticultural research and development organization. CRCV, established in 1992, is an Australia-wide joint venture of 12 core organizations and 9 supporting organizations. The CRCV has three research programs, including one for sustainable vineyard systems; an education program; and the Viticare program, which delivers information and research outcomes to the industry (www.crcv.com.au).

The sustainable vineyard systems research program addresses: Water use efficiency; Diseases and pests; An integrated crop management approach to grape production; Grape berry development; Biodiversity and Environmental Management Systems (EMS) (Broome, 2003).

CRVC has released a discussion paper, "Framework for a Wine and Grape Industry Approach to Environmental Management." It references a 2000 National Wine Industry Environment conference, where industry leaders announced support for a Code of Environmental Practices and development of Environmental Best Management Practice (BMP) protocols based on issues identified in the Viticare environmental risk assessment tool.

The Australian EMS for Winegrapes has seven sections: Water use management; Chemical and pesticide management; Soil and fertilizer management; Equipment, vehicle, and machinery management; Waste management; Vineyard establishment and Biodiversity. CRVC is also drafting BMPs for pest, disease, water use, soil and nutrient management (Broome, 2003).

In August, 2001, the government announced a $4.5 million grant to the Australian wine industry to develop a National Wine Industry Research Cluster to support the wine export industry. Among other things, the facility will seek to research and identify sustainable viticulture methodology to further reinforce Australia's international leadership in wine production (Truss, 2002).

European Programs on Sustainability

Modern-day advancements in sustainable viticulture can be traced to the European Integrated Fruit Production Systems initiated in 1977. Integrated production (IP) standards were adopted in 1993. According to Broome (2003), wine grape-specific regional guidelines were developed by E. F. Boller in Switzerland (2nd edition, 1999, www.iobc.ch.IOBCGrapes).

The 10 sections of the European IP standards are: Definition and objectives of IP; Commitment of the grower; Conserving the vineyard environment; Site, rootstock, cultivars, planting system; Alleyways and weed-free strips; Irrigation; Canopy management; Integrated plant protection; Efficient and safe application methods.

The European IP system is the basis of sustainable viticulture programs in two of the New World wine-producing countries described above: 1) The New Zealand Winegrowing Program (SWNZ), and 2) South Africa's Integrated Production of Wine program.

Another impressive European effort occurred in France in 2001. Here the Comité Interprofessionel du Vin de Champagne (CIVC) announced the intention of Champagne producers to avoid further harm to their environment by reducing the use of chemical fertilizers, pesticides, and fungicides by as much as 50% with adoption of "viticulture raisonée"(WineNews, 2002/2003). In announcing a commitment to more responsible vineyard practices, the region's 15,000 farmers acknowledged what wine growers in other countries have come to recognize and embrace: consumers care *how* the product is made.

United Nations Environment Program

As more agricultural programs participate in the United Nations Environment Program's Global Reporting Initiative, information should become more readily available, and more standardization of sustainable viticultural practices could be expected. While the programs referenced here are not inclusive of all sustainable viticulture programs, this sample reinforces the importance of assuring that wines in the global marketplace are produced to meet consumers' expectations for environmentally, economically, and socially responsible practices.

Sustainable Winegrowing Practices: The Next 5 Years

The global wine community faces a historic "tipping point" where it can become a leading model of sustainability in practice or the current international efforts could unravel and turn into public relations campaigns lacking on-the-ground actions. Other major economic sectors have been investing in sophisticated sustainability marketing campaigns—such as the energy, automotive, and electronics sectors—where the messages are on target but transparency, particularly science-based accountability, have not been the focus. The global wine community has the opportunity to establish and maintain a higher standard of conduct that, if fully executed, could thrust the wine sector into an international leadership position, demonstrating that sustainability pursuits can lead to measurable improvements in environmental, social, and economic results.

Key elements for the success of the sustainable wine-growing practices in the next 5 years will include:

- Leadership by wine growers and vintner to ensure the widespread adoption of sustainable practices by small-, medium-, and large-scale producers.
- Transparent systems that allow for credible, yet efficient, collection and reporting of information on the true status of sustainable practices on a regional, national, and international scale.
- Improved science, technology, and management systems that improve the effectiveness and efficiency of sustainable practices.

- Increased national and international market-based competition for wines produced and distributed with sustainable practices.
- Increased performance-based local, state, and national regulatory systems that create real incentives to improve environmental and social performance and reduce public and private regulatory costs by utilizing improved technology and management systems.

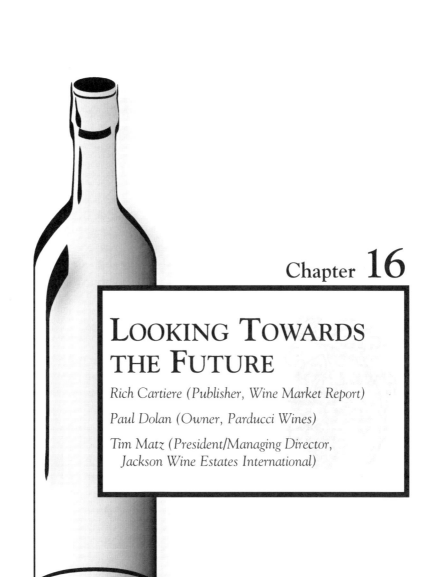

Chapter 16

LOOKING TOWARDS THE FUTURE

Rich Cartiere (Publisher, Wine Market Report)

Paul Dolan (Owner, Parducci Wines)

Tim Matz (President/Managing Director, Jackson Wine Estates International)

The global wine business today has the same growth potential and offers to change both our world and our everyday lives as much as the high-tech industry had and did in the early 1980s. In fact, the numerous parallels between the two industries are remarkably striking. Both are global industries that eventually matured to the point of facing competition from overseas producers, emerging country upstarts, and numerous domestic rivals. Both are based on products that require specific instructions to use and enjoy, requiring at times a level of additional education that can be nearly overwhelming and daunting.

So it is easy to see that, like computers and other high-tech inventions that have revolutionized our lives, the seemingly simple act of drinking wine is bringing about an evolution in how we live. It ushers in "il dolce vita," or the good life of food and drink. This includes an appreciation for hand craftsmanship and products that reflect the regionality of where they are produced, as well as opportunities of conviviality and camaraderie.

This chapter explores some of these revolutionary and evolutionary changes in wine by presenting a vision for the future of global wine. It begins by examining existing competitive and strategic conditions within the industry that are moving us from a supplier-driven to a customer-driven perspective. Then the chapter describes several different consumer trends that currently are—and will continue to—impacting the future of global wine. Finally, it presents a fairly positive forecast of how the global wine industry may look in the future.

From Supplier to Consumer Driven

For the most part, the global business of wine has most often been viewed from the supplier perspective rather than from the perspective of the consumer. It is most often reported upon, interpreted, and projected based upon how the producer, either grower or winery, sees the future.

But the reality today is that it is the consumer driving the global wine industry; suppliers are no longer in the driver's seat. High levels of production of both wine grapes and wine itself, and hypercompetition from the seemingly ever-booming number of brands from around the world, have given the consumer an unprecedented level of power of choice at the retail end. The result is that the consumer is, and will be for the foreseeable future, the primary driver of evolution in the global wine industry.

That said, we should examine key consumer trends to understand the future of the wine business, both domestically and globally. We should remember that wine consumers also are buyers of many products. They live in a rapidly changing retail world that affects how they make decisions and how they view both products and the supplier sources of those goods.

It is extremely difficult to find similarities between, and make generalized statements about, consumers in different countries. Indeed, most wine trade exporters look to find the differences so they can focus on adjusting their domestic approaches in that manner. But herein we will seek to identify some of the major emerging traits that are found in virtually all consumers in modern, industrialized nations. These trends and influences may allow a more uniform approach to describe the new consumer—one shaped by the latest influences on modern life rather than the latest developments in the vineyard and/or in the cellar.

Trend 1: Thirst for Innovative Products

The most successful wine companies in the 1990s were those vintners who sought out consumers and found out what their preferences were. The spent time discovering what their penchants for wine styles and flavors were and, based upon that, sought out innovative ways to deliver value, quality, and simplicity to them in a premium product.

Kendall-Jackson, Beringer Blass, Rosemount, and Southcorp are good examples of wineries that have produced wines targeted to specific consumer tastes. All have produced new product lines of wine that are more fruit forward, have names that are easy to pronounce, and are priced competitively. Consumers have responded positively by buying these brands and making them top sellers.

A good role model of this premise is Coca-Cola, in the soft drink industry. When Coke saturated the US and Western Europe three to four decades ago, one of their next big growth strategies was to go into less developed markets. They have proven successful in India, China, the continent of Africa, Russia, and other countries. All of these markets were consuming beverages of some kind prior to their entry, yet they were able to penetrate, educate, and develop an entire new consuming public.

The wine industry can follow suit, as long as the suppliers and wineries produce products and brands that meet the consumer needs, palates, and styles, for each market. It is important to note that Coca-Cola, while the branding is similar around the world (although in different languages), the formula or blends of the product vary depending on the consumer taste profile preferences in each market. Some markets have consumers with a slightly sweeter palate than others. We have already seen the trend in China over just the last few years and really have only scratched the surface. This market alone could exceed all other markets combined in Asia.

There is still ample opportunity to expand in innovation for wine, especially around consumer taste preferences. However, there are other areas of innovation as well, such as packaging, simpler labels, easier openings, more portability, and other taste additives. Some of this has occurred in Australia and Chile, but there is still more room for expansion.

Trend 2: Focus on Health

The trend of focusing on healthy eating habits is increasing rapidly in many nations, and is expected to continue to do so. More and more consumers are conscious of the types of food and beverages they consume, and want to be reassured that they are healthy, organic, and not made from steroids or artificially created products. Consuming less fatty foods, exercising on a regular basis, and getting tested for various diseases or illnesses are common patterns and behaviors in many people's lives today.

Fortunately, wine has a reputation for being a healthy drink in most parts of the world. Since the advent of the now famous "French Paradox" on *60 Minutes* touting the health benefits of drinking wine in moderation, many consumers have looked to wine as a health additive (Perdue, 1999). Even though it is basically illegal for vintners themselves to advertise the health benefits of wine in the US, many consumers are still aware of the benefits of reduced heart disease linked to wine consumption.

This linkage of health and wine is still growing around the world. For example, the Chinese government has communicated to its citizens that wine is healthy. Countless doctors in Japan, Northern Europe, and the US prescribe some wine for people over 50 as a preventative aid. Every year new medical research is published that corroborates this fact.

Now new health care diets recommend the addition of moderate amounts of wine, emphasizing its low fat, low carbohydrate, low calorie benefits. However, the wine industry has done little to emphasize these benefits. There is also opportunity to link the trend for innovation with the health trend and create new types of wine with vitamin additives, herbs, or other health-related flavorings like the bottled juice and water industries have done.

Trend 3: Environmental Concern

Consumers around the world are becoming more aware of environmental issues. They are concerned about air, water, and soil pollution, global warming, wildlife, tree, and plant protection, and many other ecological issues. Because of this they are worried about how products are made, and want to be assured that the environment was not harmed from any farming, harvesting, or production practices (Dolan & Elkjer, 2003). They are concerned about recycling of waste products, use of pesticides, and packaging that is biodegradable. Recently consumers have actually boycotted products they perceived as not being environmentally friendly.

As described in Chapter 15, some wine businesses are being very proactive in pursuing sustainable wine-growing practices. However, there is ample opportunity for others to expand on this theme and for the whole industry to communicate their efforts better. In addition, more innovative designs in packaging, which are reusable and recyclable, are needed.

Trend 4: Value Experiences Rather Than Possessions

The events of September 11 and the resulting financial woes that impacted global markets drive the next trend—that of valuing experiences rather than possessions. According to Leinberger (2003), these events have created a "once-in-a-generation confluence of events" that have left consumers, on the one hand, disillusioned and wary of corporate claims and, on the other hand, "more focused than at any time in modern history" on enriching their home life with family and friends through quality products and experiences. They have a new definition of self—one based on valuing experience rather than possessions, and sharing them rather than holding them.

It is critical that wine sellers and producers understand this trend, because there is much opportunity to link the benefits of wine—camaraderie, relaxation, living life to the full—with this new model of thinking. As a result of the distrust of outside social forces, but also an internal optimism, many consumers have turned to their homes, family, and friends. There is now more of an opportunity than ever for wine to be at the table as part of this picture and new trend.

Trend 5: Desire for "Value Chic"

Related to trend 4 is a focus on getting the best deal for your money—also referred to as "value chic." Consumers have a "big appetite" for discounts and deals as a result of their distrust of corporate claims and government regulations. But at the same time, consumers are searching for "affordable approximations," luxury items that they believe provide the highest quality at the most affordable price. For example, according to Leinberger (2003), 54% of Americans say they want to stay in a luxury hotel, up 17 points since 2000, and 47% want to eat in an expensive restaurant, up 11 points.

This provides an opportunity for wineries to prove they deliver value and capitalize on their brands as being such approximates of "the good, the very best in life." This doesn't mean that wineries should only sell cheap, inexpensive wine; they should produce and market a high-quality wine at a perceived good value, or price.

Trend 6: Trust in Word of Mouth

A referent group refers to a group of friends or influential people that consumers respect. If the reference group recommends something, then other will follow. Due to the lack of trust in society today, the number of consumers who report that "word of mouth" is an important source of information and ideas is increasing. Because of this wine producers and marketers would do well to concentrate on "influentials"— key decision makers in the marketplace. Also, product placement of wine in relevant media advertising, movies, radio, etc., can capitalize on this trend of referent groups.

Trend 7: Democratization of Luxury (Mastige)

There is another consumer "mega-trend" that is directly and dramatically affecting wine drinkers. The Boston Consulting Group (BCG; http://www.bcg.com/home.jsp), one of the world's leading management advising firms, has dubbed it "The New Luxury Demand of Middle America." They report that middle-class American consumers are now willing to pay up to 10 times traditional prices in exchange for premium quality and a sense of value obtained. And, despite the recession since the start of the new decade, the shift to what they called the "democratization of luxury" has been mounting and constant.

This trend suggest that consumers want products that deliver benefits and satisfactions on a level previously attained only by super-premium products, but at prices and in volumes previously thought impossible or unrealistic for such exceptional goods. According to BCG (2003), this trend is driven by such concepts as: 1) *Taking Care of Me*—or consumers who are looking for ways to manage the physical, emotional, and spiritual stresses of their lives; 2) *Investing*—or viewing the purchase of high-quality durable goods as one way to achieve safety and security; and 3) *Quest-*

ing—or wanting to experience as much as possible of the incredible offerings of the world.

Though this trend seems in direct opposition to the "Value Chic" trend, it actually has some similar components, in that consumers want a good-quality product, but at a fair price. The difference with this trend, however, is that more consumers are seeking luxury products than they were in the past. Another term for this new trend is "mastige," which means that the "masses" are now trying to achieve "prestige" with products. Wine is a perfect product to support this trend. According to John Butman (Director of Research and Development for BCG, personal interview, 2003): "Wine is one of the categories that fits very strongly with the 'new consumer,' and connects on almost all of their emotional needs."

A good example of a company capitalizing on this trend is RoundTable Pizza, an American pizza chain. They adopted an approach to selling a new pizza product— the "Napa Pizza"—in the spring of 2003 that illustrated to the wine industry how to market wine more easily. Roundtable accomplished this by: 1) tapping into the hugely positive feelings that Americans have about Napa (the best wines); 2) poking fun at the snobbishness, and thus making "Napa" and the associated product both of higher quality and more approachable; and 3) assigning an affordable value to what otherwise is seen as too costly and beyond economical reach.

The trend of mastige will provide more opportunities for the wine industry, because luxury wines will always be a component in the global scene. However, the trend opens up new possibilities for the extension of new labels within a strong brand, which may retail for a lower price but still provide the cachet of a luxury product. A good example of this is Pavillon Rouge, which is the second label of the famous Chateau Margaux in Bordeaux. If a consumer cannot afford to purchase Chateau Margaux, they can still afford the next best thing: Pavillon Rouge, made by the same producer but at a slightly reduced quality and price point.

Trend 8: Online Purchasing

We now live in a virtual society—having moved from the rural to industrial; from postindustrial to digital. This started with radio, then TV. It has now moved to the Internet, cell phones, and PDAs. Consumers are more comfortable with researching and purchasing produces via technology. This includes wine, and although the growth of wine sales through the Internet has been slower than other industries (Thach & Eaton, 2001), it is still growing. It is expected that it will continue to increase in the future.

As the trend of purchasing products via the Internet continues to expand around the world, so will opportunities to purchase wines virtually. There are opportunities for savvy wine businesses to establish partnerships with wine retailers in multiple countries who can ensure that wine is shipped directly to foreign addresses. Furthermore, current legal and tax restrictions on trade across all borders will continue to dissipate as consumers persist in pressuring global legislators to open trade borders. The rise of international wine clubs is a testament to consumers' desire to purchase wines from around the world and have the convenience of having them shipped to their door step.

Future Forecasts for the Global Wine Industry

By examining these eight trends, it is possible to make some predictions on the changes that will occur in the global wine industry in the future. Some of these are just beginning to occur, due to economic and competitive pressures that are forcing the more traditional wine businesses to change. Others are driven by innovative players in the industry who are listening to consumers and making changes based on their feedback. Still other companies are focused on cultivating new wine consumers, which creates additional opportunities and new directions. Taken together, we have used these activities, trends, and forces to forecast some of the following changes in the global wine industry.

Growth in Wine Consumption

In the 1990s, wine consumption began to fall in Old World countries, such as France and Italy. However, in the 2000s, consumption rates have slowly risen in New World countries such as the US, Canada, India, and China. It is predicted that wine consumption rates will continue to rise around the world, especially with a new focus on identifying new wine consumer segments. Indeed, recent data indicate that wine is one of the fastest growing consumer beverage categories within grocery stores in the US (Byck, 2004).

Introduction of More Innovative Wine Products

As more wine businesses focus on understanding and meeting new consumer needs, intriguing new wine varietals will be introduced. New wine products may include ingredients such as vitamins, herbs, and other types of flavors targeted at matching consumer preferences. We predict that some wineries may focus on the health benefits of wines and promote the low carbohydrate count found in wines. Others may pursue younger consumer segments with tastes for sweeter, fruit-flavored wines, with bright and humorous labels and names. Already the forerunners of such innovative products can be seen in the market with their fruit-forward wines and brightly colored labels with animal motifs. Successful examples include Yellow Tail (with a kangaroo), Rex Goliath (with a 47-pound rooster), Smoking Loon, and Leaping Horse.

At the same time, there will always be a place for the luxury wines produced by the traditional châteaux of both the Old and New World. The old, venerated labels should be able to hold their specific market niche, as long as they continue to focus on high-quality wines with a mystic of scarceness and allocation.

Novel Wine Packaging

The traditional glass wine bottle with a cork closure will continue to exist, but we predict that many new packaging options will continue to be introduced into the global market. Innovative packaging is already available in many countries, such as Australia, Chile, and France, but has not yet reached all parts of the New World. Consumers are asking for portable wine packaging, and it is expected that more wineries will introduce PET bottles for wine (plastic bottles, similar to the bottled water industry). In addition, more boxes, bags, and closures that do not require a cork screw will be introduced. Also smaller size packaging, such as wine in one- or two-glass servings, will become more available to all markets.

Emphasis on Environmentally Friendly Wines

Related to the area above will be more wineries that emphasize and communicate their environmentally friendly practices. The consumer expects wineries and suppliers to take responsibility for their respective roles in contributing to these causes. Hence, recyclable packaging will become more important. We predict more wineries will include information on their labels regarding sustainable and organic farming practices, which means it could be a marketing hook when promoting individual brands. Because the wine business is an agriculture-based business, the sustainability of the land, the protection from pesticides and chemicals, and the promotion of organic soils and grapes are all positive and prevalent behaviors expected in the future.

Continued Consolidation, But More Newcomers

With all the recent mergers and acquisitions (e.g., Fosters buying Beringer Blass; Southcorp emerging with big brands on three continents; Constellation purchasing BRL Hardy's in Australia and Mathew Clarke in the UK; and Gallo setting up business and JVs in other markets around the world) one wonders if consolidation will ever stop. We predict that it will continue for awhile, not only on the winery side, but also on the distributor and retailer levels. Due to competitive cost pressures, the large global players will need to combine to achieve economies of scale.

At the same time, we see more newcomers entering the market. One of the most interesting and sometimes perplexing trends in the wine industry is how small wineries/companies and small brands can continue to penetrate through the entire system and end up in consumers' hands, growing exponentially without heavy advertising or even distribution clout. Most recently, Yellow Tail is a brand that has grown from nothing to over 4 million cases in less than 3 years. Blackstone Merlot is another success that is a virtual brand that did not exist 10 years ago and now sells over 1 million cases.

Due to the fragmentation of brands in the wine industry, the consuming behavior of experimentation, discovery, and trial, and the gatekeepers, there will always be small brands that penetrate through the distribution and retail/restaurant tiers to the consumer. This, while challenging to many companies, is actually one of the very refreshing nuances of the wine industry. The small player has a chance to make it. In the soft drink or beer world, while it has and does occasionally happen, more often than not the small new entry gets squashed before it is given a chance.

The other phenomenon in the wine industry is the ability for a very small brand to niche themselves, and sell just a few cases at a very high profit, to ensure their sustainability and existence. While wine quality must be there, and getting it into the right hands of wine enthusiasts and public relations contacts is necessary, there are many wines out there that have done that and not been successful. Hence, it is another strange yet rewarding nuance of the wine industry that a small winery can quietly have a very small niche of consumers willing to pay a very high price for a quality wine, which allows that winery to stay and prosper in their existence. This will not change, because it has been done in the Old World of wine and the New World of wine for the entire history of the industry.

Introduction of a Global Brand

This is and has been a popular buzzword for a decade now, although one could argue it did not reach the wine industry with much relevance until the last 5 years. With all the recent mergers and acquisitions, it is inevitable that the wine industry becomes truly global in its behaviors. Therefore, we predict the emergence of a global brand; however, it could arrive in several different guises. The most popular model is the one discussed in Chapter 5 wherein a wine brand would be developed that would be sold around the world, but would source its grapes from a variety of countries. At the same time, it would be consistent in taste, quality, and price. This has not yet been accomplished, but there is a distinct possibility that it may occur in the future. More likely is our second model, which is a wine that carries strong brand recognition, such as Kendall Jackson Chardonnay or Lindemans Shiraz, but would be made and labeled with grapes from the country of origin (e.g., KJ Chardonnay from South Africa or Lindemans Shiraz from Chile). A third model could be the development of a very strong brand from one country that is sought out and coveted around the world, but with strong availability to all consumers, unlike luxury châteaux wines. When and who will develop this global brand is not clear, but we predict that it will occur in the future, taking form in one of the ways described above.

Increased Cost and Efficiency Focus

As the global wine industry continues to become more competitive, we predict that wineries will need to focus more on reducing costs and increasing efficiency in vineyard, wine production, and marketing efforts. More sophisticated software that tracks and analyzes production, finance, and marketing program results will become more common. Even small and midsize wineries will begin to focus on these issues, as the rise in consolidation and new entry wineries continues to put financial pressures on the industry. The wine industry will need to adopt the more sophisticated business and technology practices of their brethren in other beverage industries.

More Direct to Consumer Sales

We predict that consumers will continue to demand the ability to purchase wine directly via the Internet and other direct sales methods. This is already occurring at low levels via the Internet (6–10%) (Cartiere, 2003), but is expected to increase in the future. As global wine consumption rises, consumers will demand the right to purchase wines from a variety of appellations around the world. Many wine consumers are "discovery oriented" and enjoy trying a wine from a different country, or a unique style or grape varietal. Related to this is the rise of more international wine clubs, with shipments being sent around the world to arrive directly on the consumer's doorstep.

Rise in Asian Wineries and Consumption

As described in other parts of this book, we forecast that wine consumption in Asia will increase, especially in China, Japan, and India. Likewise, we predict the rise of more vineyards and some very good wineries in this part of the world. Driving forces of this forecast include low labor costs, current French and Australian winemaking consultation in these regions, an emphasis on wine as a prestige and health-related product, as well as governmental support of the Asian wine industry. The rise of this new Asian market force will create both positive and negative impacts on the global wine industry. On the positive side, wine consumption will increase; on the negative side, we see this driving more fiercely competitive cost issues for the industry.

Increased Wine Tourism

A final positive prediction for the wine industry is the continued popularity and rise of worldwide wine tourism. As the "mastige," innovation, and environmental trends among consumers expand, the idea of visiting winemaking regions, participating in harvest, and even blending a wine in a "wine boot camp" will appeal to a certain segment of consumers. Already, European countries are capitalizing on this trend and creating a range of appealing vacation formats for wine tourism. We predict this will increase and be available to consumers in all the major wine-producing regions of the world.

Editors

Elizabeth "Liz" Thach, Ph.D., is a wine business and management professor at Sonoma State University in Rohnert Park, CA. In addition to her academic experience, Liz has worked for more than 14 years at the management and executive level within Fortune 500 companies, as well as doing consulting and research in the wine industry. She currently teaches the Introduction to Wine Business Strategies class at SSU; conducts research in wine industry management and human resource practices, consumer behavior, and marketing strategies; and serves as a liaison between wine business students and industry. Liz has a doctorate in Human Resource Development from Texas A&M University, has published extensively, and has traveled to many wine regions of the world. She is very active in wine industry associations, such as WineVision, WineSpirit, and planning committees for Unified Wine Symposium. She is also on the Board of Directors of PASCO, Napa NCHRA, Women for Wine Sense, EXCN, and is on the Advisory Board of Benchmark Consulting. Liz lives in Sonoma County and spends part of her time tending a hobby vineyard on Sonoma Mountain.

Tim Matz is President/Managing Director for Jackson Estates Wine International—the corporate division for Kendall-Jackson Wines. In this role, he is responsible for all international operations, marketing, finance and sales functions, including wineries and offices in Chile, Australia, Italy, France, the U.K., and Ireland. Prior to this role, Tim was Vice-President & General Manager for Imports at Beringer-Blass Wine Estates where he managed all of their international wine brands in the US and Canada. Other experience includes heading up Sales and Marketing at Southcorp before moving into the position of President of Americas. Tim started his career in the wine industry in 1985, with Brown-Forman with management and executive positions in sales, marketing, strategic planning, and international. He has an MBA from University of Kentucky and a BBA from Kent State University. Tim has served on the Wine Market Council, the Australian Wine bureau, and Wine Vision task force.

Contributors

Jon Affonso is Assistant Winemaker at Dry Creek Vineyard. He is committed to producing wine of absolute integrity and quality from the winery's 200 acres of extensive estate vineyards, which stretch throughout the Dry Creek Valley, Russian River Valley, and Alexander Valley appellations. Jon holds a Master of Science degree from California State University, Fresno, in Agriculture Chemistry with a concentration on Enology and a Bachelor of Science in Geology from California State University, Sacramento. His winemaking career has included positions at Trinchero Family Estates as a research enologist, Château Angélus in St. Emilion, France, and at the Viticulture & Enology Research Center at California State University, Fresno, as a research assistant.

Jean Arnold is President of Hanzell Vineyards, a small family-owned winery that crafts Burgundian-style wines in the foothills of the Mayacamas Mountains in Sonoma Valley. Prior to joining Hanzell Vineyards, Jean was CEO of Jackson Family Farms and its nine independent wineries. She has over 22 years of experience in business leadership, executive management, marketing, and sales with notable wineries such as Chateau St. Jean, Chateau Montelena, Jordan Vineyards & Winery, Chalk Hill Estate, and Williams Selyem. In 1999 she founded her consulting firm, the Jean Arnold Group, to offer luxury positioning and management to private wine industry clients including Laurel Glen Vineyards, Rudd Vineyards & Winery, and the management firm of Motto, Kryla, & Fisher. At this time, The Jean Arnold Group includes Chalk Hill Estate Vineyards & Winery, independent private clients, and Jean's partnership in a new wine venture, Ottimino.

Dr. Thomas S. Atkin is Assistant Professor of Operations Management at Sonoma State University, where he teaches Wine Business Operations, as well as general business operations. In addition, he is active in wine business research and has published several articles in this area. He joined Sonoma State in 2001 after receiving a Ph.D. in Operations and Sourcing Management from Michigan State University. His job experience encompasses 13 years as general manager of a manufacturing plant and 12 years in restaurant management.

David Beckstoffer is President and CEO of Beckstoffer Vineyards, an independent grape grower that owns approximately 3000 acres in the North Coast of California, including over 200 acres in the prestigious Rutherford Bench appellation. David has worked in this family business for the past 6 years, taking over the reins of daily farming operations from his father. Prior to entering the vineyard management business, David worked for 9 years at Bechtel in their Project Finance and Development group. He holds a B.S. and M.S. in Civil Engineering from Stanford, and an M.B.A. from the Wharton School of Business at the University of Pennsylvania.

Kari Birdseye is Vice President of Sustainability Programs for SureHarvest, a company that offers software and services for sustainable agriculture. Prior to coming to SureHarvest,

Kari was the Director of Communications at the Wine Institute, where she oversaw the Communications Committee and Sustainable Winegrowing Practices Joint Committee with the California Association of WineGrape Growers. Kari also spent 11 years working for the Cable News Network (CNN) where she held several positions before becoming an Emmy award-winning Executive Producer. She has a B.A. in Journalism from San Francisco State University. Kari was also first author on the Code of Sustainable Winegrowing Practices.

Dr. Linda Bisson is a Professor of Viticulture & Enology at UC-Davis where she teaches classes in wine production. She is the holder of the Maynard A. Amerine Endowed Chair in Viticulture and Enology. Dr. Bisson is also a member of the advisory boards of the American Viticulture and Enology Research Network and has just accepted the position of Science Editor for the *American Journal of Enology and Viticulture*. She is lead principal investigator on the multidisciplinary, multiprincipal investigator program in stuck fermentations funded by the American Vineyard Foundation. She received her Ph.D. in Microbiology from the University of California at Berkeley.

Lillian Bynum is the Vice President of Human Resources for Delicato Family Vineyards in Manteca, California. Delicato is currently the 10th largest wine company in the US, with over 10,000 acres of vineyards and five major brands. Lillian oversees all human resource activities, including training and development, compensation, and safety. She is a certified Professional of Human Resources (PHR), member of the Society for Human Resources Management, and Past President of the San Joaquin Human Resources Association. Lillian is also a member of the wine industry's Western Management Group Compensation Advisory Board and certified trainer of Franklin Covey's "7 Habits of Highly Effective People."

Richard Cartiere is publisher of *Wine Market Report*, which reports on the "inside story on the wine business for more than 5,000 wine industry executives worldwide." In addition, he is also editor of *Global Wine News e-Monitor*. Rich has many years of experience in wine business writing, is a frequent presenter at wine conferences, and is one of the founding members of WineVision. His journalism career spans 25 years, including stints as the West Coast editor of *Wine Enthusiastic* magazine, as content editor on *Smart Wine*, and as assistant business editor at the *New York Times* Regional Newspaper Group's wine country newspaper in Santa Rosa, CA.

Tony Correia is an Accredited Rural Appraiser, and specializes in the appraisal of large, complex, agricultural properties, and difficult appraisal assignments. He is the president, and owner, of Correia-Xavier, Inc., and is an instructor of appraisal courses and seminars throughout the nation and Mexico, and is also a frequent public speaker on agricultural, appraisal, taxation, and estate planning issues, and the vineyard and wine industries. He has been a guest speaker for many organizations, including the American Bar Association and the Appraisal Institute. Tony is a founding member of the World Association of Valuation Organizations, and a graduate of CSU-Fresno, with a major and postgraduate work in English, and a second major in Russian.

Jon P. Dal Poggetto, CPA, is Managing Partner of the Santa Rosa accounting firm of Dal Poggetto Company LLP. He has 29 years of public accounting experience in the wine industry. He served as National Director of Winery Services for the international accounting firm of Touche Ross & Co. before starting his own firm in 1992. He is the author of *A*

Practical Guide to Winery Cost Accounting and served as chairman of the 1992 Wine Industry Conference for the California CPA Foundation. He was also a founder of the Deloitte & Touche Wine Industry Financial Survey.

Jeff DeLott is Owner and President of SureHarvest, a company that offers software and services for sustainable agriculture. The previous name of the company was RealToolbox. Jeff received his Ph.D. in 1993 in entomology at UC Berkeley where he combined ecological field research with social science program design and evaluation tools to understand and extend sustainable agriculture systems. Jeff continued his natural and social science sustainable agriculture research and taught insect ecology and agricultural ecology at UC Berkeley from 1994 to 1995. In 1996, Jeff founded Collaborative Research and Designs for Agriculture, a sustainable agriculture research and educational 501(c)3 nonprofit focused on the design, implementation, and evaluation of large-scale projects to improve the environmental performance of agricultural ecosystems. Jeff is also one of the authors of the Code of Sustainable Winegrowing Practices.

Paul Dolan is the new owner of Parducci Winery. He was formerly the president and CEO of Fetzer Vineyards since 1992. A native Californian descended from a family of winemakers, he has successfully integrated his personal interest in sustainable business practices into day-to-day operations at Fetzer. Paul is very active in the California wine community, and a founding member of WineVision. He recently published the book *True to Our Roots: Fermenting a Business Revolution*, which describes how sustainable winegrowing practices have been applied at Fetzer. He holds a Master in Enology from CSU-Fresno.

Megghen Driscoll is Director of Public Relations & Corporate Communications for Allied Domecq Wines, USA. She has more than 15 years of experience in the wine industry. Her prior positions include Director of Public Relations at Diageo Chateau & Estate Wines, as well as Vice President of Public Relations at Southcorp Wines for more than 6 years. Megghen began her wine career at the Sterling Vineyards School of Service & Hospitality.

Curtis Eaton currently works as National Sales Manager for The California Wine Company and assists with sales and marketing efforts for the direct to consumer, domestic, and international markets. Previously Curtis has worked with Buena Vista Winery, internationally with the Maison des Bordeaux et Bordeaux Superieur, and prior to that with the Ashbury Market in San Francisco. Curtis spent nearly the first decade of his career working in the food & beverage department for country clubs. He started out in his native Los Angeles but moved up to the Bay Area so that he could follow his passion for wine while completing an Associates Degree of Science in Hotel and Restaurant Management at the City College of San Francisco. It was upon his return from France that he completed his B.S. in Wine Business Strategies at Sonoma State University and began his current position in the wine industry.

Dr. Robert Eyler is a Professor of Wine Economics at Sonoma State University in California. He earned a Ph.D. from the University of California, Davis in 1998. He has published several scholarly articles on the California wine industry, and has acted as a consultant in winery litigation for free trade advocacy across states and in a trademark damage case. His academic fields of specialization are macroeconomic and monetary theory, applied econometrics, and economic history. He is also the director of the Center for Regional Economic Analysis at Sonoma State University, concentrating on providing information and doing research for the North Bay economy in Northern California.

Peter Gago is Chief Winemaker at Penfolds Wines Pty Ltd in South Australia. He joined Penfolds in 1989 after graduating from Roseworthy College with a Dux of the Bachelor of Applied Science (Oenology). He also holds a B.S. in Education from the University of Melbourne, and was a math and science teacher for over 8 years before becoming a winemaker. Peter has traveled extensively, and has written three books on wine: *Discovering Australian Wine—A Taster's Guide*; *Australian Wine—From the Vine to the Glass*; and *Australian Wines—Tastes and Styles*. Peter is currently head winemaker for the famous Penfolds Grange.

Denis Gastin is a wine writer who grew up in Australia's northeast Victorian wine regions and has had a lifelong interest in wine. He is a feature writer and Australian Correspondent for Japan's liquor industry newspaper, *The Shuhan News*. Over the past decade he has been a contributor to various other journals and wine reference books, including *The Oxford Companion to Wine*, *The World Atlas of Wine*, *Wine Report*, *Wine Companion*, and *The Pocket Wine Guide*, among others. Currently, Denis resides in Australia and is working on a new book about the growth of the Asian wine industry. He holds a B.Com degree from the University of Melbourne and was a Postgraduate scholar at Concordia University, Montreal.

Dr. Don Getz is Professor of Tourism and Hospitality Management in the Haskayne School of Business, University of Calgary, Canada. He is author of the book *Explore Wine Tourism: Management, Development, Destinations* and conducts research on wine consumers and wine tourism development. His other major interests are reflected in his books: *Festivals, Special Events & Tourism*, *Event Management & Event Tourism*, *The Business of Rural Tourism*, and *The Family Business in Tourism and Hospitality*. Don travels extensively, and having a doctoral degree in Geography (University of Edinburgh) he always explores new wine regions.

Dr. Armand Gilinsky, Jr. is Professor of Business at Sonoma State University, where he teaches Strategy and Entrepreneurship. In recent years he has served as Director of SSU's Entrepreneurship Center, Wine Business Program, and Small Business Institute. He previously held teaching appointments at the Harvard Business School, CSU Hayward, and Northeastern University. Dr. Gilinsky has had extensive consulting experience with more than 30 companies, including members of the wine industry. His areas of specialty include strategic planning and venture planning. He has authored numerous business case studies and several articles on entrepreneurial strategy. He holds Ph.D. in Business Policy from Henley Management College/Brunel University (London), an M.B.A. in Finance from Golden Gate University, an A.M. in Education Administration and Policy Analysis from Stanford University, and an A.B. (honors) in English from Stanford University.

Dr. Mark Greenspan is Manager of Winegrowing Research and Development at Ernest & Julio Gallo Winery. He has been working out of the Gallo of Sonoma facilities since 1996 and currently oversees R&D projects in more than 5,000 acres of wine grapes. Dr. Greenspan received his doctorate from UC Davis in Agricultural Engineering in 1999 and has a master's degree in Horticulture, also from UC Davis. His areas of expertise include grapevine water relations, developmental physiology of the grape berry, agricultural meteorology, and vineyard technology.

Bruce Herman is Senior Vice President and General Manager of the Estates Group, the fine wine division of Young's Market. Prior to forming the Estates Group, Bruce was Senior VP of Sales for Schieffelin & Somerset Co. where he spent 14 years. Bruce began his career as a merchandiser for United Vintners, before taking a position with Mirassou Vineyards as National Sales Manager. He has a B.A. degree in History from Marietta College in Ohio and an M.B.A. from Dominican University in California.

Tor Kenward is Vice President of Public Relations at Beringer Blass Wine Estates. He first joined Wine World Inc.'s (Beringer Vineyards, Los Hermanos, Cross and Blackwell Imports) marketing department in 1977. In 1980 he was promoted to Director of Public Relations. Over the following two decades Tor has remained a core member of the company's management team as Beringer Blass Wine Estates evolved into one of the world's premier wine companies. For a quarter of a century Tor was responsible for building and running the company's Public Relations Department.

Armen Khachaturian is a Corporate Retail Specialist with The Henry Wine Group, which represents hundreds of wineries from around the world to various markets across the US. Armen maintains accounts in Northern California and is responsible for the distribution of Henry wines to retail establishments throughout the North Bay. Armen has over 7 years of experience in sales, specializing in the wine and hospitality industry. He holds a B.S. in Wine Business Strategy from Sonoma State University, and was the Student Commencement Speaker of his graduating class.

Walt Klenz is Managing Director of Beringer Blass Wine Estates. He joined Beringer Vineyards in 1976 and was Chairman and CEO when Foster's announced its 2000 acquisition. Under his leadership, Beringer grew into a market-leading company with a strong stable of premium brands, culminating in a successful public float on the US market in 1997.

Dr. Terry Lease is an Assistant Professor of Accounting in the School of Business & Economics at Sonoma State University, where he teaches Wine Industry Accounting and Finance course and conducts professional development seminars in the Wine Business Program. He is a licensed CPA in California and Florida. His primary areas of interest in accounting are Taxation and Management Accounting.

Wendell Lee is counsel for The Wine Institute, headquartered in San Francisco, California. The Wine Institute is the public policy advocacy association of California wineries. It brings together the resources of 624 wineries and affiliated businesses to support legislative and regulatory advocacy, international market development, media relations, scientific research, and education programs that benefit the entire California wine industry. As counsel for the Wine Institute, Wendell focuses on the myriad of legal issues impacting wine around the world. He is also the Wine Institute Webmaster and manager of WineLaw.

Dr. Larry Lockshin is Professor of Wine Marketing, Director of the Wine Marketing Research Group, and Director Post Graduate Programs in Marketing and Wine Marketing at the University of South Australia. In this capacity he teaches "Managing the Wine Business for Profit; Optimising the Wholesale/Retail Relationship in Wine; and Retail Marketing

Management." He, along with Tony Spawton, conducts seminars and executive programs in wine marketing in most of the wine regions of the world and consults with major Australian wine companies. Larry is also a very prolific writer and researcher in wine marketing, with over 60 academic articles and an equal number of trade publications on the topics of wine consumer behavior, wine business management, and wine distribution and retail. Larry holds a Ph.D. in Marketing from Ohio State University, an M.Sc. in Viticulture and Agricultural Economics from Cornell University, and a B.A. in Humanities from Ohio State. He served on the Strategy 2025 and the Marketing Decade Committees of the Australian Wine Industry and he currently holds a committee position on the Domestic Marketing Taskforce for the Australian Wine and Brandy Association.

Dr. Linda Nowak is an Associate Professor of Marketing at Sonoma State University, and teaches in both the Wine Business Strategies and General Marketing programs. Her major classes are Wine Marketing, Principles of Marketing, and Marketing Management. Linda has published four articles in *The International Journal of Wine Marketing* entitled "Building Brand Equity: Consumer Reactions to Proactive Environmental Policies by the Winery"; "Effects of the Dietary Guideline Label Statement on Wine Purchase Intentions of Young Adults"; "Country of Origin Effects and Complimentary Marketing Channels: Is Mexican Wine More Enjoyable When Served with Mexican Food"; and "The Importance of Non-Financial Performance Measures in Wine Business Strategy."

Dr. Janeen Olsen holds the position of Professor of Wine Marketing at Sonoma State University. Her international background has provided her the opportunity to conduct export seminars for business executives in many Latin American cities. She has published extensively in marketing and international business journals and presented papers at conferences in Europe, Asia, and Latin America, as well as in the US. She has developed international trips for the Wine Business Program at SSU and takes Wine Business students on a wine industry tour of Chile. She has served on the Global Task Force for Wine Vision. She is active in conducting marketing research for the Wine Business Program at SSU and has published and presented her research in industry publications and seminars. She is working towards a certificate in Vineyard Management.

Cyril Penn is editor in chief of Wine Business Communications, headquartered in Sonoma, California. He joined the firm in September 1998 as editor of *Wine Business Insider*, and in January 2000 he was named editor in chief of *Wine Business Monthly*. Mr. Penn has over 15 years of wire service, magazine, and broadcast experience. Mr. Penn began his career as a journalist in New York at Reuters in 1987, where he covered the energy industry for more than 3 years. He moved on to become a freelance reporter specializing in energy, high technology, and biotechnology. Prior to joining Wine Business Communications, Mr. Penn was managing editor of the California Energy Markets newsletter in San Francisco. Mr. Penn holds a bachelor's degree in media studies from Fordham University in New York.

Karen Ross has been president of the California Association of Winegrape Growers since 1996. She is also the executive director for the Winegrape Growers of America, a national organization of state wine-grower organizations, and executive director of the California Wine Grape Growers Foundation, which sponsors scholarships for the children of vineyard employees. Karen is a co-editor for the Code of Sustainable Winegrowing Practices, and one of the founding members of WineVision, where she currently leads the Sustainability Taskforce. She graduated from the University of Nebraska-Lincoln, the Nebraska Agricultural Leadership Program, and the Graduate Institute of Cooperative Leadership, University of Missouri.

Mack Schwing is the Director of the Wine Business Program at Sonoma State University. He has a strong passion for and knowledge of wine, which, coupled with his business background, makes his current position as Wine Business Director a good fit. He worked for more than 30 years at Deloitte & Touche, with his most recent position as senior partner and global director of Programs and Initiatives. He has also lived in Japan, where he was the chairman of the wine committee at the Toyko American Club and was active in the Japanese wine import market. He holds an M.B.A. in Production Management and a B.S. in Mathematics from Michigan State University.

Tony Spawton is Associate Professor of Wine Marketing and the International Director of the Wine Marketing Research Group at the University of South Australia. He was instrumental in developing much of the contemporary wine marketing curriculum while at Roseworthy College in the mid-1980s. Tony is a key contributor to programs, seminars, and workshops in wine marketing locally and in most of the wine-making regions of the world, as well as a teacher in the Masters In Wine Marketing offered by the University of South Australia worldwide via its online delivery platform. Tony teaches the Applied Wine Marketing and Global Wine Marketing courses. Tony was an economics and marketing expert at The International Organisation of Vine and Wine (OIV) from 1990, and was unanimously elected President of the Expert Group "Market Analysis and Networks" in 2000. He is a member of the Scientific and Technical Committee of the OIV, holding specialist subgroup positions in wine industry development, and consumer and professional education. He has published numerous papers and articles on wine marketing research and applications.

Jeff Sully, CPA, CMA, is a founding partner in the accounting firm of Dillwood, Burkel & Sully LLP. He has spent more than 30 years in the wine industry. He has served in all facets of the business, having been a grower, winemaker, and retailer. In addition, he was Chief Financial Officer for a large Sonoma County winery. He has also been a consultant to the State University of New York, Binghamton, for wineries in New York State. He has lectured extensively in New York, Oregon, and California. He speaks regularly for the California CPA Education Foundation, having chaired several of their Wine Industry conferences.

Dr. Roy Thornton is a Professor of Enology at California State University, Fresno, where he teaches classes in viticulture and enology, and conducts research on wine genetics and yeasts. Before coming to California, he taught for 20 years in New Zealand at Massey University, and also worked for Gallo as a Senior Research Microbiologist. Roy has published numerous research articles on enology and viticulture. He holds both B.S and Ph.D. degrees in Applied Microbiology from Strathclyde University in Glasglow Scotland.

Richard Thomas is a Professor Emeritus, Viticulture & Wine Education, Santa Rosa Junior College, Santa Rosa, California. He has taught and consulted in Northern California vineyards for more than 30 years. Currently he is a viticultural consultant and continues to teach and coordinate courses at Santa Rosa JC in viticulture and wine tasting. Rich has written numerous articles on viticulture and is author of a monthly column for *Vineyard & Winery Magazine*. He is a professional wine judge and coordinator for several major US wine competitions. Rich holds a master's in Viticulture and a B.S. in Vocational Agriculture from UC-Davis.

Paul Wagner is a Professor of Wine Marketing in Napa Valley College's Viticulture and Enology department, as well as the founder of Balzac Communications & Marketing. In his role at Balzac Paul has many wine clients, including Diageo Chateau & Estate Wines, the Canandaigua Wine Company, the Union des Grands Crus de Bordeaux, Vinitaly, The L.A. County Fair International Wine Competition, Pernod-Ricard USA, Trinchero Family Estates, The Court of Master Sommeliers, and a host of other wine and food specialists. Before starting his own firm, Paul was general manager of Barson/Armstrong, a communications agency. He is a frequent guest lecturer at Golden Gate University, Sonoma State University, The University of Trieste, The University of Beaune, and UC Berkeley extension in the fields of wine, wine marketing, and wine production.

Bibliography

Agrain, P. (2003). Note de conjuncture mondiale. *Bulletin d'OIV, 76*(876-868), 424-453.

Anderson, K., & Norman, D. (2003). *Global wine production, consumption and trade, 1961-2001: A statistical compendium.* Adelaide: Centre for International Economic Studies.

Birdseye, K., Ross, K., & Delott, J. (Eds.). (2002). *The code of sustainable winegrowing practices.* San Francisco: The Wine Institute.

Broome, J. C. (2003). *Sustainable viticulture programs around the world.* Available: http://www.sarep.ucdavis.edu/production/viticulture/asev2003.htm

Byck, P. (2004, January). *State of the industry: Setting the stage for 2004.* Presentation made at the Unified Wine & Grape Symposium, Sacramento, CA.

Cartiere, R. (2003). Wine Internet Purchase Survey results. *Wine Market Report.*

Chaney, I. (2002). Promoting wine by country. *International Journal of Wine Marketing, 14*(1), 34-42.

Charters, S., & Ali-Knight, J. (2000). Who is the wine tourist? *Tourism Management, 23*(3), 311-319.

Coppla, C. J. (2000). Direct marketing sales boom with proliferation of wine clubs. *Wine Business Monthly, 7*(6).

Cox, J. (1999). *From vines to wines.* North Adams, MA: Storey Books.

Davison, B. (2003). Reviewing corporate financials show how HR measures up. *Employee Relations Today, 30*(1), 7-17.

Dodd, T., & Bigotte, V. (1997). Perceptual differences among visitor groups to wineries. *Journal of Travel Research, 35*(3), 46-51.

Dolan, P., & Elkjer, T. (2003). *True to our roots: Fermenting a business revolution.* Princeton: Bloomberg Press.

Duijker, H., & Johnson, H. (2000). *The wines of Chile.* New York: Spectrum.

Eccles, R. G., Lanes, K. L., & Wilson, T. C. (1999). Are you paying too much for that acquisition? *Harvard Business Review, 77*(4), 136.

Ferguson, S. (2002). Taking it direct. *Wine Business Monthly, 9*(1).

Gallagher, N. (2003, August 11). Squeezed by grape market. *The Press Democrat,* p. D1.

Gastin, D. (in press). Asia. In T. Stevenson (Ed.), *Wine report.* London: Dorling Kindersley.

Getz, D. (2000). *Explore wine tourism: Management, development, destinations.* New York: Cognizant Communication Corp.

Gilinsky, A., & Campbell, N. A. (2000). RJM Enterprises, Inc.—romancing the vine. *Case Research Journal, 20*(3), 132.

Gilinsky, A., McCline, R. L., & Eyler, R. (2000, March/April). Best business practices in the northern California wine industry. *Industry Analysis*, 30-37.

Gimeno, J., & Woo, C. Y. (1999). Multimarket contact, economies of scope, and firm performance. *Academy of Management Journal, 42*(3), 239-264.

Goold, M., & Campbell, A. (1998). Desperately seeking synergy. *Harvard Business Review, 76*(5), 70-83.

Grist, J. (2003, July). *Ancient vintage: Wine in ancient Israel and Mediterranean lands.* Presentation at the WineSpirit Meeting, Napa.

Haleblian, J., & Finkelstein, S. (1999). The influence of organizational acquisition experience on acquisition performance: A behavioral learning perspective. *Administrative Science Quarterly, 44*(1), 29-57.

Handfield, R. B., & Nichols, E. L., Jr. (1999). *Introduction to supply chain management.* Upper Saddle River, NJ: Prentice Hall.

Harrison, J. S., Hitt, M. A., Hoskisson, R. E., & Ireland, R. D. (2001). Resource complimentarity in business combinations: Extending the logic to organizational alliances. *Journal of Management, 27*(6), 679-691.

Howell, J. (2001). *Chile experience travel guide.* Los Angeles: Turiscom Publishing.

Johnson, H. (1985). *The world atlas of wine* (3rd ed.). New York: Simon & Schuster.

Johnson, H. (1989). *Vintage: The story of wine.* New York: Simon & Schuster.

Johnson, H., & Robinson, J. (2001). *The world atlas of wine* (5th ed.). London: Octopus Publishing Group, Ltd.

Keller, K. L. (2003). *Strategic brand management.* New York: Prentice-Hall Publishers.

Khanna, T., & Palepu, K. (1999). The right way to restructure conglomerates in emerging markets. *Harvard Business Review, 77*(4), 125-135.

Laforet, S., & Saunders, J. (1999). Managing brand portfolios: Why leaders do what they do. *Journal of Advertising Research, 39*(1), 51-65.

Leinberger, P. (2003, July). *Consumer trends in the global wine industry.* Presentation made at the WineVision Conference, Napa, CA.

Lukacs, P. (2000). *American vintage: The rise of American wine.* New York: Houghton-Mifflin.

MacNeil, K. (2001). *The wine bible.* New York: Workman Publishing.

Manktelow, De., Renton, T., & Gurnsey, S. (2002). *Technical developments in sustainable winegrowing New Zealand.* Available: www.nzwine.com

Markides, C. (1997). To diversify or not to diversify. *Harvard Business Review, 75*(6), 93-101.

Marshall, J. (2001). Are mergers paying off? *Financial Executive, 17*(2), 26-33.

Monczka, R., Trent, R., & Handfield, R. (1998). *Purchasing and supply chain management.* Cincinnati, OH: South-Western College Publishing.

Moulton, K., & Spawton, T. (1997). Can the wine industry survive regulation. In L. T. Wallace & W. R. Schroder (Eds.), *Government and the food industry: Economic and political effects of conflict and co-operation.* Boston: Kluwer Academic Publishers.

Noe, R. A., Hollenbeck, J. R., Gerhart, B., & Wright, P. M. (2004). *Fundamentals of human resource management.* Boston: McGraw-Hill.

O'Neill, J. (2004, January 27). *The wine industry at the beginning of the 21st century: A fast ride in a new direction?* Presentation at Unified Wine & Grape Symposium, Sacramento, CA.

O'Neill, M., & Charters, S. (2000). Service quality at the cellar door: Implications for Western Australia's developing wine tourism industry. *Managing Service Quality, 10*(2), 12–122.

Office International de la Vigne et du Vin. (1995–2000). *The state of viticulture in the world and the statistical information in 2000.* France:Author.

Palich, L. E., & Gomez-Mejia, L. R. (1999).A theory of global strategy and firm efficiencies: Considering the effects of cultural diversity. *Journal of Management, 25*(4), 587–607.

Peng, M. W. (2001).The resource-based view and international business. *Journal of Management, 27*(6), 803–830.

Perdue, L. (1999). *The wrath of grapes: The coming wine industry shakeout and how to take advantage of it.* New York:Avon Books, Inc.

Perreault, W. D., & McCarthy, E. J. (2002). *Basic marketing.* New York: McGraw-Hill Publishers.

Porter, M. (1985). *Competitive advantage: Creating and sustaining superior performance.* New York: Free Press.

Professional Friends of Wine. (2004). *Regions and wineries.* Available: www.winepros.com

Rabobank International. (1999). *Report on global market share of the 3 largest drink firms.* (Internal company document).

Rabobank International. (2002). *The major wine companies.* Internal company document.

Handfield, R. B., & Nichols, E. L., Jr. (1999). *Introduction to supply chain management.* Upper Saddle River, NJ: Prentice Hall.

Monczka, R.,Trent, R., & Handfield, R. (1998). *Purchasing and supply chain management.* Cincinnati, OH: South-Western College Publishing.

Robinson, J. (Ed.). (1999). *The Oxford companion to wine* (2nd ed.). New York: Oxford University Press.

Seth,A., Song, K. P., & Pettit, R. (2000). Managerialism or hubris? An empirical examination of motives for foreign acquisitions of U.S. firms. *Journal of International Business Studies, 31*(3), 387–404.

Shanken, M. (2003). *The U.S. wine market: Impact databank review and forecast* (2003 ed.). New York: M. Shanken Communications, Inc.

Sharples, L. (2002).Wine tourism in Chile:A brave new step for a brave new world. *International Journal of Wine Marketing, 14*(2), 43–54.

Simon,A. (1967). *The wines, vineyards, and vignerons of Australia.* London: Paul Hamlyn.

Spawton,A. L. (1990). Development in the global alcoholic drinks industry and its implications for the future marketing of wine. *International Journal of Wine Marketing, 2*(1). Reprinted in *European Journal of Marketing, 24*(4).

Spawton,A. L. (1997). *Globalisation and its implications to strategy development as the key to future success.* Paper presented at XX11eme World Congress of Vine and Wine,Argentina, December 1–5.

Spawton,A. (2003a). Supply chain management in the wine sector. *Bulletin d'OIV, 76*(876–868), 389–424.

Spawton,A. L. (2003b). *Will globalisation commoditise premium wine* (Working paper). Wine Marketing Group, University of South Australia.

Spawton, T., & Juniper, J. (2001). *Regional competencies and global trends in firm concentration within the wine industry.* Paper presented at XXVIth World Wine Congress, Adelaide, Australia.

Stevenson, T. (2004). *Wine report.* London: Dorling Kindersley.

Thach, L. (2001, September). Short report outlining publicly available data on wine human resource issues. WineVision Sustainability Taskforce. Available: www.winevision.org

Thach, L. (2002, July). Social sustainability in the wine community. *Wine Business Monthly.*

Thach, L., & Eaton, C. (2001, May). E-Commerce adoption in the wine industry. *Wine Business Monthly, 8*(5), 31-33.

Thach, L., & Shepard, J. (2001, November). The importance of supervisory & management training in the wine industry. *Wine Business Monthly.*

Thompson, A. A., & Strickland, A. J. (2003). *Strategic management: Concepts and cases* (13th ed., chap. 6, 9, 10). New York: McGraw-Hill/Irwin.

Tromp, A. (2003). *The South African system of integrated production of wines.* Available: http://www.ipw.co.za/

Truss, W. (2002). *Government releases final report on wine exports and wine tourism.* Available: http://www.affa.gov.au/ministers/truss/releases/02/02305wt.html

Ulrich, D. (1997). Measuring human resources: An overview of practice and a prescription for results. *Human Resource Management, 36*(3), 303-320.

Voss, R. (2000, May). *The New South Africa.* Available: http://www.wineenthusiast.com/

Walker, L. (2002, November). Tasting room survey: Selling at the cellar door. *Wines & Vines.* Available: http://www.winesandvines.com/feature_nov_02_tasting.html

Wall, S. J. (2001). Making mergers work. *Financial Executive, 17*(2), 34-35.

Western Management Group. (2001/2002). Wine Industry Salary Survey. Available: http://www.wmgnet.com/wi/wi01.htm

Wildfeuer, S. (1995). *What is biodynamics?* Available: http://www.biodynamics.com/biodynamics.html

Williams, P., & Kelly, J. (2001). Cultural wine tourists: Product development considerations for British Columbia's resident wine tourism market. *International Journal of Wine Marketing, 13*(3), 59-77.

Wine Diva. (2002). *Australian wine: Geographic indication system.* Available: http://www.winediva.com.au/regions/regions2.asp

Wine Market Council. (2000). *Consumer research data.* Available: www.winemarketcouncil.com

Wine News. (2002, December/2003, January). *Comments.* Available: www.thewinenews.com/decjan0203/comments.asp

WineVision. (2003). *Global exporting.* Available: http://www.winevision.org/globalexporting/Export101.html

Yahoo Finance. (2003). Factiva databases. Available: http://www.lib.uwo.ca/database/secure/jumpstart.shtml

Yeung, A. K., & Berman, B. (1997). Adding value through human resources: Reorienting human resource measurement to drive business performance. *Human Resource Management, 36*(3), 321-335.

Index

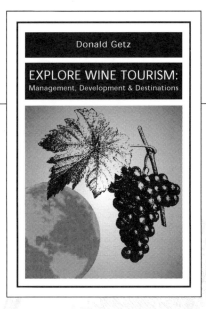